# CATCHING
# BIG FISH

# CATCHING
# BIG FISH

## AN ANGLER'S CHALLENGE

## BOB RICH

CATCHING BIG FISH
*An Angler's Challenge*
Copyright © 2025 by Bob Rich

All rights reserved. No part of this publication may be reproduced, stored in a retrieval system, or transmitted in any form by any means, electronic, mechanical, photocopy, recording, or otherwise, without the prior permission of the publisher, except as provided by USA copyright law.

No patent liability is assumed with respect to the use of the information contained herein. Although every precaution has been taken in the preparation of this book, the publisher and author assume no responsibility for errors or omissions. Neither is any liability assumed for damages resulting from the use of the information contained herein.

Published by Forefront Books, Nashville, Tennessee.
Distributed by Simon & Schuster.

Library of Congress Control Number: 2025910376

Print ISBN: 978-1-63763-381-6
E-book ISBN: 978-1-63763-382-3

Cover Design by Bruce Gore, Gore Studio, Inc.
Interior Design by Mary Susan Oleson, BLU Design Concepts

Printed in the United States of America
25 26 27 28 29 30 [RR4] 10 9 8 7 6 5 4 3 2 1

**FOR MINDY**
*My first female friend*

"THE BEST THING for being sad," replied Merlyn, beginning to puff and blow, "is to learn something. That is the only thing that never fails. You may grow old and trembling in your anatomies, you may lie awake at night listening to the disorder of your veins, you may miss your only love, you may see the world about you devastated by evil lunatics, or know your honour trampled in the sewers of baser minds. There is only one thing for it then—to learn."

—M<small>ERLYN ADVISING YOUNG</small> K<small>ING</small> A<small>RTHUR</small>,
from T. H. White's *The Once and Future King*

# CONTENTS

ACKNOWLEDGMENTS ............................................................ 11

INTRODUCTION: *I, Aquarius* ............................................... 13

1. THE HUNT ........................................................................ 15

2. THE CONCH .................................................................... 27

3. FISH #1: *The Sailfish* ..................................................... 37

4. FISH #2: *The Tarpon* ..................................................... 65

5. FISH #3: *The Barracuda* ................................................ 89

6. FISH #4: *The Permit* ..................................................... 109

7. FISH #5: *The Bonefish* .................................................. 123

8. FISH #6: *The Bass* ........................................................ 141

9. FISH #7: *The Wahoo* .................................................... 165

10. FISH #8: *The Dolphin* .................................................. 203

11. FISH #9: *The Marlin* .................................................... 223

12. FISH #10: *The Snook* ................................................... 259

EPILOGUE: *The Calendar* ..................................................... 323

# Acknowledgments

FOR ME, writing a book—like catching big fish—has always been a team sport. Besides those mentioned in this book, my thanks on the fishing side go out to former International Game Fish Association biologist and Hall of Fame member Glenda Kelley and IGFA President Jason Schratwieser, who were always there to answer my scientific questions.

On the writing side, my thanks to the good folks at Kevin Anderson & Associates who also helped me make my stories come to life, starting with Stephen S. Power for his advice, counsel, and sense of humor.

No one brings books together better than the Forefront Books team led by Jonathan Merkh, and my thanks go out to Jen Gingerich, their managing editor, and Billie Brownell, production editor, as well as Becky Nesbitt, the acquisition manager. Janna Walkup, my lead

## Acknowledgments

copyeditor, deserves special thanks for helping me "temper some of my terser" language, and Mary Susan Oleson did her usual great job on the interior design.

Bruce Gore has again designed a wonderful cover, this time incorporating an incredible Dave Magnum photo of a leaping tarpon. Thanks to both of these gents. My pal Tim Borski deserves thanks for his wonderful paintings of each of my ten target species at the beginning of each chapter. My only wish is that we had more time to fish together.

Thanks also to my manager, Bill Grieshober; my publicist, Kevin Aman, and his associate Jennifer Gmoser; Mary Butin and our digital team at Butin Public Relations; and to my assistant Courtney Kabala and to Judy Roth, who was my first non-angling proofreader.

Big thanks as well to Kevin Anderson, an accomplished writer on his own behalf for, again, turning loose the full strength of the fine company of his own name to assist me, starting with his wonderful assistant, Erica Niven.

It is also reassuring to draw on the distribution skills of the incomparable Simon & Schuster.

Finally, thanks to Miguel de Cervantes, whose writing in the seventeenth century influenced my philosophy, and to Mindy, my muse!

INTRODUCTION

# I, Aquarius

I AM DRAWN to water. My fishing rod acts the way a divining rod does in the hands of a sun-drenched farmer. Like many others, I'd always wanted to write a book but could never decide on the subject. As a businessperson, I've had many offers to write about my vocation. I turned them down because doing so seemed like spending just another day at my desk.

Also, as an angler, I've looked for a chance to test my fishing prowess against the best fishers and fishes.

Both opportunities came to me in the form of the world's largest fishing tournament, the Metropolitan South Florida Fishing Tournament. Started in 1936 as the Miami Met, the tourney offered prizes to men, women, and children for catching a variety of fish. At its height, the Met numbered one hundred thousand entrants per year!

*Introduction*

Begun by a man named H. H. (Hy) Hyman and the Miami Rod and Reel Club and sponsored by the *Miami Herald*, the Met had been fished by many of the nation's most famous sportsmen like Ted Williams and Curt Gowdy as well as celebrity anglers like Al Pflueger Jr., Bob Stearns, and Vic Dunaway. Joe Brooks and Lefty Kreh, both fly-fishing legends, each served several years as tournament directors.

What caught my eye was their Hall of Fame, which was started in 1976. It required an angler to catch ten specific species using a variety of tackle, including spin, plug-casting, and fly fishing. Since its inception, no one had qualified!

This was my chance—an opportunity to compete against some of the very best anglers in the sport. Could I do what no one else had been able to do? Could I be the first person ever to find and catch these ten fish?

Why not?

And so I decided to give it a try. Also, I would write about it and keep a diary chronicling my attempt. Who knows what agony and exaltation I would go through along the way. Also, who knew then if the storied old Met would survive the millennium. Whether it did or did not, I believed that my quest to catch some very big fish would be of interest to both anglers and would-be anglers and that my stories would entertain readers of all kinds.

This, then, is my first book written with chapters that honor each species. One need not be a Hall of Famer to enjoy it.

# CHAPTER 1

# The Hunt

*"There can be no doubt, Sancho," he said,*
*"that this is going to be a very great*
*and perilous adventure in which*
*it will be necessary for me to display*
*all my strength and valor."*

—Miguel de Cervantes, *Don Quixote*

---

Call me Bubba. It's not actually my given name. It's my chosen name—chosen upon embarking not only on my quest to qualify for the Metropolitan South Florida Fishing Tournament Hall of Fame (also known to some as the Miami Fishing Tournament) but also on my life's larger adventure of becoming a grandfather.

In the spring of 1996, my son Bob III (aka Three Sticks) informed me that I was going to be a grandfather come winter. Bobby, as he's known, is a hardworking and conscientious young man. I knew that he would be a great dad. He then asked what I wanted to be called by the little one. "Bob" was deemed out of the question, and thus began my monthslong search for an appropriate grandfather name.

As luck would have it, the Met Fishing Tournament came along in November 1996, affording me a chance to settle on a good, solid, Southern redneck fishing name that could also be easily pronounced by a toddler. Now the race was on! Could I catch the tournament's ten required fish species before my first grandchild called me Bubba? And would this time-consuming pursuit preclude me from having to change a diaper? Time would tell.

My fishing quest started in November 1996 over breakfast at the Islamorada Fish Company Restaurant and Bakery, formerly known as the Lovin' Dough. Located at mile marker 82 in my new hometown of Islamorada in the Florida Keys, this popular little sixteen-table roadside restaurant had been serving delicious, cholesterol-packed breakfasts to the locals for ten years.

It was a mandatory first stop of the day for fishing guides, anglers, shopkeepers, and insomniacs. Breakfast clubbers, beware! Neither the low-fat craze nor decaffeination, let alone no-smoking sections, had reached the Fish Company yet. Serious breakfast entrées such as omelets, eggs Benedict, and corned beef hash, along with sides of hash browns, grits, sausage, and greasy bacon, were the order of the day. The servers were pleasant. Harry, the King of Coffee, never let your mug run dry, and most of the stories you heard there were lies about yesterday's fishing. For a special treat, the homemade eight-ounce cinnamon roll was generously smothered in cream-cheese icing. It could be ingested orally or applied directly to the hips. The Fish Company no longer serves breakfast, but those huge and delicious cinnamon rolls have moved across the street to the iconic Green Turtle Inn.

On this particular weekend morning, my wife, Mindy, and I squeezed around a four-top table with two of my fishing-guide pals and their wives—Ron Wagner and his wife, Carol, and Lee Baker and his wife, Suzan (or Sue). Ron and I go way back. Like myself, Ron is getting to be one of the old-timers who has fished offshore and in the backcountry. On the boat, he developed a reputation for being calm, patient, and able to find fish. On shore, he exuded good humor and a passion for $5 wagers on football teams, especially his beloved New England Patriots. Ron had become my No. 1 betting buddy. It never ceased to amaze me that for all our weekend wagers over the years, we seemed to be about even in the win–loss column.

Lately, Ron had been honing his writing skills with cranky letters to the editor on every subject from poorly outfitted fishing skiffs to ill-conceived tournament functions that precluded guides' wives from attending. It was still too early to tell if his new penchant for poison pen letters would see him ostracized or lionized in the community or if he would leave guiding to accept an editorial assignment with the *Keynoter* newspaper. At any rate, thank God for Carol. She quietly corrected his grammar and toned down his rhetoric. The woman was a saint.

Like Ron, Lee Baker was an experienced hand at guiding in the Florida Keys. He had a loyal following—including well-known tournament anglers such as Billy Pate, with whom he fished for years—and was well respected by all the other guides. Lee was quiet and unassuming, and he often served as a foil for his friend Captain Ron.

Sue Baker was well known throughout South Florida for her role as executive director of the Met, which was free to the public and ran from late December through May. She'd started there twelve years earlier and had become the driving force behind the tournament. She was the chief cook and bottle washer and, along with limited part-time help, managed every aspect of the tournament, including administration, publicity, marketing, event planning and coordination, applications, and catch registration. To give you some idea how large a job this was, Sue had processed more than thirty-five thousand catch reports for the previous year's tournament.

At breakfast, Sue gave us some details on the Met. That year's tournament would be the sixty-second, making the Met the oldest continuously running fishing tournament in Florida. According to Sue, the Met was the brainchild of Miami entrepreneur and avid fisherman Hy Hyman, who felt, correctly, that the tournament would be a great and unique way to promote tourism in South Florida.

The format had remained largely the same over the years. Anglers registered their South Florida catches throughout a five-month period from January through May, competing in a variety of classes defined by tackle and species of fish. Weekly catch updates appeared in the *Miami Herald*, which had been a generous sponsor of the tournament since its inception. The tournament boundaries included eleven counties in South Florida as well as the western shores of the Bahamas (which was within the circulation area of the *Herald*). In addition, the *Herald* housed the tournament offices up until 1999, when they moved to a new address.

*The Hunt*

*The Metropolitan South Florida Fishing Tournament logo was highly recognized by experienced anglers as well as visitors to South Florida.*

When the tournament ended in May, the entries were tabulated and the results announced, with the winners honored at an annual banquet in Miami. In addition to awards being presented in all categories, citations were mailed out for hundreds of notable catches.

Another special feature of this free public tournament was that it encouraged fishing competition at all levels, from the grizzly old pros to the newest novices. One of my favorite features was that it also promoted fishing as a healthy outdoor activity for children through its establishment of two specific divisions: "junior" and "peewee."

While two divisions were for the kids, the tournament fathers (and mothers) wisely did not separate the entries by sex. Men and women competed against one another, and a quick review of the annual results indicated that women were every bit as successful as men. This is a nice feature of fishing itself, a sport where all are equal.

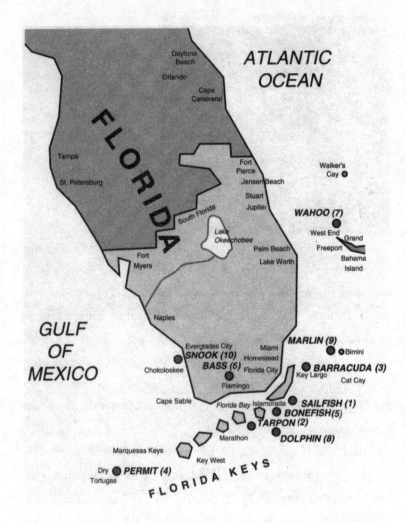

*MET tournament fishing boundaries include the South Florida counties of Broward, Collier, Dade, Glades, Hendry, Lee, Martin, Monroe, Palm Beach, Okeechobee, and St. Lucie as well as the western Bahama Islands. Locations of the ten species caught are shown.*

*The Hunt*

The fact that there was no charge to enter the tournament made the Met nonexclusionary, meaning it could be enjoyed by young and old, rich and poor, seven-day-a-week regulars and weekend warriors. There was also no residency requirement, so vacationers could participate too.

Most of the funding for the tournament came from cash and in-kind contributions from several large sponsor companies, some of which had vested interests in fishing equipment and/or South Florida tourism, and all of which shared an affection for the uniqueness of the Met and its positive impact on the quality of life in Florida's communities.

Over a plate full of scrambled eggs and sausage, Sue told us about some of the categories that had produced no winners in the previous year's Met. For example, the prize for tarpon master went unclaimed, meaning that no one registered the catch and release of six 48-inch-or-larger tarpon—two on fly equipment, two on spin, and two on plug. This might seem to be a modest feat, unless you have ever tried to land one of these big silver kings.

That's when Sue told us about the Metropolitan South Florida Hall of Fame, created by the Met in 1976. Inclusion in the Hall of Fame required catching ten specific species—which, Sue told us, no one had ever done. When I heard this, my eyes lit up. A fishing challenge, a first, a Hall of Fame—what more could anyone ask for? A quest!

Sue went on to list the fish and the tackle requirements. To make the Hall of Fame, you had to complete a series of ten challenging and specific catches, as listed on page 22.

*Catching Big Fish*

# QUALIFYING CATCHES

| FISH | TACKLE DIVISION | WEIGHT *(in pounds)* |
|---|---|---|
| Tarpon | Fly | 100 |
| Bonefish | Fly | 9 |
| Trout | Plug | 8 |
| or Snook | Plug | 18 |
| Black Bass | Plug | 6 |
| Permit | Spin | 20 |
| Dolphin | Spin | 25 |
| Sailfish | 8-pound test | Any |
| Barracuda | 8-pound test | 25 |
| Wahoo | 20-pound test or less | 25 |
| Marlin, white | 20-pound test or less | Any |
| or Marlin, blue | 50-pound test or less | Any |

No substitutions were allowed. And unlike the Met itself, there was no five-month time limit on this accomplishment. It was, in fact, a lifetime award.

So how was it, we were all wondering, that no one had been able to qualify yet? Sue explained that a few people had come close.

## The Hunt

One chap, John Lee Still from Punta Gorda, had registered nine out of ten qualifying fish and was still searching for his 8-pound sea trout or 18-pound snook on a plug. Sue herself and a few others were only two fish short.

I was hooked. Knowingly or not, Met executive director Suzan Baker had provided the bait, and I had bitten. What fun it would be to try to catch all these great fish and become the first entrant into the Hall of Fame. The challenge reminded me of Ernest Hemingway's remark that firsts are the only records that matter. And it sounded so easy. Why hadn't anyone done this yet in all that time? How difficult could it be? What was the catch? There was only one way to find the answers to those questions.

"C'mon, Sue, what's the catch?" I asked. "There's got to be more to this than meets the eye."

"No," she said, "the rules are all there on one page. There are no tricks. But to prove your catches, you do have to weigh each fish at an official Met entry station."

Aha—there it was: the catch, the fly in the ointment. The entry stations were *on land*. I'd have to kill each fish, and I don't do that. For me, fishing is catch and release. As Captain Gary Ellis said in the literature for the Redbone Tournament series that he and his wife, Susy, ran to benefit the fight against cystic fibrosis, "Release the fish. Save the memory—it's bigger." Words to live by. The only fish I've ever killed have been the occasional dinner snook during snook season.

Killing fish to make a Hall of Fame seemed so contrary to the movement in all of fishing, saltwater and freshwater alike, toward catch and release. Author Howell Raines, the editorial page editor of the *New York Times* and an accomplished fly fisherman who grew up in Alabama, might have characterized the Met Hall of Fame rules as part of the "redneck way of fishing," which he referred to in his wonderful book *Fly Fishing Through the Midlife Crisis*. In the first chapter, Raines said, "I was born in the heart of Dixie and raised in the redneck way of fishing, which holds that the only good trip is one ending in many dead fish. These fish might then be eaten, frozen, given to neighbors or used in fertilizer. But fishing that failed to produce an abundance of corpses could no more be successful than a football season in which the University of Alabama failed to win a national championship."

Sue explained that weighing the fish, which may mean killing them, went back to the old days in the Keys, before anglers became conservationists. Catch and release was unheard of back then. Weighing was part of the rules, and it was impossible to change that rule, as it would have been perceived as unfair to previous participants.

There was also the question of the need for verification in order to avoid the cheating that could occur in any tournament. The Met had gone to a release format, in addition to its classes of weight fish, for awards and tournament size records. The board, however, had been reluctant to change its Hall of Fame requirements, although there was mounting pressure to do so.

Enter the always reasonable Lee Baker, he of the calm and rational demeanor. "Weighing doesn't have to mean killing," Lee chipped in. "Most of the qualifying fish can be kept alive in a live well and released after weighing. Just like many of the bass tournaments, where fish are weighed alive and released, you wouldn't have

## The Hunt

to 'stick' these fish."

OK, release was possible for most of the species, especially the smaller ones. But what about the larger fish—the sailfish, marlin, and tarpon? What live well would be large enough for them?

I had a real moral dilemma on my hands. I wanted to begin a Hall of Fame quest, but killing my catch was out of the question. I consulted with my pals. Catch and release prevailed in Islamorada, although almost everyone I talked to said they would stick one billfish, especially given their relative abundance. Not so with tarpon. Like many of my friends, I had spent too much time hunting this magnificent fish to kill one, let alone one that weighed 100 pounds or more.

To participate, I needed a plan, a set of conditions by which I could start the quest without compromising the tournament or my beliefs. Here is what I arrived at:

- I'd compete.

- I'd try to catch, weigh, and release all species except the billfish.

- I'd stick a sailfish and a marlin, which I'd smoke, eat, and have mounted (for those of you who think eating and mounting fish are mutually exclusive events, I'll explain later).

- I'd try to band, photograph, and release a 100-pound tarpon and submit the photographs and bands to the Met. (What makes the tarpon special among these species? While I'm sure that all the other nine species have dedicated followers as well, I'm simply a tarpon follower.)

- I'd chronicle my endeavors and use the story to support a personal lobby for a change in rules at the Met to catch and release.
- I'd hope that the Met board would reconsider its position during my quest.

Now, I know this plan will sound far from acceptable to a lot of people who are reading this book. I also know that many anglers release all of their catches, without exception.

Many old-timers and meat fishermen would say, "Kill everything—don't turn this into a moral dilemma." Or, in the words of an Irish proverb, "It is not a fish until it is on the bank."

Others, including the once wildly popular Sea King, Jacques Cousteau, would have rejected my plan in total, no doubt condemning catch and release and reminding us that, as far as he is concerned, all sportfishing is "a perversion."

Well, if I'm compromised, so be it. You can't please everyone. I don't have all the answers, but if Cousteau was right and catch-and-release fishing, or a modified version of it, is my perversion, at least it's not as perverse as some other pastimes that you and I could pursue.

The ground rules were now laid. Let the hunt begin!

CHAPTER 2

# The Conch

*The strange collective nickname may have been used disparagingly at first, but today a Conch, a lifelong resident of the Keys, descendant of conchs, is proud of the shrewd and stubborn individuality the name represents.*

—Joy Williams, *The Florida Keys: A History & Guide*

---

IN MANY OF the books written about fishing, especially fly fishing for trout, the authors speak of their adventures in almost religious terms and always in the first person—as if truly great fishing can only be done alone. Sure, there are references to some fathers and/or unrelated old sages who initiated the authors into the wonders of angling a long time ago, and there are periods of camaraderie over cold barley sandwiches (beer) or old Scotch and fresh fish lovingly fried over a campfire at the end of the day, but, by and large, the hunt is portrayed as a solitary event.

Not so my quest. I took along a good fishin' buddy. So many of the species I was after required pursuit that I thought it imperative to have someone along to help move the boat, whether by push pole, motor, or even canoe paddle in the case of bass. Don't get me wrong—I do enjoy the solitude of fishing. A quiet walk on a bonefish flat, for instance, has to be likened to wading a good trout stream.

But for the Met, I wasn't too proud to admit that I needed some help—and besides, the Met Hall of Fame catches needed to be witnessed. Even if they didn't have to be, who would hold the camera and take pictures of all my victims? So, I took along my good fishin' buddy, Everett Russell Albury III, better known as Rusty.

Rusty was a sixth-generation resident of the middle Florida Keys. Known as a Conch (pronounced *konk*) by all and as Super Conch by Mindy and me, he was a lean, good-looking guy about six feet tall with short reddish blond hair and green eyes. Astride one of his motorcycles, he resembled a young Steve McQueen.

Rusty's ancestors had moved south from America's mainland to the Bahamas to avoid fighting the British during the Revolutionary War. Families like theirs took refuge in remote locations, kept to themselves, and developed their own brand of fierce independence and a goodly dose of isolationism. These characteristics led them to be called *Conchs*, after the nautilus-shelled mollusk that withdraw into their shells to avoid conflict.

The term *Conch* was reborn in 1982 during a curious affair that came to be known as the Revolution of the Conch Republic. Transportation of illegal drugs on Highway 1 from Key West to Miami was running rampant at the time. As a deterrent, the powers

# The Conch

*Slightly bemused, Captain Rusty Albury cleans his polarized lenses.*

that be in Washington decided to create a checkpoint along the highway to screen cars for illegal substances.

You can imagine the reaction of the locals, given not only their heritage but also their need to use Highway 1, the only road offering access and egress to their homes. Add to this the weekly commuter traffic to Miami, plus the tourist traffic, and you can see how inconvenient such a checkpoint would be—almost like clearing customs to enter another country every time you went to work or to the store.

The locals protested, but the barriers remained. In frustration, Dennis Wardlow, the mayor of Key West, devised a plan. Feeling ostracized and acutely aware of what long "border delays" would do to tourism, Wardlow—with the support of the town council—declared the Keys to be known as the Conch Republic, announced its secession from the United States, and then declared war on the US.

The next day, under Mayor Wardlow's generalship, the Conch Republic surrendered and immediately requested foreign aid from Washington. This rapid chain of events, strikingly similar to the famous Peter Sellers movie *The Mouse That Roared*, worked. The feds relented and the barricades were dismantled. Chalk one up for the Conch Republic.

Today, the pride remains, along with the republic's colorful flag—a pink conch before a golden sun against a field of blue. I fly one on the port halyard of my offshore boat.

Rusty Albury grew up in a family where fishing was a way of life and the Conch mindset a way of being. His dad, Russ, ran the local tackle shop in Islamorada and found plenty of time to teach his two sons the mysteries and joys of backcountry fishing for bonefish, snook, tarpon, redfish, permit, trout, and snapper. Rusty told some great stories of living in their vacation stilt house near Key West and fishing with his brother, John; his dad; and boyhood pals Craig Brewer, Rick Moeller, and Glenn Flutie, all of whom guided in the familiar waters of their boyhood.

Rusty's dad never wanted his son to become a fishing guide, even though the two loved to fish together. The senior Albury once even held an IGFA record for four years, with a 13-pound, 2-ounce

*The flag of the Conch Republic, founded in Key West in 1982.*

bonefish taken on 6-pound test line. I'm sure that neither Russ nor anyone else was surprised when Rusty started guiding full-time at age twenty-seven. It was a profession for which he had a talent and an obsession. His brother, John, by the way, became a pilot for American Airlines.

We first met in the early 1980s when Rusty was considered one of the young hotshot guides. I remember fishing with him, my wife, and our young son, Barney. A first-time fisherman, Barney caught more than fifty snappers, had the time of his life, and made a new friend of this young Florida guide whose enthusiasm for fishing was pervasive. Little did any of us know then of the changes that were sweeping the Florida Keys, which would affect so many young people's lives, including that of Rusty Albury.

Drugs were inundating the post–Vietnam War United States. Incredible demand spurred supply-side entrepreneurs, who seemed to operate with impunity, beyond the reach of overworked and understaffed local, state, and federal law enforcement agencies.

The Florida Keys became a strategic thoroughfare for the import of illegal drugs. Comprising 150 miles of connected islands, ribboning their way from Key West to Miami, the Keys are surrounded by mudflats and channels, hidden coves, reefs, and beautiful deserted beaches offering sanctuary to thousands of species of birds and safe harbor to importers of illegal drugs, mostly marijuana pressed into 100-pound bales.

Young Keys guides became natural targets for traffickers looking for help in moving their deadly wares. Consider a young guide, single and strong, pushing his skiff and clients through the Everglades for $150 a day. OK, no pity here—it's not a bad wage for a day's work. Plus, you're outdoors and you're your own boss.

Now introduce the drug lords, who needed people who could navigate small boats through the Keys—smugglers willing to risk running drugs for huge rewards.

And the rewards were very real. One old-timer, who shall remain nameless, told me that before he got caught, he once made $700,000 for one night's work guiding a small freighter through a fifty-mile stretch of Florida Bay backcountry. While such a windfall was the exception, not the rule, a lot of young men did enjoy substantial benefits from a new profession.

Suffice it to say that Rusty eventually was seduced and inevitably was caught, tried, and convicted. He served thirty-four months in a federal prison camp in Eglin Air Force Base in North Florida.

## The Conch

Rusty accepted his punishment and learned from his mistakes. He became a hardworking father of two, but eventually, he and his wife, Therese Marie ("Terry"), would divorce. While married, they complemented each other. While Rusty was usually cool and laconic, Terry bubbled over with warmth and wit. Rusty often searched for words, which came very easily to Terry. Together, these two made a good team.

When Rusty got out of Eglin, he took up pressure cleaning with one of his cousins. I hired him on to take care of my two boats, a backcountry skiff and an offshore center-console walkabout. He did a great job and eventually had his captain's license reinstated by the Coast Guard.

Rusty's character on the boat could best be described as *focused*—focused on fish. Mindy once said that Rusty could talk for hours on any subject as long as it had fins, scales, and a tail. He prepared assiduously for every trip and always had a game plan. He constantly used his longtime knowledge of his environment to give his team an advantage.

People with a fragile self-image and a fishing technique that was a little off should have been warned *not* to hire Rusty Albury for a day on the water. Gratuitous compliments to struggling anglers were not part of his portfolio. He made no pretenses at unctuous civility, as do so many other successful guides or teaching pros in other genteel sports. Rusty was focused on finding and catching fish, and there was an inherent honesty in his straightforward approach to this pursuit.

Rusty's response to questions on the boat could be monosyllabic at most and silent at least. His critique was harsh and pointed.

He even criticized my technique after I landed a 9 ½-pound bonefish on fly, a catch that won the grand angler championship at the Little Palm Grand Slam Tournament in the fall of 1998!

Rusty's brusque approach to his job and his customers was well rooted in the guiding tradition. Some of the best-known Islamorada guides, such as Jim Brewer, Jack Brothers, and Jimmie Albright, could reduce a grown angler to tears or early retirement from the sport. The stories are legendary. One of my favorites is about Jim Brewer, one of the premier guides of the 1960s. One day Jim had an older couple in his skiff. It was scorching and breezeless on the flats, and the guide's frustration level was mounting as his client made errant cast after errant cast. As Jim's insults became more and more frequent, the angler finally put his rod away, sat down, and reached into his pocket for a small box of pills. "What are those?" Jim asked. The angler replied, "It's hot, I have a heart condition, and your constant yelling has given me chest pains. These are nitroglycerin." With no show of contrition, Jim simply said, "Give me one of those!"

Knowingly or not, Rusty Albury was keeping the time-honored tradition of surly Conch guides intact. I vowed that if he ever complimented me on anything I did on the boat, I would be looking for some nitroglycerin myself. But I do know he sometimes bragged about some of Mindy's and my fishing accomplishments to some of the other guides. I knew that if I ever mentioned that to him, he'd deny it. And I also knew that if I were lucky enough to catch the ten species and thereby make the Met Hall of Fame, my good fishin' buddy Rusty would help keep me humble and remind me that I was "still reeling against the drag."

*This hard-fighting 9 ½-pound bonefish eventually won the Little Palm Grand Slam for me.*

*The Sailfish*

CHAPTER 3

# FISH #1
# The Sailfish

*He jumped broadside quartering away,
probably to see what had him,
and we saw him again in slow motion
against the drag of all the line through the water.
He hung a full second slightly bowed in the air
as if already mounted.*

—Kenneth Kirkeby, *The Tournament*

My offshore boat was a 31-foot Ocean Master with twin 250-horsepower Mercury outboards that I had purchased two years before in Fort Lauderdale. I'd found the boat while browsing through the classified ads one Thanksgiving. It seemed that its owner was awaiting the arrival of a new inboard sportfishing boat and had to make some dock space available fast. There's nothing like a motivated seller! We struck a deal, and I went to pick up the boat the week after Thanksgiving.

Halfway through the Super Bowl on January 26, 1997, I started to feel ill. It wasn't the same upset stomach that had seemed to accompany the Buffalo Bills through four straight Super Bowl losses, but a much more violent malaise. Even though I felt comfortable with my $5 bet on the Green Bay Packers (although I had to give Ron Wagner fourteen points on his Patriots), I could not watch the second half and snuck upstairs to bed, abandoning the guests and family members who had gathered in our Islamorada living room to watch the game. Leaving Mindy to make excuses for me, I took to my bed with a severe case of the flu, which put me out of commission for two and a half days. Half that time, I remember lying in bed worrying that I was going to die; the other half, I worried that I wasn't going to die.

By midmorning on Wednesday, I was starting to rally, perhaps out of sheer boredom and frustration. Then Dr. Rusty called to tell me that I had been in bed long enough and it was time to start the hunt with an afternoon search for sailfish. With Mindy's blessing, off I went to Max's Marine and my offshore boat. This time, in deference to my queasy stomach, I wasn't loaded down with the usual picnic basket of delicious sandwiches from the deli of The Trading Post supermarket or cooler filled with lagers.

The boat was extremely well equipped with a good VHF radio, LORAN, GPS, a color fish finder, and a side-scan sonar fish finder. It was obvious that this boat had been fished hard—it had thirty-one

*Fish #1: The Sailfish*

*The mighty* Fish This!—*a real bargain?*

rod holders and bent outriggers—but it was my first offshore boat, and I was smitten. My first act of ownership was to change the name from the *Predator* to the *Fish This!* The sarcastic little title humored me, although I noticed that it took Rusty a full month to start using the boat's new name when talking to his pals on the radio. Well, maybe the name would grow on him.

After getting the boat back to Max's Marine in Islamorada, we fished it three weekends in a row and raised sailfish five out of six days. Rusty had done a lot of billfishing offshore, but I was a real novice. We seemed to be able to find a lot of volunteers from the backcountry who enjoyed a day offshore.

Rusty and I entered Cheeca Lodge's Presidential Sailfish Tournament that January. We caught two sails the first day of the two-day event and were feeling pretty good about our chances to win the outboard division of the tournament. Then disaster struck!

On the second day, our crew arrived at the dock only to find the *Fish This!* sitting on the bottom, still tied to the dock. Imagine the shock! Upon inspection, we discovered that a series of unrelated events had caused the demise of the *Fish This!* A through-hull live well plug had worked loose to start things. But the overriding cause of sinking was the simultaneous failure of two bilge pumps. Maybe Bubba hadn't gotten such a great deal after all.

Luckily, two Marine Motors executive friends of mine, Tom Ireland and Dan Schaad, were at Max's, saw our predicament, and loaned us their boat for the second and last day of the tournament. While we didn't catch a fish, I was so impressed with their thoughtfulness that I ordered two new Mercury engines as part of the total makeover for the *Fish This!* With new wiring, the two new engines, and removal of the through-hull live well, the *Fish This!* was soon ready to go back to sea for the first Met species, the sailfish.

Six weeks after the Cheeca tournament, Rusty and I headed out of Max's Marine via its westbound channel, which leads to the Intracoastal Waterway and backcountry of beautiful, desolate Florida Bay. Our search for bait this day didn't take long. Taking advantage of the shallow draft of the *Fish This!* (three feet), Rusty zigzagged twice and pulled up to the closest mangrove island before turning the controls over to me and heading to the bow with his 10-foot cast net in hand.

Catching live bait in the Keys—or anywhere else—is table stakes for the hunt of many species offshore or in the backcountry. Every time I lusted after one of those sleek 40-foot-plus sportfishing boats with twin diesels and a tuna tower that looked like a stairway to heaven, Rusty reminded me how much shallow water there is in

## Fish #1: The Sailfish

the Keys, and how many baitfish live in that shallow water, and how shallow the *Fish This!* would go to catch bait while the bigger boats were chumming offshore.

This day we were in luck. It was a beautiful, sunny afternoon, with winds blowing at twelve to fifteen miles an hour out of the northeast, and Rusty spotted a large school of razorbelly pilchards darting on and off the flat from the channel. I pointed the boat to the southwest, trimmed the engines, and idled to the edge of the flat to give Rusty a good downwind shot.

As Rusty tied the nylon drawstring around his left wrist and put the folds of the net over his right shoulder, I realized I was breaking out in a cold sweat despite the 80 degree South Florida day. Maybe I was having a relapse. I started to wonder if I should tell Rusty to bucket his net and head for the dock so I could go to bed. But just then Rusty signaled for me to put it in neutral and heaved the net in a perfect arc toward the unsuspecting razorbellies. Cast netting could be the subject of a chapter all by itself. It looks incredibly easy until you try it; then you discover how hard it is to make the net open up, let alone clear the bow rail and land in the water.

As the net hits the water in a fully open circle, it's impossible to tell how you've done until you purse the net and start to haul it back. At that point, if you're lucky, you begin to see the baitfish flashing as their normal course is redirected by the decreasing confines of the net.

And on this day, we were very lucky. Rusty crushed 'em. The net turned into a mass of silver flashes as several hundred 4- to 5-inch pilchards crashed into each other in their attempts to escape. Rusty dumped his haul into the live well as I circled the boat to give him another shot.

*Rusty makes throwing a cast net look really easy. It's not.*

Second throw, same result. Good omen—let's go fishing! I'd suck it up and give it a shot for a while. I could always give it an hour and then head back to sick bay. Bait catching usually isn't that easy. I've been out for four hours with no luck, especially when the wind is blowing. Maybe it was meant to be. Maybe there was a sailfish

## Fish #1: The Sailfish

waiting for me today. Before I knew it, we were heading for Snake Creek and the Atlantic Ocean.

As a member of the family *Istiophoridae*, the Atlantic sailfish populates the South Florida coastal waters in great numbers. Atlantic sails range from 30 to 50 pounds and are most plentiful in the area during winter, when colder waters drive them south and the warm Gulf Stream provides excellent habitat with abundant food. They are voracious feeders with few natural enemies or predators except man.

As with many gamefish, the database of accurate information on sailfish is limited, and misinformation and supposition abound. If a species is fished commercially, the industry spends heavily to uncover information to either increase the catch or manage the resource (depending on whom you talk with). Funds for research on sportfish, however, are mainly dependent on conservationists and fishermen, and are limited.

Historically, sailfish have been taken commercially, especially by Japanese long-liners, although they have never been specifically targeted as a species. Domestic drift netters also pose a threat to sailfish as well as other species. While sailfish stocks are considerable, reported catches are down worldwide.

Sailfish are found in both the Atlantic and Pacific Oceans, although Pacific sailfish run almost twice as large as their Atlantic kin, averaging 100 pounds plus. Marine biologists say this is due to several environmental differences, the main one of which is food. The Pacific, with its large upwelling zones, is much more nutrient rich than the Atlantic, leading to an abundance of baitfish, including sailfish favorites, anchovies and sardines. While the Billfish Foundation tagging program has discovered that many sailfish migrate long distances, it also indicates that many others seem to be nonmigratory and stay in one geographic region. These are called *hometown fish* or *homers*.

For many people, whether they have wet a line in salt water or not, the image that comes to mind upon the mention of deep-sea fishing is a jumping sailfish, bill flaying, dorsal fin fully fanned against an emerald sea and a cloudless South Florida blue sky. The sailfish's coloring defies description. When attacking bait or fighting against a hook and line, the fish's deep blue, purple, and flashing silver colors and eighteen horizontal stripes become more pronounced as excitement pumps his adrenaline, causing him to "light up" in a phosphorescent luminescence. It's common for a hooked fish to be lit up throughout a fight until he is brought alongside the boat or landed.

Our first oceanside stop was Davis Reef, three miles off the coast of Tavernier Creek. Rusty wanted to add some balao (pronounced *bally-hoo*) to our razorbellies. While sailfish love pilchards, they prefer these hearty little baitfish. With their streamlined shape and pointy beaks, balao are ideal for slow trolling in a straight line.

We anchored off the reef and hung a chum bag off the stern. Within ten minutes a school of hungry yellowtail snappers had almost engulfed the stern of the boat. Let me tell you something about yellowtail snappers. They are delicious deep-fried, and no one prepared them better than Rick Bond at the Hungry Tarpon restaurant just south of Islamorada on Lower Matecumbe Key. Rick was a great guy and ran a great joint. His Crazy Flamingo restaurant in Key Largo used to pack in the Gucci crowd from the Ocean Reef Resort.

So, there we were on Davis Reef. While yellowtails taste great to humans, they don't make good trolling bait for sailfish.

*Fish #1: The Sailfish*

Unfortunately, yellowtails, like sailfish, love balao, and their presence messed up our bait-catching attempts. Ten minutes later, however, a small school of balao showed up on the outside edge of the yellowtail school. A long throw of the cast net landed six.

As Rusty was preparing to make another cast, a call over the radio announced a strike by Captain Donald Jones's balao boat about two miles up the coast. Commercial balao boats work the offshore coastal waters of South Florida netting balao, which are put in brine, frozen, and sold to local bait shops. As you might imagine, the local offshore captains have a love/hate relationship with these guys, as they take a lot of bait off the reefs. On the positive side, they do stay in touch with the captains on their channel and make their catches available to the sportfish boats in the area. On a slow bait day in a tournament, this supply option can be huge. The price is always right too. With a large catch in their net, the balao boat crew is happy to sell a few dozen live balao for a couple of bucks or even a six-pack of beer.

It was 1:00 p.m. when Rusty and I looked at each other, pulled up the anchor, and headed for Jones's balao boat. Donald Jones (aka DJ) had been in the business all his life, and his family had run Plantation Fishery on nearby Plantation Key for several generations. He and his crew were a scruffy lot, dressed in yellow oilskins to stay dry from the spray as their small fishing boat bobbed and weaved through the offshore swells. Rusty was at the helm while I received a long-handled net full of about four dozen balao, which I deposited in the live well before returning the net with a $20 bill inside.

A midocean boat-to-boat transaction can be tricky. The rolling sea makes it difficult for the helmsmen to keep the boats from colliding, and it put the pressure on me, the angler/bait transferee, not to do anything stupid like dropping the heavy net. This particular transfer went well, although I do think I heard a couple of DJ's crew snickering about my George Bush Bonefish Tournament hat.

Now we were headed farther offshore in search of a sailfish, our first Met Tourney target. Along the way we spotted a few of the local captains slow trolling live bait off the outside of Little Conch Reef. Rich Helmuth was there on the *Strikefighter* and Bill White on his *Killer White,* fresh off a good win in that year's ladies' sailfish tournament the week before. In addition, Rusty's uncle Arnold Ross and cousin Paul were fishing this day in their boats, the *Start Me Up* and the *Relentless.* Captain Arnold had transferred his love of and skill at offshore fishing to his son Paul, who was also a professional captain. Even Arnold's ex-son-in-law, Rob Dixon, captained a sportfishing boat, the *Challenger,* off the shores of the Florida Keys.

The northeast wind had created a good chop, which is not good for weak stomachs but is good for catching sailfish. Sailfish are predominantly surface feeders, and the rolling seas give you a great chance to see the fish cruising on the surface or lolling around in the breaking waves. These fish take on a very different appearance than lit-up fish in battle. They appear to be black or sometimes greenish brown, with their magnificent dorsal fins folded flat against their backs. Sailfish travel in schools, and it is not uncommon to see two, three, or four fish hunting together for bait.

As the depth finder showed the bottom going down from 75 to 125 feet, we throttled back and lowered the outriggers. For tackle, we had chosen two 5-foot Loomis spinning rods and two 8-foot Randy Towe custom spinning rods, all fitted with Daiwa 1600 open-faced

*Fish #1: The Sailfish*

*DJ and his crew leave the last of their balao catch in the water to sell live to sportfishing boats in their vicinity.*

spinning reels spooled with 8-pound test Ande line, IGFA-regulation double line and leaders, and No. 2/0 Owner hooks. We baited two of the hooks with pilchards and two with balao and trolled the baits about twenty-five to forty feet behind the boat, alternating engines just enough to keep the boat rolling very slowly forward. The *Fish This!* trolled well in these moderately heavy seas, lying gently in the troughs and sliding quietly over the cresting waves.

Conditions were great. We were kind of outside the fleet, all of whose members had moved inside after reporting several morning hookups where we were now. Within half an hour, three boats were reporting simultaneous hookups. This was not uncommon in these waters. In many of the local sailfish tournaments, a channel is set up as the tournament channel and the captains call in hookups, landings, taggings, and releases to a committee boat. Many times, the catches come all at once in a particular area. The tournament channel can be quiet for hours, then all of a sudden start crackling with announcements of hookups. Is it the sun, the tide, the water temperature, the barometric pressure? Who really knows? It just serves as a reminder to me of how little we know about sportfish and their habits.

One thing is clear: Sportfishing breeds a herd mentality. As the bite hit inside, we pulled in the lines and headed for the fleet. It's also interesting how offshore captains help each other find fish and share locations and other information on the radio. It's not like backcountry fishing, where stealth and cunning prevail. Offshore captains are like comrades in arms, whereas backcountry guides would fall on their swords before giving up their own location, let alone the location of a hot bite. For some reason, this always makes me think of a comment the old man made in Ernest Hemingway's classic book *The Old Man and the Sea*: "If the others heard me talking aloud, they would think that I am crazy. But since I am not crazy, I do not care. And the rich have radios to talk to them in their boats and to bring them baseball."

So, Rusty and I set up again, this time in about ninety-five feet of water. We didn't have to wait long, as we had three strikes within ten minutes, all at once, on both flat lines and the starboard outrigger. All the lines were my responsibility, as no one else could touch a rod for the catch to qualify for the Met. I grabbed the port-side flat line, dropped the rod tip, reeled in slack, struck the fish—and nothing. I scooted over to the starboard flat line and followed the same procedure. This time there was pressure on the line. Forty feet away, a giant

## Fish #1: The Sailfish

silver barracuda broke the surface in a monster leap that would have cleared a high-jump bar at six feet. I could see the No. 2/0 Owner hook in his lip, attached to a piece of broken 8-pound test Ande line. Nice fish, maybe 20 pounds. Perhaps Rusty and I should have used some wire leader and gone after that 25-pound Met barracuda!

By the time I got to the outrigger line, the fish had taken out about seventy feet of line. I took the line off the wire, closed the bail, and started reeling without striking the fish. About 100 feet away, another big barracuda took to the air in a furious leap. This time the fish stayed engaged. He was big, angry, airborne, and still hooked. So, we went out for a sail and bagged the 25-pound 'cuda on 8-pound test—that would be a good story. Landing a big 'cuda without wire leader is a long shot, but it happens more often than you might think. The hook frequently gets into the upper lip, away from the teeth, and you can land the fish. Of course, the shorter the fight, the better your chances. Rusty and I looked at each other and he gave me a shrug, which meant in Conch, "What the hell, go for it, but don't get upset when he breaks you off." Five minutes later, that's exactly what happened. I consoled myself by figuring that would have been too easy a first catch and wouldn't have given me a chance to categorically demonstrate to you later everything I don't know about barracuda.

Rusty and I re-rigged our three broken lines and headed back out to 125 feet of water to get away from the pack-hunting 'cudas.

There is a great controversy in billfishing over whether to strike or not to strike the fish. My friend Robert "RT" Trosset from Key West, who has held more than 100 IGFA records, was a leader of the no-strike camp. RT liked to drop the tip of the rod, reel down slowly, and let the fish strike himself. Rusty, on the other hand, was from the "rip-some-lip" school. I imagine Rusty figured he would either permanently implant the hook or break the fish's neck—ending the fight either way. I tended to be in between, depending on how long the "suspected" billfish had been on the line. If it's a relatively short time, I like to strike and set. If he's been on for a while, as in the case of the third fish I engaged that ate the rigger bait, I like to come tight on him and let him set the hook himself, figuring he's had the bait for a while and might have had a better chance to ingest it, giving me more surface space for a hookup. Both RT and Rusty accepted my logic, which I am now officially titling the Bubba Compromise.

By the time we got our lines back in the water, it was three o'clock and the fleet was packing it up and heading for port. The seas were beginning to lie down, and I was starting to think that day one would not be our lucky day for a sailfish.

So far, the only good thing about the afternoon was the early bait catch. It was 3:45 p.m., and Rusty and I were both thinking about heading home as a flock of royal terns flew over our boat. I shouted, "Five more minutes!" to Rusty on the bridge, which on my boat was like a declaration of unconditional surrender. Almost immediately, a sailfish crashed our starboard outrigger bait, all lit up in neon colors and looking as if he hadn't had a meal in a week. He crashed the balao so hard that it pulled the line out of the rigger. I grabbed the Randy Towe custom rod, pointed the tip, and reeled down quickly. The fish felt the hook, felt the pressure, and went airborne so fast that I never had a chance to use the Bubba Compromise. I merely pointed the rod tip down, "bowing to the king," and hoped he had hooked himself enough to give me a chance to land him, because catch or not, I knew that this would be it for the day.

Now our quarry went ballistic, stringing together eight straight jumps that were so breathtaking and violent that Captain Helmuth called from the *Strikefighter* to see if we had hooked a double.

While the Met rule book doesn't specify a size requirement for sailfish, if we were going to land this fish, in order to weigh him on shore, the Department of Natural Resources rules would prevail and require this sailfish to be at least 57 inches from bottom lip to tail. Knowing this, I yelled up to Rusty to ask how big he thought this fish was. Believe it or not, after at least eight jumps, neither my captain nor I had a clue whether or not this fish was 57 inches. It was getting late, and the lengthening shadows and fish jumping in a mass of spray against a dipping sun certainly didn't help us make accurate size judgments. Then again, perhaps Zane Grey was right when he wrote, "In such moments one never sees the fish distinctly; excitement deranges the vision, and the picture, though impressive, is dim and dreamlike."

The sail soon gave up his aerobatics and started to peel line off my reel as he headed toward the depths. Rusty jammed both engines into reverse in pursuit as the 8-pound test flew off the reel. All I could do was hold the 8-foot rod tip up, brace myself, watch water splash over the transom, and think about how incredibly strong this fish was. I wondered if I would run out of line before I got a chance to see this creature again.

We had spooled the Daiwa 1600 with 250 yards of 8-pound test, which should have been more than enough to catch a sail, but now it seemed inadequate. I'd fished 8-pound line for bonefish, snook, and redfish, but now I found myself feeling foolish using it on such a strong (hopefully 57-inch or more) adversary. I wondered how anyone could land a fish on this dental floss. (Actually, under the category of fishing trivia, most dental floss tests out at about 10- to 12-pound test.)

By now we had the other lines out of the water, the rods were stowed, and we were settling in for the battle. The sailfish's long, deep runs became familiar to me as both he and I got used to feeling each other on opposite ends of the line.

The battle began to resemble a prizefight, with the fish and I winning alternate rounds. He would sound for three minutes, taking line as he went; then I would gather in line for the next three minutes before he took off again.

For the first forty-five minutes I could feel him shake his head as he fought to get free. Then the head shakes stopped accompanying his deep runs, making me wonder if he was dead or mortally wounded. The current was really ripping toward the southeast, and it's not unusual for a mortally wounded fish to turn sideways in the current and bring his full weight plus the speed of the current to bear against his human opponent.

Ironically, this fish would go free if he died. Eight-pound test line will not pull up a fish that weighs 40 pounds or more. The strong current certainly didn't help the situation.

I started to panic. "Rusty," I asked, "is this fish dead?"

"You'll know when the line breaks," he replied.

"Thank you, Rusty. Good consolation after coming off my deathbed to stand here for an hour. Am I winning or losing?"

*Fish #1: The Sailfish*

*Rusty did manage to get one picture of the sailfish in the air, but at this distance it was hard to tell how big the fish really was.*

"Right now, it's too close to call," he said, "but I'd have to give the edge to the fish."

"Rusty, what's your longest fish fight?"

"Two hours and forty-five minutes. A sailfish on 12-pound test—we lost it!"

Wonderful. Fishing with Rusty was just great. He really knew how to build up your ego and fortify your confidence. The thought of wrestling with this fish for another hour and forty-five minutes was not a pleasing one, especially since I was still getting over the flu.

An hour turned into two hours, following the pattern that had been set early on. The sail continually dove deep while I applied pressure, lifting up and reeling down to retrieve line against a fish that had no doubt spread his fanlike dorsal fin and turned sideways into the strong northern current.

The sun was beginning to set, and when we looked around, we realized that we were the only boat still out there. Mindy called on the cellular phone to find out where we were, and Rusty told her of the fight in progress. It was to be the first of several calls as this warm January afternoon cooled into an offshore evening. As the sun disappeared, I became aware that I had soaked through my long-sleeved T-shirt.

Rusty, on the bridge, was staying very active during the battle, trying a number of maneuvers to keep this fish from spooling us. We tried circling around the sail in both directions, hoping he might get confused or disoriented. The classic offshore move of backing down on the fish seemed to be our least successful maneuver. No matter how fast we backed up, with me reeling as quickly as I could, the fish still seemed able to take line and rest as well.

Perhaps our most effective ploy was to circle wide away from the fish. This brought him closer to the surface and gave me a chance to take in some major lineage.

By 6:30 p.m., the brilliant colors of sunset had given way to a pitch-black night punctuated by the light of what seemed like every star in the solar system. The second-quarter moon had yet to rise, and the cool night air would have made for some world-class stargazing if we had not been otherwise engaged. I thought of another Hemingway quote from *The Old Man and the Sea*: "The fish is my friend, too. I've never seen or heard of such a fish. But I must kill him. I am glad we do not have to try to kill the stars." I did glance up at my favorite constellation, Orion—the Hunter—and thought how

## Fish #1: The Sailfish

appropriate its visage was as this hunt continued. Rusty had turned on our red and green navigational lights and then added our spreader lights as a precaution in case any boats were in the vicinity.

After almost three hours, the tide of battle was turning. While the fish was still running deep, his dives didn't have nearly the speed or power and took far less line than earlier. I could also feel him shaking his head again. Our biggest problem now was seeing which way the line was going and trying to react accordingly. As if sensing our difficulty, the big fish started diving in different directions and almost crisscrossing under the boat, making it impossible for Rusty to keep me pointed at him.

It was then that I appreciated how lucky I was that the fish had chosen to eat the balao on the line connected to one of the 8-foot rods. We had originally bought these to be able to hold them high and avoid our line snagging the mangroves when fighting large Islamorada bonefish on the flats. As this sailfish blasted under the boat, I discovered that I could bend over the gunwale, reach down, and put the entire length of the rod in the water so that the line cleared the keel and the engines until Rusty could get the fish back in front of me. It was a pretty good maneuver, born of necessity. I'm sure the salt water wasn't doing the reel any good, but we could clean it later. The fish actually went under the boat twelve times, causing me to go into the rail position and get a head dip each time. If it hadn't been dark, I probably wouldn't have had to stick my rod, reel, hands, arms, and head over the rail into the ocean.

The great fish was now fighting closer and closer to the surface. At 7:10 p.m. he came up halfway out of water, twenty feet behind the boat in the eerie glow of the spreader lights, and shook his head twice to free himself of the hook firmly embedded in the base of his bill. Rusty and I both saw him. He was huge, well over the required 57 inches. Without saying anything, Rusty grabbed the gaff as I gathered in twenty feet of line on the reel. I thought of a third Hemingway line from *The Old Man and the Sea*: "Fish, I love you and respect you, but I will kill you dead before this ends."

I knew it was over. I could tell by that last exhausted half jump. The fish followed the pressure right to the side of the boat. I lifted the rod and stepped back to give Rusty room to gaff the fish. Even after all this, the fish lunged away when he felt the sharp steel bite of the gaff, half pulling Rusty over the rail. Rusty dug his knees into the side of the boat, and using both arms and all his strength, yanked the gaff and the sailfish into the cockpit.

Both Rusty and I sat down on our large cooler, as if someone had knocked our legs out from under us, neither of us saying a word. It was 7:15 p.m. The sailfish, Rusty, and I had been locked in a battle for three and a half hours, and now it was over. There was no turning back. The fish was gaffed, and the gaff had apparently hit an artery, causing dark red blood to gush onto the white decking of the cockpit. On this boat, surrounded by darkness, there were no victorious shouts of joy or macho chest poundings, only the quiet relief at the end of the fight and a sad respect for a great adversary that had never given up.

As this fish died on our deck, I knew that all tournaments, including the Met, must give up requirements that cause anglers to kill fish and that I must become part of that fight as well. Tournaments, like anglers' attitudes, had to change or be boycotted.

Rusty got a flashlight and a tape measure from under the

*Fish #1: The Sailfish*

*The sailfish measured 81 inches from the end of his bill to the fork of his tail.*

console. The great black fish measured 64 inches from the fork of his tail to his lower lip (81 inches to the end of his bill), which was 7 inches longer than required. We guessed that he weighed more than 60 pounds, but after the fight and the loss of blood by gaffing, we knew we'd never know for sure. Also, it was so late that the Met check stations would all be closed, so we would have to wait until the next day for official measurement. By then we knew that he would have lost several pounds through dehydration.

After calling Mindy to tell her the news and to see if she wanted to meet us at the marina, we started our quiet ride home. Rusty drove from the bridge, with me sitting on the cooler on the deck, alternately keeping vigil beside the dead sailfish and doing some stargazing. It probably would have been a great night for profound thoughts interspersed with some major guilt if I hadn't been so tired. The adrenaline had stopped flowing, and I realized that I was soaking wet and shaking like a leaf. Every muscle in my body was exhausted. I wondered what other adventures I would encounter in my Met quest and hoped that they might not be quite so draining.

After stowing our tackle and washing down the boat, we put the sailfish on the bed of Rusty's pickup truck and covered it with ice and a canvas tarp to preserve it until the Miami Met check station opened in the morning.

The next day we took the fish over to Islamorada Bait and Tackle, where we were met by shop owner John Preast and Lee Baker, who measured the fish and wrote up the Met entry form. Lee and I talked about ways to measure fish without having to kill them for the tournament. He told us that the tournament committee had recently approved the use of Boga grip handheld scales as long as they had been certified by the IGFA. Unfortunately, these Boga grips came in only two sizes, measuring up to 30- or 60-pound maximum weights, but they would certainly help us with the smaller fish. There was one catch—you had to be standing on land to weigh your fish. In the case of many of the backcountry fish, I was sure we'd be able to find a sand flat that would allow us to stand while we weighed the fish before releasing it. Met Hall of Fame entries still had to be weighed at entry stations, however.

The official scale at the Islamorada Bait and Tackle Shop showed that our sailfish weighed in at 53 pounds. Rusty and I told Lee that we had originally estimated the fish at 60 pounds, and Lee said that with the loss of blood and the natural dehydration, the fish could have weighed more than 60 pounds when we'd boated him the night before.

*Fish #1: The Sailfish*

*The end of a long day on the water for a sick angler.*

After registering our catch and turning in thirty feet of line to accompany the application for strength testing, we took the fish back to Max's, where Rusty filleted him on a waterside filleting table. We cut open the fish's stomach to see what he had been eating and found that balao had in fact been the *bait du jour*, at least for this particular fish. We found three other balao in his stomach, at least one of which, judging by its decomposition rate, appeared to have been consumed about the same time that our bait was taken.

Our third stop of the day was the Caloosa Cove Marina to order our sailfish mount. As catch and release has become more and more popular, the people who do fish mounts have had to adapt to survive. In the old days, when I was a boy, taxidermists would take the whole fish, gut it, and mount it by applying several coats of lacquer over the actual skin of the fish to preserve it. These were called skin mounts, and the procedure was costly and quite time-consuming.

*Catching Big Fish*

*Rusty and I watched the weigh-in of our sailfish at Islamorada Bait & Tackle.*

## Fish #1: The Sailfish

The art evolved, with only parts of the fish such as bills, tails, and dorsal fins used to create the reproductions. The waiting period, as well as the cost, escalated as the number of fish parts used seemed to decline.

Today, mounting fish has become a very different business. Now all you have to do is write down a description of the fish's length and girth, and the mounters do the rest. Their products, predominantly made of fiberglass and plastic, are lifelike, colorful, and stand up very well against the old skin mounts, which deteriorate rather quickly. Unfortunately, the time and cost have again escalated. In our case, we were told that it would take a minimum of ten weeks and that the cost would be $800. I shouldn't complain, though. Mounting a fish from memory and a mold as opposed to requiring the real fish certainly helps catch and release, and I suppose the increased wait time and dollars preserve the mystique of great craftsmanship going into the final objet d'art. It strikes me that an entrepreneur could offer up "fish mounts while you wait," although it certainly would lose some of its glamour.

On the subject of the price of mounting, fishing guides are remunerated, and generally receive half of the deposit, which is usually 50 percent of the price of the mount. In other words, if a mount cost $800, the marina will require a down payment of $400, of which $200 will go to the guide. I have no quarrel with that as long as the guide reveals to his angler that the fish can be released and not killed.

This is mostly the case in Islamorada, although I have fished elsewhere where the guides will try to sucker novice anglers into killing and mounting as many fish as they can. This practice is reprehensible, and I'm glad that it is not in vogue in the Keys. I'm all for my guide pals like Dave Borras, who refused to fish people who wanted to kill species like bonefish.

Our next stop was to drop off the fish fillets with Jeffrey Ekblom, Rusty's cousin, for smoking. He smoked all kinds of fish and meat and made flavorful jerky in his backyard smoker. His neighbors called his house Camp Buttonwood, and Jeffrey held court there every Sunday, serving up delicious samples and cold beer, along with homespun philosophy. Jeffrey's wife, Lenora, told us to come back on Sunday to join the fun. His only charge was 25 percent of the catch or kill, depending on whether it was fish or fowl.

With one species down and nine to go, it was time to move on to the next challenge. I had a nice talk with Suzan Baker, who informed me that the Met's rules committee had agreed that tarpon for the Met Hall of Fame could be qualified by submitting length and girth measurements, preferably accompanied by a photograph as opposed to weighing the fish at a check station.

This was great news for all catch and release anglers as well as, of course, the tarpon. When I asked Sue if my pending book had anything to do with the decision, she said, "Of course, but it is an obvious decision that was timely." I was proud of my role in influencing the Met and proud of them for making a good course change. Maybe I should have become a lobbyist. Seriously, I sincerely felt that going to catch and release on all species would be a realistic goal. At any rate, I felt a lot better about going full speed ahead on my tarpon hunt.

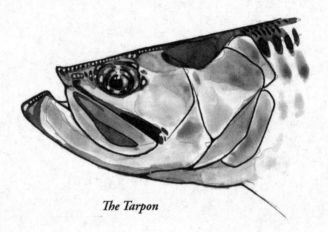
*The Tarpon*

CHAPTER 4

# FISH #2
# The Tarpon

*Suddenly the strike came . . . so quick, fierce,
bewildering that I could think of nothing but to hold on.
Then the water split with a hissing sound to let out a great tarpon,
long as a door, seemingly as wide, who shot up and up into the air.
He wagged his head and shook it like a struggling wolf.
When he fell back with a heavy splash, a rainbow, exquisitely beautiful
and delicate, stood out of the spray, glowed, paled and faded.*

—Zane Grey, "Byme-by-Tarpon," *Field & Stream* (December 1907)

---

Tarpon, or silver kings, as they are respectfully known, usually range in size from 10 to 120 pounds of pure, scaly silver power. They attract anglers from all over the world to their habitat, which seems to run from the Gulf of Mexico and the southern Atlantic Coast of the United States south to Costa Rica. A 125-pound fish is a noteworthy catch. The world record is shared by two 283-pounders, one caught in Lake Maracaibo, Venezuela, in 1956 by Mario Salazar; the other caught off Sherbro Island, Sierra Leone, in 1991 by Yvon Victor Sebag.

As tarpon have no commercial value, little research money has been spent on understanding these incredible fighting fish. Most information on their migration and spawning habits is no more than speculation.

In 1997 a group of concerned anglers came together to form the Bonefish & Tarpon Trust (BTT), a not-for-profit, science-based organization that gathered much-needed data, which would lead to knowledge about and protection of tarpon, bonefish, and permit. Their objective was to improve the long-range health and sustainability of the species.

Before then, what tarpon lacked in research, they had to make up for in public relations. These prolific creatures, believed to be prehistoric, are fished from bridges, piers, big boats, and small boats, with anglers using just about every imaginable bait—from dead fish to crabs, large lures to small flies.

Tarpon, *Megalops atlanticus*, are generally silver in color and are easily distinguished by their large, layered scales and unique low-slung jaw, which hinges up to give the fish an extremely large mouth. They will grow to well over 4 feet in about twelve years. Marine biologists have estimated 150-pound tarpon to be almost fifty years old!

Tarpon, especially those hooked on the flats, are perhaps the most spectacular leapers in the gamefish kingdom and will spend

*Fish #2: The Tarpon*

as much of their time out of water as in. Many anglers engage these fish just to see them jump before they pull hooks or break off. It is just as well that people are satisfied with this aerial display, because most of the time that's about all you get. You see, a tarpon's mouth is all bone—he has no teeth. Rusty's dad likened trying to set a hook into a tarpon's mouth to trying to snag a hook on the porcelain inside a toilet bowl. While it may not be a very appealing analogy, I think it's accurate.

The best luck I've had hooking tarpon is by trying to wait until they turn 90 degrees from me. This gives me the chance to set the hook in the softer tissue surrounding the hinge on the lower jaw. Even then it's tough. Tarpon explode out of the water when they feel a hook, spitting it immediately or breaking the line. It is not at all uncommon to lose twelve fish before you get one solid hookup.

Even after a good hookup, a catch is far from assured. Tarpon are fierce fighters that won't give an angler a minute to rest. Long tarpon battle stories are legendary, and everyone has one. My favorite is from an old pal of mine, Ron Offhaus, who went fishing for tarpon one afternoon while he was attending a grocery industry convention in Boca Raton. Ron was a bulldog of a man who had been a pretty good athlete in his youth. Fishing with a guide and a pal in an 18-foot skiff, Ron hooked up at about 3:45 p.m. with a silver king estimated at more than 150 pounds.

When Ron failed to return to his convention hotel by 7:00 p.m., his nervous wife called the Coast Guard, which was eventually able to locate the boat. The fight was still in progress. At about 9:30 p.m. the big fish broke Ron's graphite spinning rod about one foot from the reel. Then the reel seized up forty-five minutes later, causing Ron to try to handline the giant to the boat.

At 10:30 p.m., with both hands bleeding, Ron managed to pull the tired fish up to the side of the boat. As the guide reached over to lip-gaff the fish, it thrust forward in one last effort to escape, then rolled over on its side. As it did so, one of its large 3-inch scales cut the monofilament, and the big fish slowly swam away. Ron's friend and guide had all they could do to keep their tired angler from jumping out of the boat to try and wrestle his fish back.

After a battle of six hours and forty-five minutes, that fish found freedom ten and a half miles from where he had been hooked. Ron never told me about this fight. He would merely shake his head as his friend and guide filled in the details.

While tarpon have been caught as far north as New England, they are mainly known as southern-clime battlers. Rumors have spread of many large tarpon being seen off the coast of Africa. Every saltwater fly fisherman dreams of catching his 200-pounder, and many believe that Africa is the place to go do that. My pal Johnny Morris, the founder of Bass Pro Shops, had planned a trip there one spring with the legendary globetrotting angler Billy Pate. Unfortunately, the trip had to be canceled due to unrest in the area.

While you can catch tarpon year-round in the warm blue waters surrounding Islamorada, the big show takes place in May and June. This is when the giant fish converge on the area like the college kids drawn to Joe Roth's Holiday Isle—now called the Three Waters Resort and Marina—a few months earlier by the same urges, and by that, I don't mean drinking beer.

### Fish #2: The Tarpon

Tarpon come to our area from the gentle waters of the Gulf of Mexico, as well as the depths of the windswept Atlantic Ocean, to engage in the annual prehistoric spawning rites that regenerate their species. On a calm morning, it is not uncommon to see dozens of fish "daisy-chaining," or swimming in tightly knit circles, with the males fertilizing the discharge of egg-laden females. BTT biologists say that ripe females will lay as many as one thousand eggs.

While these fish are totally preoccupied, they will stop momentarily to snack on pinfish, mullet, crabs, and shrimp as well as lures or small flies stripped in front of their large underslung jaws. Their favorite food is the palolo worm, which hatches every year in the waters of the southern Keys on low-falling tides during a new moon. According to local guide Craig Brewer, this hatch is an amazing phenomenon. It generally starts in the evening when small worms emerge from the bottom of the offshore shallows and ride the falling tide out to sea. It is then that they are intercepted by the hungry spawning tarpon. These worms are thought to be an aphrodisiac and may fuel the passion of the tarpon spawn. Whether that's true or not, these large fish lose all perspective when the hatch begins. Their usual wariness disappears, and it is not uncommon to see them bouncing off skiffs as they clamor to suck down as many palolo worms as possible. It is also amazing to me that these huge fish, which grow to more than 200 pounds, will stop to scarf up small feather flies. It speaks volumes about their incredible eyesight.

The tarpon's frenetic energy during the spawning months of May and June is matched only by that of visiting anglers who flock to the Keys from around the world. The Keys' hoteliers are in heaven, not to mention the area guides, whose schedule books are filled months in advance.

As April 1998 gave way to May, I got serious about my search for a 100-pound tarpon. I fished six days with Rusty and one each with Craig Brewer, Lee Baker, and Sandy Moret's son Andrew, an excellent young guide. In spite of the unusual 20 mph winds, which were an almost daily spring nuisance to fly fishermen, we were able to catch and release several large tarpon, none of which made the stick.

The largest fish that I had up to the boat was a "guessed to be" 115-pounder that I'd hooked in The Pocket when I was fishing with Captain Craig. This big fish was exceptionally athletic and spit our hook after a nice double-jump maneuver half an hour into our fight.

Rusty and I had some long, tough days in search of the elusive silver kings. We tried all the classic Islamorada tarpon spots with varying degrees of success: The Pocket, the point at Buchanan, Ninemile Bank, Rabbit Key Basin, First National Bank, Lignum-Vitae, Palm Lake, and, of course, offshore in the ocean in spots such as Whale Harbor and Caloosa Cove. We also did some good exploring around Ox Foot, Schooner, and Rocky Channel. (The only reason I didn't like fishing the latter place early in the day was that it always got the Conch singing, whistling, or humming the Beatles song "Rocky Raccoon," which got a little tedious.)

A good angler in her own right, Mindy joined us on one of our outings, and I was lucky to put a large tarpon in the air.

We hooked this fish at First National after an early stop at Rocky Channel. It was sweltering hot, and I put a bandanna over my head for some shade. After an hour-and-a-half tussle, with Rusty and

*Fish #2: The Tarpon*

# Tarpon Girth to Weight Correlation

| Girth in Inches | Pounds | Girth in Inches | Pounds |
| --- | --- | --- | --- |
| 27 | 58 | 35¼ | 110 |
| 27¼ | 59½ | 35½ | 112 |
| 27½ | 61 | 35¾ | 114 |
| 27¾ | 62½ | 36 | 116 |
| 28 | 64 | 36¼ | 118 |
| 28¼ | 65½ | 36½ | 120 |
| 28½ | 67 | 36¾ | 122 |
| 28¾ | 68½ | 37 | 124 |
| 29 | 70 | 37¼ | 126 |
| 29¼ | 71½ | 37½ | 128 |
| 29½ | 73 | 37¾ | 130 |
| 29¾ | 74½ | 38 | 132 |
| 30 | 76 | 38¼ | 134 |
| 30¼ | 77½ | 38½ | 136 |
| 30½ | 79 | 38¾ | 138 |
| 30¾ | 80½ | 39 | 140 |
| 31 | 82 | 39¼ | 142½ |
| 31¼ | 82½ | 39½ | 145 |
| 31½ | 85 | 39¾ | 147½ |
| 31¾ | 86½ | 40 | 150 |
| 32 | 88 | 40¼ | 152½ |
| 32¼ | 89½ | 40½ | 155 |
| 32½ | 91 | 40¾ | 157½ |
| 32¾ | 92½ | 41 | 160 |
| 33 | 94 | 41¼ | 162½ |
| 33¼ | 95½ | 41½ | 165 |
| 33½ | 97 | 41¾ | 167½ |
| 33¾ | 98½ | 42 | 170 |
| 34 | 100 | 42¼ | 172½ |
| 34¼ | 102 | 42½ | 175 |
| 34½ | 104 | 42¾ | 177½ |
| 34¾ | 106 | 43 | 180 |
| 35 | 108 | 43¼ | !! |

*This chart is more a rule of thumb and not as accurate as the formula that factors in length as well as girth: $Girth^2 \times Length \div 800$.*

Mindy now singing a duet of "Rocky Raccoon," I brought the fish to the boat so that Rusty could lip-gaff him and haul him over the gunwale for girthing, photographing, and releasing.

We knew it was going be close, and it was. The tarpon's girth measured 33 inches, which meant that he weighed about 94 pounds—6 pounds too light. Rusty released the fish, and I slumped into a seat, tired and soaking wet from my battle in the hot sun.

Feeling sorry for myself, I thought of Zane Grey's reaction to losing a giant marlin after a five-hour fight. He wrote about losing his fish in *Tales of Fishing Virgin Seas*: "Whereupon I fell down in the cockpit and lay there, all in an instant utterly prostrated. When I recovered somewhat and sat up I found I was suffering in many ways—nausea, dizziness, excessive heat and labored breathing, stinging swollen hands and a terrible oppression in my breast. My arms were numb."

"What are you moping about?" Mindy asked as my fish swam slowly away.

"Are you two sure he wasn't big enough?" I begged.

"Yeah, I'm sure," said Rusty.

"Me too," Mindy joined in.

As my two fishin' pals broke into another chorus of "Rocky Raccoon," I wondered if honesty was, in fact, its own reward. I would find out the answer to that a few weeks later when fishing with my best pal in the Keys.

Gary Ellis and I started fishing together on Memorial Day weekend in 1975. He loved fishing for big spring tarpon with a fly rod as much as I did, and he was really good at it. He would say that it was sexual. I don't know if I'd go that far, but it is a rush. We fished

*Fish #2: The Tarpon*

*Gary Ellis looks back.*

*I fought a big tarpon at First National Bank on a very hot day.*

together many times over the next five years, mostly in Islamorada but also up the coast in Homosassa, where we caught some huge tarpon with 12-weight fly rods.

By 1980 the Florida Keys were changing. Drugs were everywhere. Some of the guides had become part of the supply chain.

I could see what was coming and stopped going to the Keys in 1981. Gary and I drifted apart. Our only correspondence consisted of Christmas cards.

During that time, I met and married Mindy. Gary, in the meantime, married his girlfriend, Susy Sheppard. Together they had a daughter. Soon after Nicole was born, she was diagnosed with cystic fibrosis, a deadly disease that greatly shortens the lives of its victims.

Gary and Susy were devastated but came out swinging. Wanting to help find a cure, they dreamed up the most unique idea: a charity event to benefit the cause to find a cure for cystic fibrosis. Their event would be a celebrity fishing tournament in the Keys, where the winner was the one who caught and released the most redfish and bonefish. Mindy and I now had a good reason to start visiting the Keys again. We were excited to help raise money for a good cause, especially now that the authorities had successfully helped end the area's drug epidemic.

Gary and I started fishing together again as if nothing had ever happened. The Ellis's Redbone Tournament was wildly successful, and children like Nicole who were afflicted with the disease were thriving. Mindy and I were proud that Gary and Susy had called on us to help grow the tourney into a series of tournaments around the country.

## Fish #2: The Tarpon

When Gary called me on May 13, he asked how my Met quest was coming along and wondered if I wanted to go tarpon fishing with him the next day. I told him I had some work to do around the house (shore duty). Gary said he was booked, but if I wanted to do some predawn fishing, we had a good tide for a favorite spot of his and could fish between 4:00 and 8:00 a.m.

I got up at 3:30 a.m. the next day and met Gary at his slip at the Lorelei. I brought two fly rods—a 12-weight and an 11-weight—while Gary brought a 12-weight with a Sea Master reel rigged with a clear sinking line, affectionately known as a slime line, for dredging. This is a method used for blind casting in deeper channels. You throw your line upstream and let the fly swing downcurrent. Once you have a good bend in the fly line, you retrieve it in short strips. The bite often occurs when the line straightens out. I think it's because fish watch the fly and then grab it when they think it's going away from them.

Many anglers decry the monotony of dredging, calling it "dredgery," but I call it smart tactics. About 90 percent of the tarpon fly tournaments are won by anglers who invest at least part of their time blind casting and dredging with a sinking line. Also, many times, a tarpon will roll, giving you a sight cast as well. I guess you'd call that "semi-dredgery."

So after two cups of coffee, Captain Gary Ellis and I headed out of the Lorelei Basin with Gary intermittently flashing his big million-candlepower Q-Beam at channel markers to keep us on course. Actually, we barely needed the spotlight. It was a beautifully clear night, complete with a full moon, lots of stars, and a gentle 5 mph breeze out of the northeast. We turned left and headed south down the shoreline of Upper and Lower Matecumbe Keys, reminiscing about the early morning starts in Homosassa twenty-three years before.

Gary zipped through a twenty-five-foot wide, quarter-mile-long channel called Bucky Stark's Wheel Ditch, which was cut through the mangroves, their branches overhanging to create a cathedral-like ceiling. All of a sudden, we blasted out the other end, as if we'd been shot from a cannon into the open night under a high ceiling of brilliant stars, halfway through our twelve-mile trip to Channel Five, separating Craig Key from Long Key.

"Not bad, Gary, but twenty years ago, you would have taken that channel a lot faster."

"Twenty years ago, I took everything a lot faster," he said, laughing.

We sped by Channel Two. In the moonlight, I was able to make out the massive concrete foundations of the old Flagler railroad bridge where, fishing with Gary and another friend, Robert Buck, I had caught my first tarpon and permit, and Mindy had caught her first permit twelve years later. This night held some great memories, I thought, as Gary cut his big Mercury engine, stuck the pointed end of his push pole into the mud, and tied a line from the stern to the pole.

"Where are we, Gary?"

"It's called Desperation Point."

"Appropriate," I said, and we both laughed.

If you've never done any night fishing, you should. Darkness amplifies all the sounds of the night, and if there are tarpon around, the volume and frequency is incredible. When we first shut down

## Fish #2: The Tarpon

the engine, it was so still you could almost hear your own heartbeat. Then, as if used to our presence, the tarpon started rolling all around us. We could hear them gulping air to fill their airbags or slurping up small surface baits. Occasionally the sounds were punctuated by the explosion of free-jumping tarpon as they crashed back into the depths of the channel. It sounded as if someone were dropping Volkswagens into the water from the Channel Five bridge.

Gary handed me my 12-weight Loomis and Sea Master reel with sinking fly line attached to a large black fly called Tarpon Drudgery. Don't ask me how tarpon see flies at night, let alone black flies. I think it's a combination of sight and feel, as the fly interrupts the current of the water that is pushing by them. I stripped out some line and went to work. Talk about blind casting! In spite of the full moon, it was so dark I couldn't even see the fly line in the air. I had to concentrate on feeling the pressure on the tip to know I had the rod "loaded," creating a good, tight loop in the line. Actually, it wasn't that tough; I have often practiced casting flies with my eyes closed. It makes you try to feel the rod tip and keeps you from making the classic mistake of overworking your rod. Try it, you'll like it.

For the first twenty minutes, I had limited success. I was throwing line on both sides of the boat as the big full moon falling tide rushed by us toward the bridge. The next forty minutes produced two good bumps, but I was unable to come tight on the fish.

It was 5:30 a.m. as Gary repositioned his 17-foot Action Craft about twenty-five feet to the west. He suggested I try dredging with slime line to get the fly deeper. He also recommended that I try to let the line sweep more before retrieving it: "Get a good bend in the line, then try some sharp, short strips to flare the fly."

On my second throw, I jumped a monster. He hit the fly and came straight out of the water. He looked like a 130-pounder. Gary and I gasped in unison as the fish's silver scales shimmered in the moonlight. He was awesome. He jumped again and then ran, pulling line off the deck and onto the reel. Then he was gone. Just like that. Like a ghost leaving us transfixed in the darkness, wondering how he'd freed himself.

Now we two old friends were focused. The joking and kibitzing stopped. I threw line as Gary watched, both of us in silence, feeling that something was about to happen. At ten minutes to six, a large fish rolled about sixty feet from us in my ten o'clock position, moseying left to right against the falling tide. Glad I had just collected my line, I made one false cast before laying down the fly six feet in front of him.

"Great shot! Perfect!" Gary whispered as the line swung on the big fish.

I held my breath, and I knew that Gary was doing the same. *One-a-thousand, two-a-thousand . . . Bang!* The bowed line tightened. Holding the rod in my right hand, I tightened my grip on the fly line in my left, not striking, just holding on for as long as I could to allow this fish to set the hook himself. The fly line burned my thumb and fingers until I had to let go. There was no line on the deck. This fish was on the reel and headed inshore toward the backcountry. The only sound was the taut line skimming through the water. The bow of the boat swung around and pointed toward the hooked fish running against the falling tide.

He was pulling line off the reel—50 yards, 100 yards, 150 yards, driving through the channel below the moonlit surface, deep

## Fish #2: The Tarpon

and deeper, nothing on the surface, no aerial displays—no jumps at all.

Gary and I knew that was a good sign. Some of the heaviest tarpon stay in the water. Of course, there is always that sinking suspicion before you visually ID a tarpon that it is another species. This could have been a large shark, for example. Granted, feather flies give off no scent to attract their keen olfactory senses, but sharks have been known to strike artificials, especially when bounced off their noses.

This fish was trucking. He was headed inshore and had dumped about 250 yards of backing when Gary pulled his push pole and fired up the motor to give chase. Standing on the bow angler's platform, I was able to gather about half of the line. Then I felt the line start to rise.

"He's coming up, Gary! Hit the Q-Beam!" I yelled.

Gary was way ahead of me. He flipped on his portable spotlight just in time for us to see the tarpon's unmistakable broad silver-green back as he did a slow roll in front of us, whalelike, as if the pressure on the side of his mouth were a mere inconvenience.

"That's him!" Gary blurted out, letting out the breath that he, like I, had been holding.

Our fish, now almost nonplussed, slowed down and kept heading west. It was still dark, but the sky was brightening to the point that we could soon follow the fish without the Q-Beam.

This went on for about half an hour. Gary killed the engine while I lowered the rod at an angle to the fleeing fish, trying to make him not only pull the boat but turn the bow as well in order to tire him.

Every time we got to within twenty feet of him, he would surface for a breath of air and dive again, taking a hundred feet of line with him. I pressured the line with my fingers as much as I dared without risking breaking him off.

At first light, around 7:00 a.m., an hour and ten minutes after we had hooked the fish, two boats pulled up. Guides Ricky Miller and Tad Burke knew about my quest and slid in next to us with their parties to check out the scene, offer advice and counsel, and tell a few jokes as well. Ricky and Tad had put their anglers on some big Channel Five tarpon and were now heading for other spots as the falling tide began to slow. As that happened, our fish changed direction and swam right past our boat, headed for the ocean.

"We didn't need this," Gary said. "I was hoping he'd stay inside where he had less depth to maneuver."

Ricky saw the fish's change in tactics also. We thought we heard him say something about "a long morning for the over-the-hill gang."

"Hey," Gary laughed, "since when is tarpon fishing a spectator sport?"

Tad, who was one-quarter Native American, picked up on it quickly and yelled over, "Water bad, buffalo leave, we go. And by the way, it looks like you two brave old warriors are headed for the big waters."

We all laughed. They fired up their engines and headed west as our quarry towed us east toward the Atlantic.

Gary and I knew the pending problems. We had to get close to the fish for our trip under the concrete bridge, and we were hoping that he would stay away from the cement abutments as well as the underwater pilings supporting the adjacent high-tension poles.

The fish was twenty-five feet from the bridge when the reel fell off the rod. That's right—it fell right off. There I was, my prize in sight, my rod in one hand, and my reel in the other.

"I can't touch it!" Gary yelled, knowing that our catch would be disqualified if anyone else touched my rod, reel, or line.

"It's OK, Gary," I said optimistically. "Just try to keep close to him with some gentle boat pressure. I'll try to get it back together after we clear the bridge."

As we passed under the span, I looked east. "Pretty sunrise, Captain."

"It'll be a lot prettier when we get away from the bridge and you get the reel back on."

The ring screws on the rod were locked up. I was barely able to wedge the reel on, but I did. In the meantime, the fish had taken a left and was swimming along parallel to us, about twenty feet from the pilings.

"We're screwed," Gary commented. "The tide's dying and he's getting a second breath. Lean on him."

I did, and the fish slowly followed the boat as it slipped sideways out to sea. There is only one thing harder to catch than a tarpon in a channel and that's a tarpon in the ocean, where he can dive deep and find sea fans and other outgrowths to break a line. Tarpon on the flats are easier because they have to fight on a horizontal plane, close to the surface, where an angler can gather line. On this day, however, Gary and I were happy to take our chances in the ocean away from that barnacle-encrusted bridge which would cut a line in a heartbeat.

Pulled away from the bridge by my pressure and aided by the

weight of the boat in the weakening falling tide, the fish headed out the channel.

"Thank goodness, Gary, now we can relax a bit."

"Not so fast, Bubba. He's headed for one of those crab traps on the edge of the bank."

Crabbers often set their large, rectangular wooden traps along channel edges, attaching ropes to round, plastic foam-marker buoys painted in their own patterns for easy identification. Our local fish seemed to be schooled from birth to swim around these ropes when hooked, to break the lines.

Little did this fish realize the collective experience he was up against—or, should I say, how many fish Gary and I had lost to this trick. Without saying anything, Gary fired up his engine and I grabbed his fillet knife. We beat the fish to the trap line, which I grabbed and cut as the fish swam by. The marker was painted blue and gold, colors belonging to Richie Russell, who put out some traps every year to supplement his income as athletic director and baseball coach of local Coral Shores High School. I made a mental note to call him and apologize when we got back.

Gary and I were congratulating each other on our slick move when his cell phone rang.

"Who the hell is that?" I asked.

"It's the local radio station. I've got to do my live 8:00 a.m. radio spot, 'Catch of the Day.' I'll talk about this great fight in progress."

"Oh, fine, Gary. NBC has the last episode of *Seinfeld* tonight. ESPN has game four of the Montreal Canadiens–Buffalo Sabres NHL playoffs, and Catch 100 FM is going to carry a fish fight. You

Fish #2: The Tarpon

*Captain Richie Russell shows off a nice Florida lobster.*

and I will make history—the first live-action, play-by-play coverage of a battle between a man and a tarpon. I hope they have a tape delay to bleep me out if we lose this guy."

We both laughed as Gary started his show. He told his listeners about our fight, targeted our location, and even gave his opinion on who was winning, pointing out how wet I was and even commenting on the color of my shirt, like a radio announcer describing to his viewers what color trunks each boxer is wearing.

I whispered to him, "Why don't you just say I'm the shirts and the fish is the skins?"

Then Gary asked, "Bob, how about a quote for our listeners?"

"Fine, Gary, but why don't you interview the tarpon first?"

By this time, we were both roaring. As the "Catch of the Day" segment ended, the reel fell off again. This time I couldn't jam it back on. Something was bent.

"Gary, quick—hand me some strong monofilament. I've got to try to tie this reel back on." I had to loosen the drag to do this. I knew it was giving the fighter in the silver trunks a chance to rest, but I had no choice. I put the rod between my knees and cinched up a couple of figure-eight knots around the reel seat and the rod's butt section.

We looked up to see the tarpon doing circles around another one of Richie's trap lines. Gary gunned it again and we cut another crab trap free, hoping we weren't too late. Luck was with us: The line sprang free, and the fish headed out to sea again.

My rod and reel repair job was holding up, allowing me to really burn the fish, putting low pressure over his back and making him turn the bow of our boat every time he ran.

The tarpon was now close to the boat and had started crisscrossing under us, making me run around the boat to keep from breaking him off on the trim tabs. Gary grabbed a lip gaff and prepared to boat the fish. This, by the way, is no small feat for a guide. Many anglers tell some wild stories about guides being pulled off their skiffs and dragged along for yards by large, gaffed tarpon—shades of Captain Ahab and Moby Dick.

Gary had no such problem this morning. At 8:20 a.m., two and a half hours after the hookup, I got the fish up to the boat, then

## Fish #2: The Tarpon

backed him up and rolled him over. The big fish was finally whipped. Gary got on his hands and knees, reached into the water, lip-gaffed the fish, and pulled him into the cockpit.

"Look at this," Gary said as he extracted the fly from the side of the tarpon's mouth. Our 15-pound test leader had worked its way through the bottom of the fish's gill and out the top, explaining why it had taken so long to land him. You see, any time a fish is foul hooked or hooked in a way that turns his head, as in this case, it takes away his hydrodynamics in the water, creates resistance, and makes it much more difficult to bring him to the boat. The line probably worked its way into the gill because the fish kept diving deep into the channel against my pressure instead of jumping.

Totally exhausted, the big fish lay motionless as Gary worked the line free of his gill and measured his girth at 36 inches and his length at 66 inches. (Our math, using the classic weight formula [girth x girth] x length ÷ 800, would later peg him at 108 pounds.) I grabbed a camera and took a couple of pictures of Gary and the fish before we lowered him carefully back into the water by the headpin in Channel Five, two and a half miles from where we'd hooked up. I started the motor and idled along as Gary held the exhausted fish next to the boat so that water poured through his mouth. After about twenty minutes of this, the big fish's tail started moving and he pulled away from Gary's grasp, turned around, and dove deep, headed for the bridge.

"How about that?" Gary said, giving me a big hug.

"Routine, Cappy, routine," I joked. "Never in doubt," I added as I felt the muscles in my left leg and right arm begin to cramp.

# Catching Big Fish

*Gary and my Met tarpon.*

## Fish #2: The Tarpon

Gary swung his boat around and headed for the Lorelei with both of us quietly thinking of the adventure we'd just shared—or maybe Gary was thinking of what he would tell the anglers who had booked him for an hour ago and would no doubt be standing impatiently on the Lorelei dock.

"Well, pal, you'll probably want me on 'Catch of the Day' tomorrow morning," I suggested.

"Gee, that would be great, Bob. Would you do it?"

"Forget it, Gary. I'm sleeping in."

That night, *Seinfeld* aired its final episode; the Sabres beat the Canadiens, 3–1, for a four-game playoff sweep; Ol' Blue Eyes, Frank Sinatra, died at age 82; and Marjory Stoneman Douglas, protector of the Florida Everglades, left us at age 108. It was she who wrote in her classic book *The Everglades: River of Grass*, "They are, they have always been, one of the unique regions of the earth, remote, never wholly known. Nothing anywhere else is like them." Change one word, *regions*, to *fish*, and she could have been talking about tarpon. I'm glad I didn't have to kill one that day, nor will other Met hopefuls have to in the future.

From now on, I'd just as soon trick a few tarpon into eating a fly, get a couple of jumps, and break them off. Busting a tarpon like we did that day seems a little pointless, but fish number two was in the books!

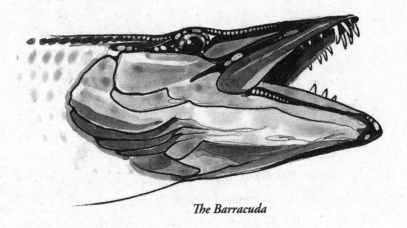
*The Barracuda*

CHAPTER 5

# FISH #3
# The Barracuda

*The truth is that the barracuda is among
the finest game fishes in the world.
Of course, it's a killer, but so is every other fish that swims;
a barracuda is only more efficient.*

—Erwin A. Bauer, *The Saltwater Fisherman's Bible*

---

I'VE NEVER LIKED barracuda. They're nasty looking, nasty smelling, and dangerous. OK, I know that they put up a great fight, and I've heard all the stories that if you don't bother them, they won't bother you, but I've seen their ferocity in attacking bait. I've also watched in helplessness as one cut a hooked bonefish in half, and another mutilated a yellowtail snapper that I needed to photograph for tournament points, disqualifying my catch.

I'll grant you that left alone on a flat or in the offshore shallows, they may be timid, but I maintain that a hooked 'cuda has obviously not been left alone, and is bothered, and is dangerous. Every year you'll hear a new batch of horror stories about hooked barracuda striking back. For example, there is a confirmed story about a hooked 'cuda that nearly killed a woman in Florida a few years ago. This was a large fish that actually jumped through the above-deck open window of a houseboat, slashing a woman on the shoulder and causing her to nearly bleed to death before she could be rushed to the hospital. The woman survived, but only after receiving more than a hundred stitches and a major blood transfusion.

I also remember fishing with Captain Tony Lay, one of the best fish catchers I know, but a guy who was a bit "out there." On the way home that day, Tony saw a huge barracuda, grabbed a rod, threw to the fish, and hooked him—while the boat was still going full speed! Tony handed the rod to my then twelve-year-old son, Barney, who was delighted. After Barney brought the fish alongside the boat, Tony reached down—barehanded, of course—grabbed the 20-pounder behind the gills with his left hand, reached into the fish's mouth, and retrieved his lure without the fish having time to react. But as Tony dropped the fish back into the water, a peculiar thing happened. You know how released fish, after a long fight, always dart away from the boat and at least seem to catch their breath before swimming off? Well, this fish did neither. As he sank back into the water, he seemed to channel all of his energy to leap upward and try to bite off Tony's hand. Fortunately, Tony was too quick and yanked his hand away from the fish just in time. With the ever-present cigarette still dangling

*Fish #3: The Barracuda*

*Tony Lay relaxing at the Lorelei.*

from his lips, he said to us coolly, "Wow, that was close." Such is the stuff of legends.

So I've developed a healthy respect for this most sinister-looking member of the *Sphyraenidae* family that heavily populates the boundary waters of the Met Tournament. Happily, there is an abundance of this species off the Baja and California coasts as well. The Pacific barracuda is a different species than its Atlantic namesake, however. The Pacific 'cuda is one of four species, all of which grow to be less than half the size of the great barracuda found in the Atlantic.

Barracuda, or great barracuda as they are also called, are unique. They are long and streamlined, predominantly silver with vertical black lines on their backs and some large, dark blotches on their posterior sections. Their mouths are full of long, sharp, pointed, almost canine-looking teeth.

Those found in deeper water (forty to ninety feet offshore) can range in size from 30 to 50 pounds, but a 25-pounder for the Met is no automatic catch, believe me. Even one of the 10-pounders that are prevalent in the Keys is an awesome-looking fish, especially when engaged on light tackle.

Despite all this, Bubba had a plan. I'd seen a lot of 'cuda hanging around the reefs, wrecks, and lights on the ocean side, off the shores of Islamorada, and I knew that these fish were suckers for baits such as pilchards, yellowtails, blue runners, and any other fish, large or small, that appeared to be injured. Those injured fish were part of my plan.

Before we went offshore in Islamorada, Rusty told me that he had an idea about how we could dispense with our 'cuda requirement. He said he knew where several large 'cuda lived in the backcountry. "Knew where they lived"—right, and he probably knew them by name if my theory was right and Rusty was part fish. He said these large fish get very territorial and live by themselves in certain channels, near wreckage, or under docks where the property owners feed them like pets. He told me that this catch would be a no-brainer.

We were coming back from a day of bonefishing in my skiff, a 16-foot Silver King with a poling platform and a forward-angling platform powered by a four-year-old Mariner 115. This boat may have been the best fishing acquisition I'd ever made. It went very

## Fish #3: The Barracuda

"skinny" in about eight inches of water, which is a prerequisite in the Keys for fishing tailing redfish on the flats unless you want to spend the night out there under the stars after the tide falls out. It also ran fast and was very stable when fishing. At that point, I'd had it for four years and could honestly say that I hadn't seen another flats skiff that I would trade it for.

Unlike the *Fish This!*, I had yet to come up with a suitable name for my skiff, although several had been suggested. As a rookie in the Keys, I used to ask some of my guide pals if I could follow them to Flamingo and back through the tricky passages of Florida Bay. I did this so often early on that Captain Gary Ellis suggested I call the boat *Bubbles*, as I was always in his wake.

After naming my offshore boat *Fish This!*, Captain Craig Brewer suggested naming the skiff *Bite Me!* Not a bad name, but Mindy opined that a double dose of bad taste might be a little much. So, the skiff was still nameless, but that was OK because nobody talked to one another in the backcountry anymore anyway.

That day, I stowed my fly rod, and Rusty produced a 5-foot Loomis and 1600 Daiwa from under the gunwale rigged with 8-pound Ande and wire leader. We started our search for a major-league barracuda.

I find it interesting that when 'cuda are young and smaller, they seem to school and hunt in packs. They are voracious eaters until they get older and larger, when they seem to become more insular and territorial and much more selective in their eating habits. I tested this theory on Rusty, who gave me one of his patented insights: "Well, they didn't get that big by being stupid." The Albury wisdom. Once again, short and never sweet.

We tried several spots that afternoon and met several single monsters, including one old codger that lived under a bayside dock and must have gone better than 40 pounds. That fish had been around so long that the residents had even named him—Mr. Snaggletooth.

This was not to be our 'cuda day. I threw everything I could think of at these fish, but the reaction was always the same: nothing. They all rejected pilchards, as well as every artificial lure I'd brought with me, including my old favorite neon-green tube lure. It's strange the way a bait that is so popular in one area can fail so badly in another.

As we headed home, we decided to save this part of my quest for an offshore adventure the next weekend, when my old college roommate Tommy Roe and his wife, Margaret, would be visiting us from Minnesota.

Saturday, February 15, dawned bright and clear, with a wind out of the northeast at 18 mph, gusting to 25 mph. Our crew gathered at the Islamorada Fish Company Restaurant and Bakery before the offshore search for Mr. 'Cuda. In addition to Rusty, Tom Roe (whom I'd nicknamed Earthquake, or EQ for short) and his wife, Margaret (whom I'd nicknamed Madge), were joined by my daughter, Kimberly. Before breakfast, noticing the wind on the flats, I suggested that the crew might want to take some precautionary seasickness pills, which everyone laughed off.

The expedition turned out to be an abbreviated disaster. The morning wind made catching bait impossible. When we finally netted some pilchards and headed to the reef, the unsettled ocean was rising and falling from three different directions.

Fish #3: The Barracuda

*Tommy and Margaret Roe compared the size of their snook.
I hate it when our wives do this to us.*

Every 'cuda-catching maneuver we tried seemed to put us broadside to a wave. After a couple of hours, I looked over at EQ, who had turned the same color green as the old Minnesota North Star hockey jerseys. The others didn't look much better.

I have a three-part theory on deep-sea fishing and seasickness: (1) For every five people on an offshore boat on even a moderately choppy day, at least one person will feel ill; (2) a great fishing day for four people at the expense of one who is seasick is not a worthwhile trade-off; and (3) at the first sign of seasickness, we return to shore.

And that's exactly what we did. For us, this was now standard practice when someone was feeling ill. Rusty kept his mouth shut when it happened, although his eyebrows told the story. I'm lucky I've never been seasick, but I don't think fishing is worth a ruined day for anyone. The Conch may or may not have agreed, but he respected my wishes.

Many believe the rough seas upset their stomachs—and the end result supports their theory. Actually, doctors tell us that seasickness is an inner ear problem caused by rolling seas throwing off a person's balance, which leads to nausea. I've heard of many recommended cures, including patches of an antihistamine called scopolamine stuck behind the ear as well as elastic bands worn around the wrists to hit pressure points. These measures may work for some. A number of friends swear by meclizine, a drug used in the popular over-the-counter Bonine pills. For years doctors have prescribed meclizine to treat vertigo and other inner ear problems. Having some food in your stomach helps, but in my experience, there is no absolute guarantee against seasickness. Just be careful what you eat and especially drink the night before.

*Fish #3: The Barracuda*

**My daughter, Kim, weathered a rough day to land her first blackfin tuna.**

We pulled into Bud N' Mary's Marina and dropped off Tommy along with Madge, who also admitted to feeling "a little queasiness." Kim decided to stay on board to witness "the big catch." As I slid the *Fish This!* into the channel and headed for Alligator Light, Rusty climbed up into the tower and stood next to me in silence. I couldn't resist. "Ready to go fishin', Everett?"

"What am I? A boat captain or a taxi driver?" he replied. I guess Rusty didn't endorse my seasickness policy.

The rest of the day was uneventful, although Kim did land a nice blackfin tuna. I was sorry we didn't get the 25-pound 'cuda that day. Kim had to go back to Buffalo the next day, and she had been looking forward to being part of this chapter. She was a gamer, but she'd have to wait for another day.

All hands were as good as new and ready for dinner at the Green Turtle, an iconic restaurant that we would purchase a few years later. The atmosphere there was dark and woody, with old fishing pictures adorning the walls. The food was good, and the entertainment was spectacular, with Tina Martin—known throughout the Keys as Tina Turtle—tickling the ivories and belting out songs from Elvis to Andrew Lloyd Webber in a beautiful alto voice. Very talented and resplendent in her many-colored, sequined cocktail dresses, Tina had become an Islamorada icon.

Turtle chowder with a splash of sherry was a must at the Green Turtle. Many of their other dishes were worth a try, but the consensus favorite was yellowtail snapper almondine.

Over coffee, EQ asked, "What time are we going offshore tomorrow?" I guess I shouldn't have been surprised. Tommy was a proud competitor, and he wasn't about to let his weekend fishing end on that day's bad note.

"Tommy, we don't have to," I said. However, his jaw was set and I knew we would be going 'cuda fishing the next day.

The next morning, Rusty and I got up early to get bait while EQ and the women went to breakfast. The plan was for us to call EQ when we had bait; he would then grab some lunches and join us. It didn't take long to fill our live well with bait, and then Rusty did a "guide thing"—one of those magic fishing tricks that leave us mere

*Fish #3: The Barracuda*

*The Green Turtle has been a popular Islamorada restaurant for many years.*

*Popular singer Tina Turtle shared the mic with young Nicole Ellis.*

mortals shaking our heads in disbelief.

We were cruising south on the inland waterway when Rusty said, "Stop!"

"What's wrong?" I asked.

"I see something," he remarked, looking up ahead.

"What?"

"Bird crashing bait, outside in the ocean."

I looked under the bridge. I could barely see the ocean, let alone a diving bird out there.

"Go to Indian Key and take a left," Rusty directed as he headed for the bow to get set up with his 10-foot cast net. Sure enough, there was a small pelican diving on bait. We idled up and in two throws and fifteen minutes, our live well was full of a few hundred razorbelly pilchards. As we sprayed down the deck, put away the net, and called EQ, I noticed that about twelve pelicans were now diving on the school of pilchards. I began to wonder if they had just joined the first pelican or if, in fact, they had been following Rusty.

We picked up EQ and headed north past Davis Reef, six miles offshore to the marker at Hens and Chickens, which my diver friends tell me is one of the most beautiful coral formations in the area. With huge, spiraling coral heads, Hens and Chickens—a popular name given to many reefs or shallows—is home to innumerable tropical fish and about thirty resident barracuda of giant size.

It was a beautiful morning. I noticed large flocks of terns floating on the breezes and diving on glass minnows. The wind had settled to 10 to 12 mph out of the northeast, and the seas seemed to be made up of gentler, more well-defined swells than yesterday.

### Fish #3: The Barracuda

We circled Hens and Chickens and, peering into the clear waters, could see that no one was home, so we moved offshore a few miles and started slow trolling north and south in about eighty feet of water just off Little Conch Reef. That morning, we had set up the same four rods and reels that we had used in the sailfish search. We had respooled with 8-pound tournament Ande, however, which tests out much more accurately than regular Ande.

Nothing happened for an hour. I consulted with Rusty, suggesting that we might move closer to the reef and get into some shallower water. The problem was, the area where we wanted to be was occupied by a dive boat, the *Lady Cyana*, which was anchored up so that its ten or so client divers could explore the wreck of *El Enfante*, a Spanish galleon that had gone down in 1733. Eventually the *Lady Cyana* pulled its hook and headed for port. We immediately changed our course and continued our slow troll around the mooring ball designating the wreck of *El Enfante*.

Our plan was for me to engage the fish, at least until we made a judgment as to whether it appeared to be a 25-pounder or not. If so, I'd try to land him and, if not, EQ would do the honors. We didn't have to wait long, as one of the Loomis rods bent over almost double. I grabbed it as the barracuda on the other end exploded in the familiar horizontal combination high jump / broad jump. "That looks like our 25-pounder!" I shouted.

I howled, EQ chortled, and Rusty snickered.

We had him in the boat in seven minutes. "Boy, that was easy," I said. Rusty pulled out his trusty Boga grip—10 pounds! I couldn't believe it. He looked like a monster, and he was only 10 pounds! This was going to be tougher than I'd thought.

We released the "monster," set up, and started again. What happened in the next hour and a half was incredible. We caught five barracuda, each one weighing a few pounds more than the previous fish. Strike, fight, land, weigh, release—12, 15, 16, 19, 23 pounds. Then we stalled. All the 'cuda started weighing in between 12 and 18 pounds.

There was only one thing to do: break for lunch, which we did, with Tommy breaking out sandwiches from The Trading Post. As we ate, we all agreed that it was a good day, but maybe not the big day. It looked as if all the 'cudas down there were too small, or at least like the smaller ones were getting to the baitfish faster.

It really didn't matter. It was a beautiful day on the water with friends. Tommy had rediscovered his sea legs and we still had a cooler full of lagers. Life was good. We set up the rods and I climbed up on the bridge to enjoy the view with an ice-cold Bud. All of a sudden, the line popped out of the right rigger as a huge silver 'cuda blasted out of the sunlit sea and started a mad dash away from the boat. His frenzied flight, punctuated by long leaps, was spectacular! I nearly fell off the tower as I grabbed the Randy Towe rod and held on for dear life. (This was the same rod I'd used for my sailfish but was now modified from 8 to 7 ½ inches after a run-in with a ceiling fan the week before.) Tommy, Rusty, and I looked at one another, smiling. "EQ, I don't think I'll be turning this rod over to you."

Tommy laughed too. If this fish didn't make the stick, he was going to be very close. We all knew it. Unlike the fight with our first fish, the 10-pounder, we now had a point of reference to work from. This was a very big, very strong, very angry fish. The fight took about twenty minutes. Like the sailfish, this 'cuda never quit. Unlike the

*Fish #3: The Barracuda*

*Tom and Bubba practice their 'cuda process.*

*Tom, Rusty, and the 25-pound 'cuda.*

sailfish, however, he stayed fairly close to the surface, which made it easier for me. We could see him the whole time.

When the 'cuda finally stopped jumping, I told Rusty to grab the gaff. We hadn't killed any of the 'cudas that morning, but I figured this was our fish. Rusty gaffed him at about 3:30 p.m. The Boga grip told the story—25 pounds, then 26 pounds, then 23 pounds, then 27 pounds. *Damn!* We couldn't get a consistent reading on the deck of the rocking *Fish This!* No wonder the Met Tournament directors insisted on dry-land weighing.

We iced the fish in the large aft cooler, and Tommy and I spent the next hour and a half looking for an "insurance" fish. Both of us landed another dozen 'cuda, but none of them was over 15 pounds.

At 5:00 p.m., we headed for Max's Marine, calling Islamorada Bait and Tackle to warm up the scale and asking Mindy and Madge to chill the champagne. Owner John Preast weighed the big 'cuda in at 25 pounds even, not an ounce to spare—but we had entry number three in the record books after a great day and another wonderful experience shared with an old friend.

There was no great postgame ritual with the 'cuda, as had been the case with the sailfish. When we got back to the boat to clean up after the weigh-in, some of the other boats were returning, and we asked the captains and anglers if they wanted some barracuda. They looked at us as if we were crazy. You see, barracuda are among the tropical species that have a history of being infected with a toxic substance called *ciguatera*, which makes them poisonous to humans. While not all of these fish are infected, enough are to argue against eating them. I used to wonder how the Bahamians ate so much barracuda and didn't seem to suffer any ill effects. I asked a pal of mine,

*Fish #3: The Barracuda*

*Mervin with dinner. Notice the tube lure.*

Mervin, a fishing guide from Deep Water Cay, about that one day.

"Mon, that's why we own de kaat," he replied.

"De what?" I asked.

"De kaat, Mon. You know, meow, meow. We feed a piece of de 'cuda to de kaat, and the next day if de kaat is still living, we have de 'cuda for dinner."

Mystery solved. With no takers for our 'cuda, I told this story to Rusty and EQ. Rusty said that in the Keys, the old Conchs used to put a penny on a dead 'cuda's eye: If the coin didn't turn green, the fish was safe to eat—or was it that if it *did* turn green, it was safe to eat? I don't remember, but I don't really care, because I'm not going to eat de 'cuda either way. We motored the dead fish to the channel outside Max's, where we threw him overboard and watched him sink to the bottom, knowing that in the Keys way, his remains would not be there tomorrow.

While I'm still not crazy about barracuda, I have a newfound respect for their strength and courage.

More importantly, on February 26 I got a wonderful telephone call telling me that I was now a grandpa to a beautiful baby girl named Jenna Christine. Baby, mother, and father were all doing

*Grandpa celebrates Jenna's first Easter with proud papa, Bobby.*

*Fish #3: The Barracuda*

well—and so was grandfather. Our family's joy in beginning a new generation was all-encompassing and made my quest seem even less important. Perhaps becoming a grandpa didn't just mean growing older but also growing up . . . however, I still had seven more fish I wanted to catch.

The Permit

CHAPTER 6

# FISH #4
# The Permit

*The brown trout may frustrate you, but a permit will drive you mad. I kissed the first one I caught; it weighed only 5 pounds.*

—Lefty Kreh, *Permit on a Fly* (Foreword)

I'M NOT GOING TO tell you that I think permit are supernatural. But I'm always surprised that the few I've seen photographed leave any image on film, somewhat like vampires, which supposedly have no images in mirrors.

We know that fish have the five senses of sight, smell, taste, hearing, and touch developed to different degrees. Well, I believe that the permit has all of those better developed than any other gamefish. In addition, permit have a well-developed sixth sense, which is the sense to stay just out of range of any angler regardless of how proficient they are or what tackle they may be using. John Cole put it another way in his book *Fishing Came First*: "Permit seem to know when every skiff leaves the dock and they do not linger to learn if it's headed for them."

The permit, *Trachinotus falcatus*, is a member of the pompano family and looks a little bit like the jack crevalle, which is found in the same warm Atlantic waters off the Florida Keys, the Bahamas, the Caribbean, Central America, and Mexico, where it is often called the Mexican pompano.

Permit are characteristically silver with a touch of yellow on their undersides, while their gray fins and scythe-shaped tails often appear to be black when they're in the water.

Like the pompano, the permit's body is oblong. Their faces are punctuated by smallish, underslung mouths and oversized eyes, leading me and others to believe that they have extremely well-defined eyesight. On many occasions when I've been lucky enough to get a fly in front of one, I've watched him tilt over to get a better look, putting his eye inches from my fly like a scientist peering through a microscope at a specimen before moving on to another bench for the next experiment. After years of trying, I've decided the best way to record a permit catch is to catch a jack crevalle and release him as quickly as possible, mentioning what a nice permit that was and hoping no one on the boat noticed that it was a jack. So far, I've had little more luck with that subterfuge than I have had catching permit.

These fish are far warier than bonefish and much larger as well. They seem to range between 10 and 18 pounds, although I have caught a few over 25 pounds, and I've heard that they will grow to more than 40 pounds.

## Fish #4: The Permit

They love swift current flowing over light-colored sandy bottoms. When you see them feeding, they are usually on the edges of a flat, bumping the bottom with their noses while looking for shrimp or small crabs. Their small mouths are incredibly strong, and they can quickly crush a crab, sucking out the good stuff and leaving the shell behind. When they feed, their tails are often exposed out of the water. Alone or in a small school, tailing permit are an awesome sight that an angler will not soon forget.

When hooked, a permit takes off like he's been shot from a cannon. Multiple long runs of more than 250 yards are not uncommon. Permit will also turn their wide, muscular bodies sideways to the current, perhaps giving them time to rest before another long flight to escape. When they use this tactic, an angler is well advised to get after them and try to keep them moving. A rested fish will take you well into the next television time slot. You have to be careful, however. With their strength and girth, these fish will break you off on any light tackle if you try to bully them. I guess by now I've made my point: Permit on the flats are damn hard to catch. As the late A. J. McClane once wrote in an article in *Field & Stream*, "First permit or last, you never forget any of them because nobody catches enough to become blasé on the subject."

Most of my success with these fish, as limited as it has been, has come from blind casting live crabs in deeper water where I think they hang out. I've now also managed to catch nineteen permit on fly and, like other fly fishermen I know, I remember every single one of them. The Met tackle requirement of "spin" meant artificial, and I knew up front that this would be extremely difficult.

While many permit are caught in Islamorada each year, the farther south you go in the Keys, the more prevalent these wonderful fighting fish become. When the Met tournament challenge emerged, Rusty and I started strategizing about how and where to catch each species, and our permit strategy was easy: "See RT."

"RT" was the nickname for world-class fishing guide Robert Trosset Jr., who fished out of Key West. We called RT and set up a day to fish for perms in his friendly home waters. Rusty said he'd love to join us, and I responded, "Great!"

While preparing for my trip to Key West, I got a call from Suzan Baker. She told me that John Still had caught an 18-pound snook to complete his thirteen-year quest for the Met Hall of Fame. Maybe I should have been disappointed that I wasn't going to be the first into the Hall, but I wasn't. I was just happy for this man I'd never met. I called to congratulate him, and he was very gracious on the phone. He was obviously a great angler and a gentleman. I told him that I would be proud to follow him into the Met Hall of Fame, hopefully sooner rather than later.

RT was one of the most popular and best-known fishing guides in the Florida Keys and had put his friends and clients onto 116 IGFA world record catches. He was booked more than three hundred days a year and was also sponsored by many fishing boat and tackle manufacturers, such as Penn Reels, to use their equipment.

When we pulled up next to RT's boat, I noticed that he was icing down two cases of Budweiser. He knew that Rusty was joining us, but I thought those provisions might be a little heavy even for the three of us. As Rusty and I climbed aboard and stowed our gear, RT laughed and said that the beer wasn't all for us and that I'd soon

Fish #4: The Permit

*Robert Trosset with a nice pair of wahoo.*
PHOTO CREDIT: Rusty Albury

understand. He cast off our lines and pushed off the dock for the start of another adventure.

So there we were, RT, Rusty, and me, motoring down the southern shore of Key West on one of the most beautiful, calm, sunfilled mornings I'd ever seen in the Keys. It was warm but not oppressive. Two night herons feeding near the shoreline caught my eye. The still waters were light blue, bordering on transparent. As we motored west past the historic sites of Key West—County Beach, the foot of Duval Street, Truman Annex, Fort Taylor—dozens of tarpon rolled all around our boat, drawing our eyes from the shores to the silken sea of which we had become a part. The morning's visibility seemed to be without boundary, and spirits on board were high in anticipation of the adventure that lay ahead.

RT informed us that we would be running about fifty-six miles from Oceanside. His target was one of the many wrecks that dot those waters. While Key West is the westernmost island connected by the Overseas Highway, there are other more westerly islands in the chain of Keys that are accessible only by boat.

Our target wreck was about twenty miles this side of the farthest group of Keys, the Dry Tortugas, named by the Spanish explorer Ponce de León, who visited there in 1513. He named them the *Tortugas*, the Spanish word for the sea turtles he found inhabiting the area. The adjective *dry* was later added by sailors who found no fresh water there.

It is on one of those islands, Garden Key, that Fort Jefferson was built in 1846. Originally designed to help defend the coast, it was used after the Civil War as a prison. Its most famous resident was Dr. Samuel Mudd, who set the fractured leg of Abraham Lincoln's assassin, actor John Wilkes Booth. Originally implicated in the crime and imprisoned at Fort Jefferson, Dr. Mudd was later exonerated and released, but not before the phrase "Your name is Mudd" became part of our country's folklore.

## Fish #4: The Permit

Our trip that day was a veritable nature walk. All types of waterfowl flew overhead, while fish of all species rippled the water's calm surface in search of food. About twenty miles out, we came upon the Marquesas, a small, circular ring of keys known for their pristine waters and abundance of tarpon, bonefish, and permit. RT said that the Marquesas were the only atolls in the Atlantic that closely resembled those found in the South Pacific, which were formed by ancient volcanoes now sunk into the sea. The Marquesas are about half a mile across and provide great sheltered fishing in their quiet lagoons, if you don't mind the usual bumpy ride from Key West. Today, however, the bumps had been flattened out as we continued our journey west.

About half an hour later, we saw two shrimp boats drifting together on the horizon. RT pointed the *Spindrift* in their direction. As we pulled closer, we could see their suntanned crews working on the decks as hundreds of pelicans and cormorants circled the boats or perched on the riggings looking for handouts. We pulled up to the *Master Mike* from Alabama, and its captain pointed RT to its sister boat, also from Alabama.

Apparently, the crew knew what RT was looking for. As we pulled alongside, the boat's captain reached over to take two six-packs of Budweiser from RT while one of the crew handed Rusty an empty garbage pail and then another pail full of sludge-like material. This was the stuff that they had netted along with the shrimp that they were sorting out on their decks, mainly small crabs and baitfish of all species.

RT explained that shrimping was a tough and isolated business. Occasionally, one of the crew working on a boat might be

*Sea birds flock around a shrimp boat trolling off the coast.*

on the lam or at least looking for a place where he could enjoy a little quiet anonymity. He told me that once when they were doing this maneuver, someone in his party had pulled out a camcorder, causing a few cursing members of the crew of the shrimper to dive for cover.

Shrimping as an industry has undergone major changes. Twenty-five years ago, companies such as Key West's Singleton dominated in the hunting, netting, and processing of shrimp. Today, companies like our SeaPak in St. Simons Island, Georgia, have revolutionized the industry by sourcing pond-raised shrimp from around the world. In other words, they've become farmers, not hunters, of shrimp in the wilds, thus leaving backward companies like Singleton fighting to survive.

### Fish #4: The Permit

We waved goodbye to the shrimpers as they popped open the Buds and wished us good luck. We covered another twelve miles in about twenty-five minutes before RT throttled back his big Suzukis and Rusty tossed the anchor in about 105 feet of water. The hook caught right away, and the current swung us directly over RT's target wreck, which he explained was a tugboat and barge that had sunk years ago in a tropical storm. I started to pick up one of my Loomis spinning rods and noticed a hurt look on RT's face. "RT," I said, "do you have one of those excellent Penn rods I could borrow?"

His eyes lit up and a huge smile came over his bearded face. *Smart move, Bubba*, I thought. RT handed me one of his 7 ½-foot Penn Sabre rods with a Penn reel spooled with 10-pound Ande. For the hunt, he had brought along two dozen yellow brush-tailed jigs. We would use all of them before the day was over.

As two adult black skimmers took advantage of the calm waters to hone their unique fishing skills, RT scooped up a pail of the shrimp boat sludge, or "unspecified protein"; took up a spot at one corner of the transom; and started scooping it overboard like Richard Dreyfuss in *Jaws*. "Watch the chum," RT said. In two minutes, the blue runners appeared, followed soon after by a school of bonito that darted in and out of the cloudy pieces of crab and other species from the shrimper's catch. Then, all of a sudden, there they were. What first looked like large, dark shadows moving in on the outskirts of the falling fragments of chum were dozens of large permit, easily discernible in the clear waters of the Gulf of Mexico above this wreck near Rebecca Shoal.

RT told me to throw the line out over the fish, leave the bail open, and allow the jig to fall about thirty feet into their midst. Then he told me to close the bail, snatch the rod up three times while lifting the jig about six inches each time, then let it fall for about five seconds before repeating the process. He said the bite would usually happen as the jig fell.

There was no wait. First throw, bail open, line falls, close bail, tap three times, let lure fall, and *bang*—the stiff Penn rod bent double. First cast, first bite, first fish on. Striking would have been redundant. The permit was hooked solidly. He took off, peeling off about sixty yards of line before taking a right turn and running again. In fifteen minutes, the fish had completely circled us, with me following him around the boat.

He was slowing down. I was taking line. "RT, this is going to be too easy," I said. "Grab the camera, Rusty." Famous last words. *Snap!* Immediately, I felt the sickening feeling of a rod with a slack line in my hand. I retrieved the limp line to find that our 5-foot, 60-pound test leader had been broken cleanly about a foot below the knot connecting it to the double line.

I looked at RT. He shrugged his shoulders. "Don't worry, Bubba, it happens. You'll get the next one," he said as he picked up his chum scoop.

But we didn't. We lost the next three permit in almost identical fashion. It was clear that these fish were fighting, then diving to the wreck and breaking us off. So we changed procedure. RT connected an anchor buoy to our anchor line. After hookups, Rusty untied the anchor, allowing us to drift off the wreck. It worked. I was able to pull six permit to the boat for weigh-ins, even though each of them made the same big circle and headed back for the wreck. None of these fish made the 20-pound mark required to qualify for the Met, although one was about 18 ½ pounds. All of a sudden, I was having flashbacks to our barracuda day, when it had seemed impossible to come up with the correct weight fish we needed.

RT pulled the hook and slid us to the edge of the wreck in the hope of finding some larger fish. The first hookup in the new location established a new pattern. The permit circled, then sprinted toward the wreck before becoming dead weight. Then, a few minutes later, the line went limp. Now the leaders were being broken right above the hook.

RT surmised that the tired permit were being chased by bull sharks hanging around the wrecks. The quickened pace halfway through the flights was the fish fleeing the sharks, running for the wreck before the sharks intercepted them and ate half the fish. This is when they turned to dead weight. The second hit leading to limp line was the shark finishing off the job, also explaining why we weren't pulling up any half-eaten fish. RT said that this was most unusual. Most days he fished these wrecks, the hooked fish fled for open water.

By now, it was 3:30 p.m., and with at least a two-hour ride home, we were running out of time—and chum as well. Rusty pulled up the anchor and RT moved down the road about 150 yards, putting us well off the edge of the wreck.

RT dumped our remaining chum, and we waited and hoped for the perms to reappear. The seas, whipped up by a fresh wind out of the northeast, were becoming a little choppy. But suddenly there they were again, dark shadows in the remaining chum.

I threw out my line and told RT and Rusty a joke. "Hey, you guys. What did the fish say when he ran into the concrete wall? *Dam*."

*Rusty and Bubba practiced getting them hooked, bending the rod, and breaking them off. As soon as the fish made it to the wrecks, they were gone!*

They both groaned as my line came tight. We guessed it to be a large permit. Rusty threw the anchor buoy overboard and the fish made a big mistake. Rather than dive deep, he made a long, shallow run, then compounded his error by continuing in a straight line instead of turning and fleeing for the wreck. By the time he tried to correct his course, we were at least 250 yards off the wreck. The fish ran up current to no avail. Half an hour after the hookup, I had him up to the boat—a beautiful permit, heavy and oblong and looking pound for pound like a Hall of Fame entry.

RT reached over and grabbed this fish by the tail. He put the Boga grip on the permit, which weighed almost 23 pounds! We had our fish. RT slid him into the live well so we could release him after the weigh-in.

We motored back to the wreck to retrieve our anchor and then headed for home. Permit on the flats are solitary and spooky—quite

Fish #4: The Permit

*RT and my permit (notice the subtle fingers on the scale).*

a contrast to the huge schools of permit we had seen and fished on this day. But they are strong and smart adversaries, no matter where you find them.

The permit did not survive the two-hour trip back to Oceanside, even in RT's giant live well. RT tried every way possible to revive the fish, short of mouth-to-mouth resuscitation, but to no avail. This is another reason why I believe the Met should go to an all-release format for the Hall of Fame. These fish, while hearty in the wild, are extremely fragile in confinement, even in the largest live well.

We weighed the fish in at the Oceanside checkpoint—it was just over 22 pounds—and filled out our Met paperwork. Rusty filleted the fish while we stowed our gear in his truck, then we headed home for Islamorada, eighty miles northeast on the Overseas Highway.

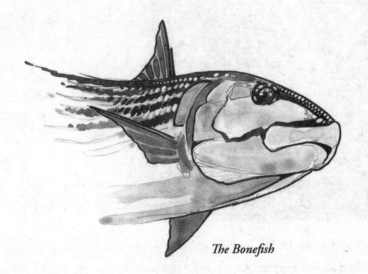

*The Bonefish*

CHAPTER 7

# FISH #5
# The Bonefish

*The bonefish is the nearest thing there is
to a perfect game fish for fly fishing.
It accelerates faster and sprints farther
than any other fish you take on light tackle.*

—Dick Brown, *Fly Fishing for Bonefish*

---

THE BONEFISH may be the single most-prized catch of the Florida Keys, the Bahamas, Panama, and Belize, not to mention Christmas Island in the Pacific. Bonefish are the only member of the *Albulidae* family, and I believe they are in a league of their own in the world of fish.

While they seem to change shades depending on the color of the bottom, the water, and the sky, bonefish are predominantly silver with greenish-colored backs, dorsal fins, and tails. In his informative book *Saltwater Game Fish of North America*, Herbert Schaffner says, "Bonefish have an armor-plated head and long pig-like snout. They are often seen breaking the surface of the water on the flats with their tails as they root in sand for shrimp and crabs. The bonefish has a single dorsal fin with seventeen to nineteen soft rays."

Bonefish commonly range from 4 to 8 pounds, but it is not uncommon to catch one of more than 10 pounds, especially in the middle Keys of Florida. I have taken many of my largest bonefish in close proximity to my hometown of Islamorada. My neighbors say there is a reason for this. Many catch-and-release tournaments are held in our area, and one of the prerequisites for winning is often recording at least one weight fish at a weigh station set up somewhere in town, like at Papa Joe's Marina or the Lorelei. These large fish are brought to checkpoints in live wells, weighed, and quickly released. Many, we believe, then settle down in the vicinity and are referred to by the locals as "downtown fish"—large but wary. Mark Twain would have gotten a kick out of this fact, which verifies his saying, "There is no use in your walking five miles to fish when you can depend on being just as unsuccessful near home."

As with other species, the larger the bonefish, the smaller the school. It is not uncommon to see schools of one thousand bonefish in the Bahamas all weighing from around 3 to 5 pounds. In the Florida Keys, however, the typical school, if there is such a thing, seems to consist of around a dozen fish. The big ones seem to hang out with one, two, or three other fish their size. In my experience, the giants tend to keep their own company.

## Fish #5: The Bonefish

None of these fish, large or small, is easy to catch. They have been described by many adjectives, from *shy* to *wary* to *invisible*. My favorite description is that the bonefish is the "gray ghost of the flats."

I have had my best luck sight fishing for bones when tide activity is the greatest, rising or falling. The fish seem to venture out of the safety of deeper water onto the edges of the flats in search of food at such times. They are incredibly sensitive to their environment and will dart away at the first sign that something is out of place.

The best way to spot fish on the flats is to wear a good pair of polarized sunglasses to cut the glare and to get up as high as possible in a skiff. Unfortunately, getting up high is also the best way to be seen by the bonefish, and once they have seen you, heard you, or felt your presence, they flee and the game is over. Captain Ron Wagner tells me that he has his anglers step quietly off their platform and into the cockpit of the boat once fish have been spotted. He says that this lowers the angler's profile and improves the odds of not spooking the fish. He's also told me about some older guides who used to insist that their anglers sit down during the hunt and then direct their casts blindly, without necessarily seeing the fish, based on the face of a clock with the bow being twelve o'clock, the stern six o'clock, and so on. In other words, the guide might tell an angler to throw thirty feet at ten o'clock. This may be so, but I don't know. It is true, however, that the clock method has become a common tool of basic communication in sight casting.

Wading for bonefish can also be very productive for the purist and is done extensively in the Bahamas, where the sand bottoms will support your weight and the smaller schooling fish seem to be a little less spookable. It's more difficult in the Florida Keys, where we seem to have limited visibility. Most of our oceanside flats are hard sand or rock-bottomed and good for wading. The bayside flats, however, are more deceptive. Most of them are made of mud or silt. Step out of the boat on one of them, and you will be up to your waist in muck, needing a hand from your friends to get back into the boat.

Two years ago, I had a bonefishing brainstorm. I ordered Rusty a pair of snowshoes from the L.L. Bean catalog, figuring he could use them for traversing the soft mudflats of Florida Bay. Can you imagine the look on the face of the UPS guy when the snowshoes showed up on his truck for delivery to an address in Islamorada? He must have thought that Super Conch had lost his marbles. We tried them, though, and they worked great, so long as there was some turtle grass on the flat. When we used them on mud alone, we sank, albeit a little slower, but just as deep. And with the snowshoes attached to your feet, it was almost impossible to extricate yourself.

Bonefish are not fished for—they are stalked or hunted. They are extremely picky eaters renowned for bumping baits and then swimming away. I suspect that what they are really doing is sucking in a bait and then blowing it out of their mouths if it does not appeal to them. This process takes place so quickly that it is practically impossible to react to. Any slack in the line will almost certainly cost you a chance for a hookup.

With bonefish, there is never a need for a violent strike. A gentle tap response is much more effective in helping this wary gamefish hook himself. The initial run of a hooked bonefish is one of the most awesome events in the fishing world. It is not uncommon to have a bonefish strip off 250 yards of line in the time it takes an angler to say, "I've been spooled."

*Fish #5: The Bonefish*

*Bubba test-drove his new pair of L.L. Bean snowshoes on the flats, just before taking a seat on the turtle grass.*

When I originally got involved in the hunt for the Met Hall of Fame, my fishing pals and I had many discussions about which of the ten required species would be the most difficult to catch. We never really talked much about which fish would be the easiest. For me, it was academic. Bonefish on the fly is one of my favorite pursuits. My other rods seemed to be collecting dust as I spent more and more time on the flats with my trusty three-piece 9-foot, 8-weight Loomis GLX graphite fly rod and single-action No. 2 Islander reel. It seemed to me that every third bone I caught on the fly was over 9 pounds. "This'll be a piece of cake," I confided to Mindy. "I won't even target this species. I'll just let it happen."

"Don't underestimate bonefish," Mindy, ever the voice of reason, warned. "They're never easy on any tackle."

Mindy was right on, as always. Four trips with Rusty for a 9-pound bonefish ended up in four oceanside fish broken off, the first at a flat called Tea Table, the second at Tavernier Creek, the third in front of Holiday Isle, and the fourth in front of Whale Harbor.

The Tavernier fish was a heartbreaker. We had him on for two long runs before my reel seized up, allowing what appeared to be a 10-pounder to break off. The Whale Harbor fish was even tougher to lose. We hooked up on a shoreline flat on Saturday morning at around eleven o'clock. The fish ran south along the beach and broke us off on a sponge growing on the bottom, right next to a channel. This one had to have been an 11-pounder. Feeling the frustration of four lost bonefish, I lost it and started cursing in my loudest voice (*voce alta*)! The next thing I knew, I was hearing the laughter and applause of about twelve people around the pool of the Chesapeake Motel who had seen the hookup, watched the ill-fated fight, and clearly heard my profane epithet. I hadn't realized how close we were to shore! Totally embarrassed, I looked back at Rusty, who was poling the boat, shrugging his shoulders and trying to look as if he had no idea who I was.

*Fish #5: The Bonefish*

So now there I was, zero for four. There was only one thing to do to change my luck—dump Rusty! Only kidding. What kind of friend was I? I wouldn't dump my pal just because he couldn't help me catch a 9-pound bonefish in four tries.

The first time I came to the Keys, I fished with a great young guide by the name of Jim Brewer, who was incredibly talented. Sadly, he died in a single-engine plane crash, leaving behind a wife and three children, one of whom, Craig, had a passion for fishing and loved to explore the backcountry with his older brother, Steve, and his fishing buddy, Rusty Albury.

Eventually, Craig put the experience of his boyhood explorations to good use and became one of the premier fishing guides in the Keys. Orvis recognized his talents and had him on their certified guide list for two years before he joined Sandy Moret's Florida Keys Fly Fishing School. You had to see Craig with a fly rod in his hand to appreciate the skill attainable in this sport. At six feet four inches tall, Craig used his height and reach to create long, fluid motion in his casts. His rhythm was incredible, and he could change direction and throw to any position on the clock without endangering himself or the people he was fishing with. He was also a great teacher, willing to quietly explain what he was doing and then dissect an angler's casting style, helping even a novice make corrections that would lead to results. Whether you needed small adjustments or an industrial-sized fly-casting makeover, Craig was your man. As a guide, he was patient, understanding, and always professional. For every fish you might lose fishing with him, you would pick up a valuable tip on what to do next time and how to improve your technique.

Periodically, Mindy would book Craig for a day of fly fishing. It was not only therapeutic but also very helpful to her in improving her fishing skills. That year, they would fish in the Don Hawley Tarpon Tournament against, among others, Rusty and me. For now, though, Mindy, Craig, and I became teammates as I wheedled my way onto his skiff in search of a bonefish weighing more than 9 pounds.

My first trip with Craig to catch my Met bonefish was to be as uneventful as my second. The wind blew at better than 20 mph both days, the first day from the west and the second from the northeast. For some reason, a west wind absolutely shuts down fishing in the Florida Keys.

Throughout North American angling circles, fishing is considered to be at its finest when the wind is blowing out of the west, giving birth to the adage, "West is best"—except in Islamorada where "West is worst." This anomaly had always puzzled me, and I was never able to get a credible answer as to why a west wind all but shuts down Keys fishing while it's great everywhere else. One day, one of the old-timers let me in on the secret. Apparently, fish are most comfortable when the conditions, including wind direction, are what they are most used to. Throughout North America, the prevailing winds are out of the west. In Islamorada, however, the prevailing winds are out of the east. When the winds blow out of the west, our fish get uncomfortable, or "whacked out," as Rusty says.

If this prevailing wind theory is true, it suggests that anglers anywhere would be well advised to experiment with different techniques when the wind blows from a nontraditional direction. We've worked this theory pretty well in our home waters and come up with

## Fish #5: The Bonefish

*Captain Craig Brewer demonstrating "Florida Keys chic."*

a bunch of productive west wind spots. So now we're catching fish on west winds but in different locations and with different bait, lures, and flies.

To Craig Brewer's credit, he put us on a lot of fish both days in spite of the horrible fishing conditions. The wind was giving me fits and I was having great trouble turning over my 16-pound tippet to make good presentations to the fish. Those I did get my fly in front of had lockjaw. We changed flies often and watched our target species reject Crazy Charlies, Clouser Minnows, Merkins, and Bonefish Specials with equal disdain. They even rejected Craig's favorite, the Tasty Toad; when that happened, I knew we were in trouble.

Besides changing flies, I also changed rods, going to a 10-weight Loomis GLX with a dual-mode Sea Master reel. Having fished the Keys for quite a few years, I estimated that the average wind speed was around 15 mph and predominantly out of the northeast. In such breezy conditions, a 10-weight rod helps you cast a sharp loop that cuts through the wind. My theory on this is supported by some of the classic anglers who have put in a lot of time on the flats—anglers like Dick Pope, who fished almost exclusively with a 10-weight. I think I could also make a good case for using this rod even on large tarpon.

During my two days fishing with Craig Brewer, I made some truly horrible casts. It was all the wind's fault, trust me! Craig never lost his patience or raised his voice; he quietly coached me through my mistakes and gave me a few ideas to work on. By the end of the second day, my technique for fishing in the wind had definitely improved, which is really important if you are going to succeed in the Keys. I managed hookups on three large bones, all of which broke me off on mangrove shoots.

My bonefish quest was put on hold for a few months over the summer as we headed up north to look after business. I didn't have a chance to do any saltwater fishing between June 22 and the end of August.

On August 25, Mindy and I dropped our son Barney off at the University of Miami, where he was enrolled as a freshman in the class of 2001. Empty nesters for the first time—Barney was the fourth of four—we headed home to Islamorada. I called Rusty, who told me that the bonefish had been biting pretty well, and we set up three days of fishing before I had to go back north.

The first two days were carbon copies of each other—heavy rain squalls at dawn accompanied by massive amounts of thunder and lightning, followed by clearing skies and temperatures in the high 80s with breezes of less than 10 mph out of the east. These were typical August days in the Keys. The early morning rain is actually great for fishing, as it cools the water to 86 or 87 degrees, well within the comfort zone for bonefish. (The bonefish temperature range is between 76 and 89 degrees. When the temperatures are above or below this range, these fish will not leave the comfort of deeper waters for the crustacean-rich flats that surround the Keys.)

Rusty and I waited on shore each day until the last bolt of morning lightning passed, then took to the boat. We didn't have to go far, as the downtown fish were out in force after the rain. While they were plentiful, they were also very wary. I threw a variety of flies at them as the sun came in and out from behind huge, billowy cumulus clouds, and egrets and herons dried their wings and searched the flats for food. We managed to catch two bonefish both days, each weighing in between 6 ½ and 7 ½ pounds, well off our target of 9 pounds.

The third day dawned like the first two, except the morning storm was much more violent, forcing us to stay home until 10:00 a.m. At 9:15 a.m., our fledgling scholar called from Miami with great reports on his first three days of academia. Actually, most of his dialogue revolved around the fraternity rush and the Miami social scene. But it was a good conversation, one that left me happy that my son was well launched into his college career. He was a hard worker, and I knew that he would do well.

When the skies cleared, the bonefish started tailing all around Islamorada. They were tailing everywhere! It was incredible—and I was atrocious. I bonked two fish on the head at Lignum-Vitae Key, pulled two hooks at Tea Table Reef, and fed one of Rusty's special $8.50 Snapping Shrimp flies to a juvenile barracuda at the Swash. By noon, the Conch had quit talking to me. I was fishing like a blacksmith. I knew that I was trying too hard, but that's tough to correct. Before he went silent on me, Rusty had suggested that perhaps I had fallen under some evil curse. As I stood on the bow in abject silence, I wondered if the sea gods, or Jim Brewer, or whoever, might remove the curse if I offered up an acceptable human sacrifice—like perhaps a sixth-generation Conch.

The silence was deafening. I decided on a bribe. "C'mon Rusty, I'll buy you lunch. Let's head for the Islamorada Fish Company." It wasn't our usual lunch place, but the new dock restaurant at the Fish Company just down the road served the best conch salad in the Keys. Happily, Rusty gave in. We pigged out on cumin-flavored conch salad and ice-cold Budweiser drafts before continuing our adventure.

I think that Rusty was most cheered by the fact that I was going to have to be on a 2:00 p.m. conference call on my cell phone, so he would get some quality time on the bow to do some fishing. We had seen some 30- to 40-pound tarpon rolling at Whale Harbor on the late-falling tide the day before, so Rusty decided to head over there to stake up and fish while I joined my conference call. He rigged up a 9-weight Orvis Trident rod equipped with a new lightweight Tibor reel for tarpon. We'd also seen some permit swimming with the tarpon the day before, so Rusty had me rig my 8-weight Loomis with a Chernobyl Crab for him, just in case.

My phone rang just before two o'clock. It was my conference call—actually a telephonic meeting of the management board of the Buffalo Sabres, a venture I'd invested in the year I'd gotten out of business school. As a small-market sports franchise in the National Hockey League, the Sabres had perpetual cash-flow problems, and it seemed like they had more board meetings than all the Fortune 500

### Fish #5: The Bonefish

companies combined. I was not looking forward to relinquishing the angler's bow platform to Rusty for the one-hour call I knew was about to start.

When I picked up the phone, I joined two other board members—Northrup R. "Norty" Knox and George Strawbridge—and waited for the others to be patched in. Norty, a close friend for many years, was a great athlete who captained several US polo teams and who, at sixty-eight years old, would still beat you in golf, tennis, squash, billiards, or just about any other sport you can think of. Norty and his brother, Seymour, who had recently died of cancer, had put together the small group of investors that bought an expansion franchise in the NHL in 1969 that eventually became the Buffalo Sabres. George Strawbridge, fifty-nine, was also an outstanding amateur athlete, well known in equestrian circles. A Pierce Brosnan look-alike, for many years he was a world-class event rider. I'm not sure what that means other than that he and his horses jumped over a lot of high fences, hopefully together. George was a member of the Campbell Soup Company Dorrance family and was a good guy. Norty, George, and I all loved to fly-fish.

As we waited for the others to join the call, I giggled thinking of Norty and George sitting in an oak-paneled boardroom in wool suits and starched shirts, not knowing that I was standing on the deck of a fishing boat, barefoot, dressed in shorts and a T-shirt with "Islamorada, every place else sucks" on the back.

Just then Rusty said, "Wow, look at that! Stay up there," and handed me the 8-weight Loomis as a giant school of forty or more large bonefish swam by our skiff, about fifty feet away. I tucked the telephone onto my shoulder under my right ear, grabbed the rod, and pulled some line off the Islander reel. I made two false casts with the phone on my shoulder and let the line fly—bull's-eye—five feet in front of the herd of fish meandering on the edge of the flat. There was no wait! The lead fish immediately dove on the Chernobyl Crab and was hooked.

There I was with a giant bonefish on the line and two fly-fishing pals on the phone on my shoulder. As the big fish got ready for the inevitable dash for freedom, I challenged fly-fishing aficionados Norty and George, "Hey, you guys, name this tune." The hooked fish played his part. As I held the reel up to the phone, the big fish fled for the adjacent channel, peeling off 250 feet of line and setting my reel whirling, creating a sound that only an angler could appreciate. On the other end of the line, Norty and George went crazy. They both started laughing at once, realizing what they were hearing.

As the other (and stodgier) board members joined the conference call, I excused myself and put the phone, still connected to the meeting, on hold on the deck so I could pay full attention to my quarry. My fish had fled to the channel with the school, so Rusty cranked up the engine and followed. The school took a left turn and headed for the ocean. The hooked bone tried to join them, but we were on him. By now, our skiff was in the channel and the bonefish was twenty-five feet away. He had run into the channel next to a mangrove island. His choices were to head left for the ocean, go right for the backcountry, or turn around and jump back up on the flat he had just left. Of course, he also had the option of diving for the bottom and trying to break off the line. Recognizing this probability, I took up the drag and really leaned on this fish to keep him off the bottom. I figured I'd rather pull the hook or break him off than have him break me off.

*Fish #5: The Bonefish*

*Bonefish on line, telephone on shoulder, and ISLAMORADA EVERY PLACE ELSE SUCKS T-shirt on the back.*

The fight was complicated by the boat traffic in the channel. At one point a vessel that resembled an oversized bass boat drove by. The driver throttled back and his buddy yelled over, "Whatcha got?"

"Snag!" Rusty responded, and they motored on. *Good response*, I thought.

The only other tense moment came when two wave runners passed us at full throttle, one on each side, about ten feet away, causing Rusty to let out the classic two-word profanity. I wondered how the Buffalo Sabres board would have enjoyed hearing that on the live phone lying on the floor of the skiff.

The rest of the fight was academic, if there is such a thing with gray ghosts. The fish went left, right, and back. I muscled him up to the surface, and Rusty netted him, removed the hook, and put him in the live well. The whole thing took about seven minutes. We applied the Boga grip that told the story: 9 pounds, 2 ounces!

As Rusty slid our fish into the live well, I picked up the phone, wished everyone on the board well, smiled at Rusty, and sat back for an hour of telephonic tedium, buoyed by the fact that Super Conch and I had our bonefish and species number five aboard.

Wanting to release our fish, we called ahead to the Met check station and next to a public beach. A volunteer named Christy brought over the official mullet scale, which verified our catch at 9 pounds, 2 ounces. She took our picture.

Before releasing him, we measured the fish to be 27 ½ inches long from nose to fork of the tail, with a girth measurement in front of the pectoral fin of 16 ½ inches. Using the classic and reliable weight measure of: girth times girth times length divided by 800 ([girth x girth] x length ÷ 800), we figured this fish should have weighed 9 pounds, 3 ounces. Who was going to quibble? I was pleased to have this one done. We gently placed the big fish in the water, and he swam away unaided, though a tad dazed and confused by his live-well confinement and sudden beachfront celebrity.

I invited Rusty over for a celebratory scotch. As I was bragging to him about my fishing style, he said, "By the way, Bubba, that fish never really ate the Chernobyl Crab. You hooked him in the nose."

There he went again—my old pal Rusty, keeping me humble.

*Fish #5: The Bonefish*

I didn't care, though. A catch was a catch, even if the fish was foul hooked. I refused to be humbled. Anyway, how many people can lay claim to catching a bonefish by the nose while talking on a conference call?

*Rusty and my 9-pound, 2-ounce bonefish.*

*The Bass*

CHAPTER 8

# FISH #6
# The Bass

*Don't think of bass as being smart because you can't catch them when you know they're there. Think of them as wary creatures that have learned to survive in a dangerous world where not detecting a predator means death.*

—HOMER CIRCLE, *Circle on Bass*

---

BECAUSE I HAVE fished in Lake Erie for bass since I was old enough to hold a rod, I was glad they were one of the ten target species.

Bass were a natural to become the most popular American freshwater gamefish. They are native to every state in the union except Alaska and are found in Mexico and southern Canada as well. These abundant, voracious feeders will strike literally any bait out of hunger or territorial protectionism. They are hearty, aggressive, and bad-tempered, three traits that make them great fighters.

Largemouth bass, *Micropterus salmoides*, average around 3 ½ pounds but have been known to range up to 20 pounds. In fact, the world record is 22 pounds, 4 ounces. Their northern, cold-water smallmouth cousins, *Micropterus dolomieu*, tend to be much smaller. From my experience fishing in the Great Lakes, a 3 ½-pound smallmouth is a dynamite catch to brag about. The record for smallmouth bass, it turns out, is 10 pounds, 14 ounces.

Both largemouth and smallmouth bass feed at all levels in the water. They tend to seek the cover of overhanging rock ledges, fallen tree branches, roots, and other debris. They seem unable to resist plugs, jigs, and other lures bounced deep by their hiding places. They are also known to crash surface plugs, lures, and flies, giving the angler an acrobatic display of their incredible talent for multiple jumps.

These hearty battlers are found everywhere from huge bodies of water such as the Great Lakes to small lily ponds on golf courses in waters ranging from 30 to 90 degrees. While they have been known to feed day or night, in clear water during the heat of the day they tend to seek refuge from predators in their safe hiding places.

Equipped with incredible sensory equipment, bass will strike lures in even the murkiest water, once again assuring their reputation as the consummate freshwater competitor.

Of the twelve fish in the Met Tournament roster, the bass is the only freshwater species, and I'm glad. I think it's a great testimony to bass and a special challenge to any would-be Hall of Fame angler, which underscores the diversity of fishing in South Florida. Having said all that, I was at a loss where to go or what to do to notch this

*Fish #6: The Bass*

*Attorney/angler Jay Levine shows off a nice 5-pound bass in Nine Mile Pond.*

one, and a 6-pounder no less. When I questioned Rusty, he was the picture of confidence. It seems that he had already consulted with a friend who was a bass aficionado.

Jay Levine was a trial attorney from Miami who represented Rusty Albury a while back when he was settling with the government for his past indiscretions. Jay's dad was a New Jersey businessman who moved his family to Miami to develop residential property in Dade County. At the University of Miami, Jay the student displayed a talent for accounting and planned to specialize in business law at the University of Miami Law School. That is, until he got his first taste of the inside of a courtroom in a mock trial. From that day on, Jay's career path was established. Like many advocates, Jay loved the competitiveness and the battle of wits with prosecutors in the pursuit of justice.

When asked a pointed question, Jay once said, "No, it's not about the defendant. It's about the challenge, and it's about the law." He mellowed a bit when he talked about Rusty's case, however. "Rusty was a guy who'd made some mistakes but was also totally honest and ready to pay his debt to society. I just wanted to make sure that he was represented fairly and that that debt was fairly assessed."

From the stories I have heard, Jay was a well-prepared, intelligent, and passionate advocate who worked long hours on behalf of his clients. He brought those same attributes to his avocations: hunting and fishing.

A five-foot, eleven-inch ball of fire, Jay was perpetual motion, with a full head of jet-black hair, a salt-and-pepper mustache, and not a pound of extra body weight. When Rusty consulted with him about finding and catching a 6-pound black bass on plug in February 1997, Jay said that he would share his favorite place with us, but only in person. He wanted to be part of the expedition. Jay told us to bring our plug rods to meet him at an A.O.K. Tackle shop in Homestead so we could pick up our freshwater fishing licenses.

My first problem was that I didn't have a plug rod. A trip to the World Wide Sportsman in Islamorada took care of that. Long story short, I made a beeline over there, where I shook several rods, feeling for I know not what before I asked for help from one of the fishing experts working in the reel department. He fixed me up with a 7-foot fast-action Loomis GL3 plug rod, which I combined with a gold Shimano Calcutta 250 reel, spooled with 10-pound test tournament Ande. I also picked up two books on bass fishing as well as some colorful lures with unusual names like *spinnerbaits* and *buzzbaits*, just as I'd seen on the bass shows on TV. Watching these programs,

## Fish #6: The Bass

I'd noticed that many of the hotshot bass guys threw with their right hand, then changed the rod to their left and reeled with their right. I selected a right-hand retrieve reel, even over the admonitions of Rusty that left-handed fishing was difficult.

Guys like Hank Parker and Bill Dance made it look easy on TV. I figured that it would be no problem, and it wasn't—until I tried it. Every cast resulted in a bird's-nest-sized backlash. Finally, I learned to roll my wrist over to the left and throw the thing more like a baseball than a spinning rod. It worked, and after several hours of practice on the dock, I was able to land a lure fairly close to an imaginary target. I figured I was ready to try my technique on a real fish.

Our destination was a small body of fresh water called Nine Mile Pond, named simply because it is located nine miles from Flamingo in Everglades National Park. After passing through the park gates, we drove through thirty miles of desolate flatland that looked like the plains of Africa, with its own style of protected wildlife.

As gray herons and smaller white egrets soared overhead, Rusty, Jay, and I drove toward our destination in Jay's four-wheel drive Chevy Tahoe with his 17-foot aluminum canoe strapped on top.

We finally pulled up to the pond, which was actually a series of several connected ponds, put the canoe on the shore, and unloaded our gear, which included a large cooler full of ice, sandwiches, sodas, and beer. As we prepared to push the canoe into the pond, I asked Jay, "Where did all these logs come from?"

"Those aren't logs," he said. "Those are alligators."

I couldn't believe it. Strewn around the pond were dozens of floating, four- to ten-foot-long alligators.

"Are we safe from those things?" I asked Jay.

"Yeah, as long as we don't bother them."

"Thanks," I said, wondering how Webster's defined the word *bother* and if paddling a canoe in their midst would qualify.

Good old Rusty, sensing my concern, jumped in to allay my fears. "Navy frogmen are taught that if an alligator is smaller than you are, he won't bother you. If he's larger than you are, he'll eat you."

Thanks, Rusty.

We got into the canoe—me in the bow, Jay in the stern, and Rusty sitting in the middle on the cooler. Jay shoved us off and the canoe started shaking like a palm frond in the wind. As we shook our way onto the pond, I distinctly thought I saw two of the closest gators perk up and lick their chops. One of them looked to be about four feet, but the other one was clearly bigger than me.

"Rusty," I suggested, "perhaps this canoe might stop shaking if you sat on the floor." He took my advice, and it worked. Both of the nearby gators slipped ominously underwater as our canoe slid down the shoreline. Let the adventure begin.

Jay had rejected all of my TV baits, explaining that they work fine on surface fish, but he wanted us to use something that would get down deep. On the shoreline he'd shown me how to Texas-rig plastic worms that, with the help of small bullet weights, would sink to bass hiding places. I soon discovered that casting while standing on a stable dock and casting while seated in a rocking canoe are two very different propositions. I finally got the hang of it, though, and we started catching fish. Jay showed me how to throw near the shoreline, let the lure sink, then lift the lure slowly, straight up, while reeling down quickly to take up slack. This causes the lure to rise slowly from the bottom and then fall back. Most of the fish we

## Fish #6: The Bass

caught struck at the very end of the lift; most were in the 2-to-3-pound range.

Jay knew his stuff. He told me that the bigger fish would be different. They would pick the bait up gently and start to slowly move away with it.

"When you see the line start to move in the water, you must reel down slowly until you feel it come tight. That's the time to whack him as hard as you can," he advised.

"Just like on TNN, right, Jay?"

"Right, Bubba, just like on TNN."

I was ready, and I didn't have to wait long. Jay had pushed us up next to an underwater rock formation surrounding a tiny mangrove island. I cast my lure in among the underwater branches and started my slow lift and quick retrieve. All of a sudden, my line started moving to the right, away from the mangroves—slowly, but very noticeably. I wound down, came tight, and struck the fish as hard as I dared without turning over the canoe. What looked to be a giant female black bass exploded straight out the water, shaking her head violently from side to side to get rid of the 2/0 Tru-Turn worm hook that was firmly embedded in her upper lip. She repeated this jump five more times, and also made some thirty- to fifty-foot runs as she tried to get free. After about seven minutes, I brought her alongside and looked for a net, which was not on board. Jay told us that nets were for sissies, so Rusty reached down, put his thumb in the fish's mouth, and pulled her out of the water by her lower lip. She was a magnificent bass, and I thanked Neptune, figuring my hunt for a 6-pound bass among the gators was history. My Boga grip told the story—5 pounds, 11 ounces. We couldn't believe it. I stepped out onto some nearby rocks, first making sure they weren't the backs of alligators, to weigh the large fish on dry land. Same weight—5 ounces too light.

We released the fish and tried for another two hours to find the 6-pounder before we gave up for the day and headed the canoe for shore. By now it was two in the afternoon. We stopped on the way home at the Mutineer restaurant for a late lunch. Over sandwiches and iced tea, we did a little debrief on our morning's fishing. Jay said that those bass were no doubt spawning and that the large fish was probably a nesting female, full of roe. He said that it might be tougher to get our 6-pounder when the spawn was over.

Jay shared with me some other things about himself. He said that while he loved the courtroom, he'd been at it for a long time and would give it up for a job working with one of the prestigious national associations representing the conservation interests of hunters and/or anglers. He would be great at it, I knew. I made a mental note to arrange an introduction between Jay and Johnny Morris. I knew that they would hit it off and that Johnny might be able to help Jay live out his second career.

While I was disappointed that we didn't rack up our species, it had been a wonderful day. Just think about it: First, I'd caught a bass that weighed well over 5 ½ pounds (at least 2 pounds heavier than any I'd caught before). Second, I'd made a new friend, whom I'll probably lose if he sees anyone fishing in his honey hole in Nine Mile Pond. Third, I didn't get eaten by an alligator. Life was good.

After that February day on Nine Mile Pond, I did go on several more bass expeditions, even though most of the experts, including Jay and Rusty, said that it would be difficult to find a 6-pounder. The

## Fish #6: The Bass

winter spawn was over, and most of the large females were "roed out" and off the beds.

The day after Nine Mile, I couldn't raise my left arm over my shoulder. I remembered reeling down and striking a large bass that had magically transformed itself into a submerged log, which sent pain shooting through my left elbow that rendered my hand numb for about ten minutes. I didn't think much about it until the next day, when tendonitis had set in. If you are like me and don't do a lot of sports left-handed, you might consider a left-hand retrieve reel that allows you to keep your plug rod in your right hand. I did just that, going over to World Wide and buying another Shimano Calcutta reel, this time with left-hand retrieve. Unfortunately, plug reels are not like spinning reels, whose crank you can change to the other side to fish right- or left-handed.

All told, I went bass fishing throughout South Florida exactly twenty times between March and October. It was really fun, and I learned a lot. Bass have done well as a species throughout most of the Met region. Every time out, I caught at least one fish of more than 4 pounds, but I figured I'd have to wait for November or December to find my 6-pounder.

Some of the watery venues we tried were fun but not very productive. One of my pals, Glenn Flutie, told me about a great canal for bass behind his house in Fort Lauderdale. Glenn grew up fishing in Islamorada before he moved north and set up his own advertising agency. He still found lots of time to fish and, in fact, won the prestigious Gold Cup Tarpon Tournament four times in a row before he turned professional by becoming a part-time guide. I don't believe his Gold Cup four-peat will ever be accomplished

*Glenn Flutie, cousin of the former Buffalo Bills quarterback Doug Flutie, and his dad, Al.*

again. I figured if Glenn knew tarpon, he must know bass, so I tried his spot. At the end of the day spent on Glenn's canal, I had been chased by a dog, cursed at by a neighbor, bitten by a hundred angry red ants after I stepped on their hill, and totally ignored by the resident bass population.

While I always felt that I could land my 6-pounder in the heavily populated bass waters of the legendary Lake Okeechobee, I really wanted to find the fish in an area closer to home in the Keys and a little bit more off the beaten track. I believe that some of the best bass fishing in South Florida can be done in the canals that crisscross the region, bringing fresh water to the agricultural fields around Homestead.

## Fish #6: The Bass

It was on my twentieth day in pursuit of a large bass that I found success in one of those canals—a canal known as the Aerojet. The canal, or actually system of canals, in Homestead takes its name from the Aerojet Company, which dredged it. Aerojet was one of the first and largest vendors to NASA, manufacturing solid-fuel booster rockets for use at Cape Canaveral. Way back before the cape was ever known as Kennedy, Aerojet dredged coral to form canals and built a variety of production facilities, all of which have since been abandoned. (Ironically, the solid-fuel rockets they manufactured for sending astronauts into space, at a cost of millions of taxpayer dollars, were never even used!) The thirty-foot-deep, steep, rock-walled canals provide a great habitat for freshwater fish and other wildlife. As some of the rocks fell and trees along the edges of the canal grew in, nature provided better and better cover for a growing bass population.

There is great bass fishing throughout the Aerojet, which is easily accessible and open to all anglers. The canal network can be reached by many of the public roads in the area. Any good map (including road maps) will show you spots that are near roads, so you can fish the shores on foot or carry in a canoe or small fishing boat. Public ramps are also available for those who want to trailer in high-powered bass boats, which, while legal in these waters, may be a tad excessive.

On Sunday, November 2, 1997, Rusty and I borrowed a 12-foot aluminum boat from Rusty's cousin Paul Ross, which we strapped down in the back of Super Conch's pickup truck, and headed for Homestead. It was a beautiful fall day as we started our drive up the Overseas Highway at 7:00 a.m.

After nineteen unsuccessful trips to find my 6-pounder, I had decided to try some new tackle. For my birthday, Mindy had surprised me with the one and only Banjo Minnow—actually, the complete 110-piece Banjo Weedless Fishing System, with "everything I need to catch any game fish in the world! Freshwater, saltwater, in any condition." What a gift!

The night before, I had watched the introductory video that came with the package. It featured Banjo inventor Wayne Hockmeyer feeding his invention to dozens of starving bass. I listened in awe as he explained how his Banjo products triggered the fish's "genetic response," which sounded to me like it had more to do with reproduction than feeding.

On the road to Homestead, I read the twelve paragraphs of directions on the Banjo System to a skeptical Rusty, who listened patiently. As we drove, I rigged up some of the Banjo Minnows with their Banjo Nose Hooks, Banjo Baitweights, Banjo Corkscrew Rattles, and Banjo Weed Guards.

By now we were passing the Last Chance Saloon in Florida City. Rusty took a left turn on Palm Drive, and we headed past the Circle K convenience store. We soon arrived at the first canal. Rusty pulled up to the makeshift boat ramp. There were two trucks parked there with empty trailers, but being third on the canal was no problem. There were miles of canals out there and hopefully enough bass for all; plus, I only needed one.

Cousin Paul's rectangular aluminum boat was light and easy to handle. It had two seats, one forward and one aft, with room in the middle for a medium-sized ice chest. Rusty showed me the modifications he had made with Paul's consent. He had added

## Fish #6: The Bass

oarlocks to hold a pair of wooden oars, and some rod holders. Also, he had brought along a 10-pound anchor on forty feet of line so that we could stake up and really work an area hard, as opposed to the run-and-gun method we had used last winter on the shoreline of Nine Mile Pond with Jay Levine.

As we slid the boat into the canal, a pair of brown freshwater birds called *anhingas* craned their necks to get a better look at us from some nearby shrubs. A light 10-knot wind out of the northeast and a slight haze combined to cool the landing and make the morning quite comfortable. Rusty said, "Get in, Banjo Bob, and let's get started." I think that as far as Rusty was concerned, the jury was still out on my new birthday tackle.

Rusty rowed us south on the canal for about a quarter mile before anchoring up next to a promising shoreline with good overhang and shelter. I rigged up a chartreuse Banjo Minnow while Rusty went with a more traditional Texas-rigged artificial black worm.

The first fifteen minutes weren't pretty. Rusty landed three small bass while I got "skafats." Perhaps I wasn't following Wayne Hockmeyer's video retrieval instructions. Rusty struck his fourth bass and said, "Hey, Bubba, Banjo this," triggering my "genetic response" to change bait. I tied on a Texas-rigged plastic worm, pitched it to the shoreline, and promptly whacked a 4 ½-pounder that gave us a great aerial display. Now we were getting settled in.

As we covered the shoreline, we changed rigs often, and just about everything we tried worked. Rusty threw a bunch of topwater lures with good success, while I was finding some larger fish with light-colored plastic lizards.

By 10:00 a.m., we'd caught about twenty fish, but none larger than my 4 ½-pounder. I began to get that old sinking feeling that there were no 6-pounders out there. I was also frustrated that the highly touted Banjo Minnows had struck out. When we stopped to snack on some of the spicy boneless chicken breasts that I'd picked up earlier at The Trading Post Deli, I reread the Banjo instructions and noticed that my kit included some animated-looking plastic frogs called Banjo Frogs. I rigged one up as Rusty looked on with raised eyebrows.

We repositioned the boat about thirty feet from shore as an annoyed great blue heron gave up its perch on a fallen Australian pine branch and squawked its way down the canal. I could see that some shoreline erosion had created a very irregular wall, which might provide good cover.

The morning had clouded over a bit and the water in this spot was a little murkier than the rest of the canal, so, following the instructions, I chose a bright chartreuse frog. I threw it up on the bank and gave it a small tug so it plopped into the water, just as a live frog might hop off the shore. I let it free-fall, twitching it a little to get its back legs moving, yet trying not to retrieve the frog away from the jagged wall of the canal.

The lure sank for about ten feet and then stopped—didn't move, just stopped. I reeled up the slack, came tight, and whacked it as hard as I could. Nothing happened.

"Snag?" Rusty asked just before the line moved to the left about two feet. "No," I said. "It's alive!" Whatever had the frog had apparently chosen to hunker down instead of fleeing to open water. I tightened the drag and leaned on the fish. I'd spooled my reel with

## Fish #6: The Bass

12-pound Ande. While it was well below the allowed 15-pound test, I knew that I could put a lot of pressure on the largest bass without much fear. I pulled, and whatever I'd hooked pulled back! I was locked into an Aerojet tug-of-war, which seemed to amuse Super Conch greatly.

After about five minutes of this, my adversary abandoned her cover and skyrocketed for the surface, going airborne and showing herself as a large, angry black bass, clearly the largest we had engaged this year. If she wasn't over 6 pounds, she wouldn't miss by much, or, as Zane Grey said of a fish he hooked, "A blind man would have known this bass to be enormous, for when he fell he cut the water as a heavy stone."

"Is that her, Rusty?" I asked.

"I'm getting the net out, Bubba," came the response.

This fish had a lot left. Now out in the open, she swam right past our boat, making a beeline for the safety of the other shore and pulling drag as she went. For the most part she tried deep dives and jumped only twice more, the second time as Rusty reached down and netted her. The whole thing took about ten minutes. Our Boga grip scale read just over 6 pounds! We had done it, on my twentieth try!

"Rusty," I said, "I want to keep her alive. Let's clear out that ice chest."

"I've got a better idea," he said as he slipped some braided line into the fish's mouth and through her gill, tossed her back into the canal, and tied off the line on the stern cleat.

We were concerned about the accuracy of the Boga grip aboard the rocking boat, so we decided to stay on the canal to see if we could

*Bubba and his bass and a healthy fear of big gators.*

catch a larger fish. We planned to give it a couple of hours. If we didn't find one, we would put this fish in our ice chest full of canal water and take her over to the closest Met check station—which happened to be the A.O.K. Tackle shop—for a weigh-in. Then I wanted to bring her back to this spot and release her.

"I've got a better idea," Rusty said. Why wasn't I surprised?

"Let's release her in Islamorada."

Now I knew the Conch had flipped. I wasn't aware of any substantial body of fresh water south of Homestead.

"That's just a great idea, Ev! Where shall we release her, in the Cheeca swimming pool?" I asked.

"Nope," Rusty replied. "In Johnny Morris's thousand-gallon freshwater tank at World Wide."

## Fish #6: The Bass

*Johnny doing what he does best—
catching big largemouth bass and advertising his wares.*
PHOTO CREDIT: Bass Pro Shops

There you had it. You didn't get to be a Super Conch just by showing up. What a great idea!

Johnny had opened the new World Wide Sportsman the previous Saturday with a special benefit fundraiser for the IGFA amid pomp and pageantry, surrounded by celebrity guests from the sportfishing world, including Ted Williams, Curt Gowdy, and Jimmie Albright.

It was a beautifully designed and constructed destination location that would greatly impact Islamorada while underscoring our claim to be the Sport Fishing Capital of the World. Down on the first floor were two huge aquariums. The larger, which held 2,500 gallons of salt water, showed off permit, snook, bonefish, tarpon, redfish, and a variety of colorful tropicals in their natural habitat, complete with artificial mangrove roots that climbed over the three-inch-thick wall of glass to touch the salesroom floor. The smaller, 1,000-gallon freshwater tank next to it, also authentically completed, held three garfish and two smallish bass. The beautiful lunker that now swam on a line behind our aluminum boat could certainly find star status in those elegant surroundings, where I could show disbelieving visitors one of my Met species—not mounted, but living in luxury as a celeb. Who knows, with the feeding program they had, she might even bulk up by a few pounds.

So, there we were on the Aerojet, quite a threesome, with Rusty rowing, me casting, and our big fish dutifully following along behind. Our plan to spend two hours to try and find a larger insurance fish had been cut short. About an hour after catching our fish, I heard some splashing and looked down to see her in a very agitated state. It didn't take long to see why. We had company. What looked to be a 9-foot alligator was swimming up behind us, closing ground on my fish.

"Don't worry, he won't bother us," opined Rusty, whom I truly believe knew absolutely nothing about alligators.

"Rusty, that may be so, but it will definitely bother me if that

## Fish #6: The Bass

gator eats my fish or causes her to die of fright!"

"OK, OK," said Rusty as he started rowing us back toward the landing. While feigning some disgust with my concern over a "little" gator, I noticed that he was pulling quite a wake with those oars. He wasn't fooling me this time. The big gator turned off, and the big bass calmed down and let us pull her for a while.

We hit the shore, loaded the boat into the back of the truck, and transferred our fish to the ice chest sans drinks plus canal water, being careful that she didn't jump out the way John Lee Still's Met fish had in the Everglades twelve years before.

Here, Rusty and I got into a heated argument. He wanted my fish to ride in the closed ice chest back in the boat. I, however, demanded that she ride in the cab with us, with the top open so I could keep an eye on her. Rusty finally deferred. It was a little cramped up there in the cab of the truck, and Rusty's bad humor didn't improve every time we hit a bump or went around a curve and some canal water sloshed out on our laps. I suggested he slow down and enjoy the ride, to which he mumbled something unrepeatable under his breath. I finally relieved the tension when I promised I would pay for a truck wash.

"And an interior shampoo?"

"Yes, Rusty, and an interior shampoo with any fragrance you want," I replied.

The Conch smiled.

We carried the cooler into A.O.K. to meet the young clerk who would serve that day as the weighmaster. As water sloshed onto the floor and display case counter, he started grumbling like my fishin' buddy. What was it about these guys? Didn't they like a little bass water? I wondered if he would withhold certification until I promised to pay for a floor shampoo.

The big moment came. Our fish weighed 6 pounds, 1 2/3 ounces. She was more than big enough, although I think she may have lost a few ounces when that big gator zeroed in on her. I know I almost did. I bought a portable aerator for $10 and attached it to the cooler so we could close the top for the one-hour ride home to Islamorada. This appeased Rusty, even though I demanded that our fish continue the ride home in first class.

Before leaving the A.O.K. parking lot, I called George Hommell, manager of World Wide, to make sure that he would accept our *piscine largesse*. George laughed and said, "Sure, bring her down. We need a big bass in that tank." So off we went with water mysteriously still managing to slosh out of our cooler, especially on tight turns.

Noting that the pickup driver was in somewhat better spirits, I suggested that if our bass was going to join Johnny Morris's cast, she should have a theatrical stage name like some performer who joins the circus. We finally settled on a name that combined the monikers of her new grandpa, George Hommell, and her previous home, the Aerojet. As I lifted the cover to see how Georgetta was doing, the tires hit a bump, water splashed onto our laps, and Rusty introduced me to a few new Conch words.

We made two quick stops on the way to World Wide—one at Paul's to return his boat, and the other at Lee and Suzan Baker's to turn in our paperwork and the required thirty feet of line sample. When we finally got to World Wide, we carried the cooler to the aquarium and deposited Georgetta. She swam around twice, looked

Fish #6: The Bass

*Introducing Georgetta to her grandfather George Hommell and Jeff Frazer at Johnny Morris's World Wide Sportsman.*

at the other fish, and settled quietly under an overhanging rock, no doubt exhausted from her travels. She had found a new home. I watched as the two male bass in the tank looked at her before they took off for parts unknown, probably to rent tuxedos and buy Georgetta some candy or flowers.

We'd called Mindy, and she arrived with a smile and a camera. As I stood next to the freshwater aquarium with a huge crowd of two rather disinterested shoppers, I looked around and there it was—not ten feet away—a giant end-aisle display fully stocked with the incredible Banjo Minnow System. I posed next to the display, holding one of the boxes, and smiled broadly as I began to prepare my heartfelt product endorsement remarks for the testimonial ads that Wayne Hockmeyer would no doubt be calling me to do on his TV infomercials.

Now that Georgetta had entered the scene, I knew that life would be good, especially because we were past the halfway point in my quest.

The next morning, before flying up north, we stopped by World Wide to see how Georgetta was doing and ran into Donald Chittick, the official aquarium manager. She was doing great; he was not doing quite as well. It seems that our aqua deposit had violated some procedure that Don had put in place—namely, a ninety-day quarantine on fish, to be sure they were disease-free before joining the aquarium population.

Don mellowed a bit when we suggested that Georgetta looked healthy and, if not, three gars and two scrawny bass could be easily replaced. He smiled and said, "I agree. If I'd have been here, I'd have had you bring her right in too." The quarantine rules would be important as the collection grew. He went on to explain that the saltwater tank was especially sensitive to organisms.

As it would turn out, the World Wide aquarium manager should have had no fears about the two small bass in his tank contracting a disease from Georgetta—she ate them both.

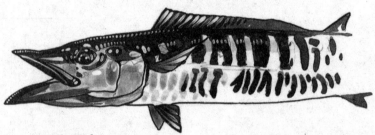

*The Wahoo*

CHAPTER 9

# FISH #7
# The Wahoo

*If the wahoo were as plentiful as the tarpon,
it might well top the latter in popularity.*

—BYRON DALRYMPLE, *Sportsman's Guide to Game Fish*

---

LIKE MANY ANGLERS, I've caught several wahoo but have never actually fished for them. Wahoo are the largest member of the mackerel family. Unlike their cousins the Spanish mackerel, wahoo, *Acanthocybium solandri*, don't seem to school up with a lot of other fish but range the ocean with a few others of their species or by themselves, leading to their nickname, the lone wolves of the ocean.

Wahoo are incredibly fast. With streamlined, torpedolike bodies, they are reported to be capable of speeds up to 60 mph, making them very efficient predators and worthy opponents for light-tackle anglers. Offshore fishermen say that they are light-years faster than the bonefish and able to change directions quicker as well. They are also known for making incredible leaps when hooked and for fighting until completely exhausted.

Following warmer waters, wahoo migrate to the ocean around South Florida in the winter and then head north toward Bermuda in the spring. They tend to range between 10 to 25 pounds, though many are caught each winter that weigh more than 50 pounds. A few catches better than 100 pounds have been recorded. Their appearance has been likened to that of the kingfish or mackerel. Their coloring is dark blue or greenish gray on the back and sides, silvery on the underside. They are distinguished from mackerel by the dark bars that run horizontally around their girth. They become a dark iridescent blue in battle but fade quickly when boated. Their long, low dorsal fins always remind me of marlin. Instead of bills, however, they have sharply pointed heads with upper and lower rows of very sharp, flat teeth, making it necessary to fish them with wire leaders at least. Anglers and guides are cautioned to handle them carefully, as they have incredibly fast reactions and movements and can cut a hand or arm in the water or on a boat.

Wahoo are often found in 100 to 350 feet of water, especially over wrecks or other protrusions on the ocean floor that lift the current and attract bait. They love the Gulf Stream, and during the early winter months they're found off the east coast of South Florida, throughout the Bahamas, and down to the West Indies.

Most wahoo seem to be caught by anglers fishing for something else, such as sailfish. Slow trolling with live bait or fast trolling with skirted lures and dead bait are both effective ways to catch these

## Fish #7: The Wahoo

gamefish. They love fish and squid and will feed on almost anything smaller than themselves. Thread herring, balao, pilchards, mullet, strip baits, or squid work great, as do feathered jigs or shiny lures. When trolling dead baits or lures, you never have to worry about going too fast. These speed merchants will get your offering if they want it.

The seasonal scarcity of wahoo is the only reason I can think of why more people don't fish for them. Besides being world-class battlers, they are also one of the most delicious fish on the table. With limited commercial fishing of wahoo, they are usually plated only by sportfishing captains and anglers. In the Keys, a wahoo dinner is a must-attend event.

Rusty and I went fishing for my 25-pound wahoo three days in February 1997 with minimal success. We did catch and release two small ones (10 and 12 pounds). Upon the advice of Rusty's uncle and cousin, we then put off our wahoo hunt until fall, when the larger fish were supposed to return to the offshore waters of the Keys. We did try the waters off Bimini for two days in June with local legend and IGFA Hall of Famer Captain Bob Smith; we were looking for marlin or wahoo, with equal lack of success.

In mid-September, the word went out that the wahoo had arrived in the waters off Key West. Almost every year there is a two-week window called a "mini season" when these fish show up, apparently on a southern migration. While they weren't in as great abundance as they had been in November, December, and January, it was reported to be a good bite with several large fish being caught.

I called RT, who, unfortunately for me, was halfway out the door on his way to a two-week vacation with his wife, Lisa, to go fishing (what else?) for blue marlin in the Azores. (He would later report that they had more than fifty fish hookups each day.)

When I asked RT for a recommendation, he suggested that I call Captain Kenny Harris, an experienced Key West guide who knew how to catch wahoo. I talked to Kenny on the phone, and Rusty and I drove down to meet him the next day. Apparently, September was a rather slow month in Key West, as Kenny was able to enjoy a few days off.

We met him at Oceanside Marina at 7:00 a.m. He was standing next to his boat, the *Finesse*, a Conch 27 powered by a 200-horsepower Yamaha outboard. When we arrived, Kenny was in mid-kibitz with some of his pals, and it was obvious from the spirited banter that I had found myself another character and this trip would be anything but boring.

As we climbed aboard his boat, Kenny greeted us. "Hi. I've got three rules on this boat. Don't touch my windshield. Don't lean on my canopy supports. And make me look good. You follow the rules, and we'll get along fine." I figured I could follow the first two rules. I wasn't sure how to achieve the third, but I reckoned that I would learn.

Captain Harris was a bulldog of a guy, five feet, one inch tall, with graying hair and a barrel chest. He weighed more than the 120 pounds he maintained when he was an All-Florida high school wrestling champion in his native Fort Lauderdale. In spite of his expanded waistline, you could see the power in this man's frame as well as his personality. As we talked on the way out the channel, it was apparent that Kenny had transferred his competitive nature to the sport of fishing. He was a guy I wanted on my side if a fight broke out.

Fish #7: The Wahoo

*A giant barracuda learns not to mess with Captain Kenny Harris.*

Kenny had moved to Key West from Fort Lauderdale with his wife, Doris. They had two teenage sons, and Kenny was a good dad who took an active interest in his sons' pursuits, whether they were playing roller hockey or baseball. As we motored offshore, I told Kenny about my Met quest, and he shared with me some of his experiences guiding customers over the years to Met grand angler championships. Apparently, Key West was the place to go for notable catches of different species to win the annual Met championship. It seems that three Key West guides—RT, Kenny Harris, and the legendary Ralph Delph—used to battle for this prize every year, with various anglers as clients. Ralph was Kenny's mentor for many years until the two drifted apart and Kenny went off on his own. Now, Kenny Harris was a star in his own right, having put his anglers on fifty-seven IGFA records.

Our first stop was a channel marker just outside Key West Harbor, where we anchored up to catch thread herring for bait. Kenny handed Rusty and me rods set up with tiny Sabiki rigs. I could see the competition setting up immediately between Kenny and Rusty as we each tried to catch the most bait, with half a dozen laughing gulls keeping score overhead. In twenty minutes, his 100-gallon live well was churning with good-looking thread herrings—a hearty wahoo bait just a little larger than razorbelly pilchards.

The final catch count: Kenny—40; Rusty—25; Bubba—4.

As we pulled the hook, Kenny laughed and said, "You backcountry boys are just too used to fishing for the holy trinity."

"What's the holy trinity?" I asked.

"Bonefish, permit, and tarpon," replied Kenny as Rusty stared out to sea and pretended not to be listening.

Let me make a few comments here about catching bait for offshore fishing. Many northern anglers arrive in the Keys pumped and anxious to "catch the big one" and are annoyed when their captain stops in the shallows or just offshore to catch live bait.

"What's going on here?"

"Why are we stopping?"

"Why didn't you catch our bait before the charter began?"

"Why am I paying all of this money and the captain isn't prepared?"

### Fish #7: The Wahoo

First, live bait improves your chances to catch fish immensely. Most baitfish will not survive overnight in captive live wells. Finally, most fishing trips begin too early to allow captain and crew to catch bait and still be on time.

I would suggest that if an angler doesn't want to stop for bait, he should tell his captain beforehand and then be prepared to fish with dead baits or lures, realizing that this impatience may cost him some fish. A better option may be to look at bait catching the same way you look at fishing itself. Support the crew and ask what you can do to help. Bait catching can be challenging and fun. Many captains will rig up a rod for their anglers to try to catch some bait. If they are throwing cast nets, many captains will show their charter clients how to throw after they have netted some baits. One word of caution here: It's really difficult. Try not to fall overboard.

With bait in the live well, we headed for a favorite spot of Key West guides, the south point of the bar about ten miles offshore. Here, the water ranged about 120 to 150 feet and had good currents, creating water activity that wahoo love. I always enjoy a fishing trip to Key West, and it never ceases to amaze me how many different species of waterfowl we see there. This morning was no different. Along the route to the bar, herring gulls, sooty terns, and storm petrels all flew overhead.

When we reached the end of the bar, Kenny turned off the engine and rigged two 7-foot Penn rods with bait, one on the surface and the other with a breakaway weight designed to drift the thread herring at about thirty feet, a depth wahoo prefer. He tied 2/0 Owner hooks to 1-foot wire leaders. Our target species, the wahoo, has razor-sharp upper and lower teeth that would immediately cut monofilament line.

We didn't have to wait long for some action. Unfortunately, most of it was of the barracuda variety. We got constant hits by barracuda ranging in size from 10 to 15 pounds, in addition to several kingfish and a few large Spanish mackerel. Boating these fish was fun, albeit tiring.

A statistical study from a University of Florida marine biologist noted that many Florida fish species are dwindling as the barracuda population grows. The guides I have shared this information with disagree, but my offshore experiences to date seem to be supporting this research.

After lunch, we changed our location and were drifting over the wreck of a WWII submarine. Wrecks provide shelter for many species, and if you want to succeed as a Key West guide, it behooves you to know the location of as many as possible so that you can find them on your LORAN or plug their coordinates into your GPS. Kenny Harris could find them as well as anyone. Ten minutes into the drift, I had a giant takedown below. I had the bait-casting reel in free spool and was using my thumb to prevent backlash. All of a sudden, line was flying off the reel, being pulled much faster than during any of the barracuda or kingfish attacks. I counted to five and flipped the handle, setting the drag. Then I turned the handle twice, taking slack out of the line and coming tight on the fish before striking the fish with three quick lifts of the rod. The fish was hooked solidly and took off directly away from us at an incredible rate of speed.

"That's him!" Kenny shouted as he jumped to the helm and

### Fish #7: The Wahoo

prepared to start the engine. Rusty moved over to reel in the other line. But Kenny didn't start the engine. Instead, he told Rusty, "Leave that other line out, he's not big enough. Maybe his mate is close by." How in the world did Kenny know not only what species this was but also how much he weighed? He wasn't even holding the rod. Obviously, the answer is *experience*.

I fought the fish for about fifteen minutes, during which time he stayed mainly near the surface. He made three beautiful long runs, one of which was sideways to the boat and gave us a good view of how fast he moved through the water. I was amazed by his ability to change directions during the middle of a run. I'd never seen a fish do that before. Most will run in a straight line. This fish was running straight away from the boat and all of a sudden turned about 150 degrees on the fly and was almost swimming back toward us. (This ability to change direction is a well-known fighting characteristic of wahoo. Many anglers feel their line go limp and think the fish is off when he is really speeding right back toward the boat in a characteristic move that I have dubbed "the old wahoo buttonhook.")

When the long runs stopped and the fish began to dive deep, I knew we had him. As I pulled the fish alongside, Kenny gaffed him and slung him into his forward cooler. While I would just as soon have released the fish, I knew that wahoo steaks would have value to Kenny and his family, especially during these slow days of September. Rusty had told me that wahoo is a delicacy, and I knew he would probably take some as well.

"Are you sure he's not 25 pounds, Kenny?" I half asked and half pleaded.

"Naw, man, he's around 18 or 19 pounds," he said as he put

the lines out again.

About five minutes later, after the wahoo had stopped kicking, I put my Boga grip scale on him, being careful to avoid the neat rows of sharp upper and lower wahoo teeth.

Eighteen and a half pounds! I hate it when fishing guides do that. As I washed my Boga grip and put it away, Kenny told me about the 48-pound wahoo that he'd caught two days ago. I also hate it when fishing guides do that—you know, the old "you should have been here yesterday" thing.

Fishing in the afternoon was slow. Kenny shared with us his passion for catching world-record sharks on all kinds of tackle, including fly. One of the catches he was proudest of was a 567-pound tiger shark on 20-pound test!

I tried the wahoo maneuver with Kenny two more days that month with no success, as the few wahoo in the area became fewer. And I vowed to return in November during the peak of the season.

When I got back to Islamorada after having had no wahoo success in Key West, I ran into my friend Alex Adler, a successful offshore guy whose 48-foot boat, a Marine Management hull, the *Kalex*, was a familiar sight off the Atlantic coast of Islamorada. Alex had built a fine reputation in these waters as well as in the Bahamas, where he often captained Johnny Morris's 42-foot Merritt, the *Tracker*.

Alex felt that we were a little early in the season for wahoo and might have better luck beginning in November, confirming my plan. He invited Rusty and me to join him and his mate, Joe Melazzo, and said he would give us a shout in a few weeks when conditions were right. Alex was waiting for the last three days before the full moon,

*Fish #7: The Wahoo*

*Captain Alex Adler, Tracy, and a monster Bahamian bluefin tuna.*

hopefully with a wind out of the northeast.

Why those were the right conditions will have to remain a secret that resides with Alex, but they lined up perfectly on November 14, and we went fishing for wahoo with Alex and had about as much success in the Islamorada waters as we'd had off Key West with Kenny Harris. As always in fishing, I learned a lot. Alex liked to fish for wahoo by slow trolling live speedos, a member of the mackerel family. He and Joe filled their live well with these critters by lowering a 6-foot hoop net and dropping snowball-sized handfuls of chum mixed with sand over the hoop. When the speedos swam over the top, Joe raised the monofilament net quickly, netting a dozen or so baits at each try. The speedos proved effective on kingfish and 'cuda, but no wahoo showed up.

Alex Adler was an energetic and precise captain, and great company offshore. When I said goodbye to him at the dock, he was busy weighing both sides of whether or not we should have trolled lures.

Wahoo frustration was setting in. About a week later, I ended up filing a protest with the Met against a fish—not against a rule, not against an official, another angler, or Rusty, but against a specific wahoo whose name I never knew.

Here's what happened. Rusty and I bought some new lures at World Wide and went wahoo fishing on the *Fish This!* the weekend before Thanksgiving. The Conch had done some homework and gotten the coordinates of a Coast Guard cutter that sank in 138 feet of water on Molasses Reef, eight miles off Key Largo. Wahoo are reported to love wrecks, fast-trolled colorful lures, and winter in the Keys. I figured we were lookin' good!

Saturday was ideal, with scattered clouds, temperatures in the mid-70s, and winds out of the northeast at 10 to 15 knots. We motored through Snake Creek and out to Molasses, with dozens of brown and white gannets swooping overhead.

## Fish #7: The Wahoo

When we neared the wreck, we put two lines out on the riggers and two on the downriggers. There was no waiting on this morning. The second downrigger bait was no sooner set at about thirty feet than something struck it with ferocity. I grabbed the Penn standup rod and watched in awe as a large creature on the other end stripped off 250 yards of line before Rusty could even get the boat stopped. We knew it was a wahoo. No other fish hits so hard or peels line so quickly.

All of a sudden, he slowed and then off he went again in a new direction. By now, Rusty had the other lines in and was giving chase, motoring downwind to intersect the fleeing fish, allowing me to retrieve some 20-pound Ande line off a badly depleted supply on my reel.

The fish stayed fairly close to the surface, and after about fifteen minutes and five runs of decreasing length, we brought the wahoo clearly into sight. "Does he make the stick?" I asked Rusty.

"Probably," Rusty said as he grabbed the gaff. "But I'd rather have the one that's swimming with him."

I looked in the water and saw what Rusty was talking about. Swimming next to our hooked fish was a giant (60-plus-pound) wahoo. Both fish were all lit up with their characteristic luminescent stripes shining in the clear offshore waters under the winter sun.

I reeled down to the leader and stepped back so that Rusty could gaff the 'hoo. Just then, as we watched, the 60-plus-pound swerved in and bit the tail section off our fish just above its anal fin. I mean, this was a bite! As the gaffed fish hit our deck, we could see that he was missing about eight to ten inches of the end they don't eat with.

That fish was immediately disqualified. You see, the Met, like all other fishing tournaments I know of, has a rule against mutilated fish.

So if you land a fish that's been bitten by a shark or hit by a propeller, it doesn't count. It's a good rule and ensures that an angler fights a healthy fish to the net or gaff with no help from anyone or anything else.

There is an interesting exception to this "mutilated fish" rule that not many people know about. If the fish is mutilated after he is gaffed or netted, it is still a legal catch according to IGFA governor George Hommell. The point being that the fish was healthy throughout the fight until the gaffing, which technically ends the contest. It really didn't matter in our case, as our target fish was bitten before Rusty gaffed him.

Actually, it's not uncommon for a hooked fish to be attacked by a predator, usually a shark or barracuda, but that was the first time I'd caught a fish that was attacked by one of its own species. After this bleeding fish stopped flopping around in our cooler, we put the Boga grip scale on him, and there it was, 25 pounds, even with eight or nine inches of his tail gone. I'd caught my weight wahoo, but he wouldn't count.

After a fast start, the rest of the day was uneventful. We did manage to catch four schoolie dolphin and a few "maybe that's him" kingfish.

After we put the boat away and cut up some 2-inch-thick wahoo steaks, feeling like I'd just snatched defeat from the jaws of victory, I called Sue Baker to protest that unnamed 60-pounder—and all living wahoo, while we were at it.

"Sue," I said, "how am I supposed to catch a member of a species that will eat its own to avoid their capture?"

Sue met my mock anger and real frustration with genuine laughter. I even heard her husband, Lee, giggling in the background.

## Fish #7: The Wahoo

Then she promised me that the rules committee would get back to me on my protest, but I shouldn't let waiting for their response dim my enjoyment of competing in the Met, which translated to, "Sure, we'll review it, Bubba, but don't hold your breath."

"Yeah, right," I replied, and headed for home, where I'd have a grilled wahoo dinner—my consolation prize.

So, let's review the bidding. I'd struck out on wahoo in Key West and Islamorada. There was only one thing to do—go north!

A friend of Sue Baker who heard about my wahoo quest suggested that I call a young offshore captain he knew in Jupiter named Chris Kaczor. I called him and he gave me a date and I planned to meet him at the Sea Sport Marina.

Monday dawned cool and clear with a steady wind out of the northwest at 16 knots. I started my drive north to Jupiter at 6:30 a.m., picking up a large coffee at our favorite Burger King along the way. Chris was set to go when I arrived at the dock. He had a smile on his face and two dozen freshly caught thread herrings in his live well. Apparently, he liked the offshore breeze, as did I, and felt that our chances were good.

Chris shared some facts about his life on the way offshore. Born in Cleveland, Chris had moved with his family to Jupiter when he was in elementary school. As the youngest of four sons in a sports-minded family, he had to build himself up to deal with his roughhouse siblings. He played halfback in high school, where he met his future wife. They had a one-year-old son, and Chris said he would bring the boy on board when he was old enough to mop the decks. Although he was relatively young, Chris had been working on offshore boats for twelve years.

*Captain Chris Kaczor carefully releases a tail-wrapped sailfish.*

Chris loved smaller boats that he could work alone and disdained the big boats from Palm Beach and their captains who, he said, spent most of their time on the radio "bitching about fishing and their charters." On this Monday morning after a vacation weekend,

## Fish #7: The Wahoo

he wouldn't have to worry about them. As we pulled up to a nice color change about five miles offshore, I noticed that there were no other boats in sight. It made me think how happy this would have made Daniel Webster, who said, "The day was fine—not another hook in the brook."

Chris turned off his 200-horsepower Evinrude and watched as the northbound current seemed to ease us over the gentle swells created by the moderate offshore breeze. I had brought four rods, two with spinning reels and two with offshore reels, all spooled with 15-pound tournament Ande. I drifted two lines back at different lengths while Chris rigged up a weight to drift a third line back at about thirty feet deep.

There would be no waiting on this day. Within five minutes, a large Atlantic sailfish devoured the first thread herring we rigged. He gave us two great jumps before pulling the hook on the third. Soon after, a large kingfish hit our sinker bait and did a pretty good wahoo impersonation, at least until we could see him.

After releasing the king, we got covered up by schoolie dolphin. I had brought along a rod rigged with tournament 10-pound and a feather in case one of these dolphins was more than 25 pounds. Once we identified the hooked fish as a dolphin, we would reel him to within 25 feet of the boat and leave him there in the hope that a larger fish would follow. A great plan, but it didn't work this day.

The action was constant, and all of a sudden it was 11:00 a.m. and our stomachs were growling. I'd made some leftover turkey sandwiches from Thanksgiving dinner, complete with dressing and cranberry sauce. Chris said that they weren't bad, but being Polish, he would have preferred sausage sandwiches.

I shared with him that Buffalo had the best kielbasa sausage in North America and that I would overnight him some on my next trip north.

Halfway through lunch, one of the lines went off and a sailfish at the other end made a postcard leap. As I picked up the rod, Chris apologized and asked if I wanted to break him off. "C'mon, Chris, the day I break off a sail to catch another target species will be the day I quit the Met Tournament." I had the beauty up to the side in about fifteen minutes, even though he felt strange. We thought he was foul hooked until we got a good look at him and realized he wasn't hooked at all. The wire "wahoo" leader had bent and literally tied around the fish's tail.

"Lassoing sailfish, eh, Chris? Is that a Western-style catch or a Polish technique?"

Chris laughed and said, "Either way, it's a first." What made it doubly strange is that when the fish first jumped, he was hooked the traditional way in the mouth; somewhere during the fight, the hook had come out of his mouth and he'd gotten lassoed around the tail. We wondered if he had twisted himself around and pulled the hook, or perhaps another sail had been with him and gotten tangled up when the first fish spit the hook.

In the meantime, we weren't fishless. We went on to catch a dozen more dolphins, two more kings, three large barracuda, and two more sailfish, with Chris apologizing for each hookup that wasn't a wahoo. In short, it was a spectacular day of fishing!

Captain Chris Kaczor was an outstanding offshore professional, despite his young age. We drove toward shore, listening to two late-arriving older Palm Beach guides complain about their bad

*Fish #7: The Wahoo*

fishing afternoon with charters who didn't want to go in until they caught "at least one fish." I kidded Chris that he could turn into one of those guys when he got older. He promised that when he got older, he would keep his enthusiasm. I promised that I would call him to go fishing again soon.

Panic was setting in. I had chased wahoo in their favorite waters of Jupiter, Key Largo, Tavernier, Islamorada, Marathon, and Key West with some of the best captains in the business—Chris Kaczor, Rusty Albury, Alex Adler, Paul Ross, Kenny Harris, Robert Trosset, and Ralph Delph—and I'd been zapped. The 25-pounder (with all of his body parts attached) had eluded me.

It was March. Most of the local wahoo tournaments were over, and these big, fast cannibals seemed to be migrating north toward spring wahoo hotspots like Bermuda—well out of the Met territory. Advice was coming in from around Islamorada. Rusty told me that a local captain, Allan Starr, had been whacking wahoo on Cay Sal Bank in his boat, the *Reel Quick*, fifty-six miles from Islamorada toward Cuba. Of course, there were unconfirmed reports of hostile gunships out there, but, as Rusty said, "They probably won't bother you." Mindy suggested I go on sabbatical until I get this fish. The guys at the tackle shop had started calling me Wahoo Bob. Tara, the cashier at The Trading Post Deli, had started patting my hand and saying, "Maybe today, Bubba, maybe today."

Then a breakthrough. My next-door neighbor Johnny Morris called me. He said that he'd been bonefishing in Freeport and was docking his boat when some guy pulled up and tossed eighteen large wahoo onto the dock.

"Who is he, Johnny?"

"I'm way ahead of you, buddy. His name is Pete Rose and here's his telephone number."

It would turn out that Pete Rose was a citizen of the Bahamas and a commercial fisherman, not the ex–baseball player. I called him immediately to talk wahoo. At first, Pete sounded a little standoffish as I begged him to let me tag along on a wahoo expedition. He finally agreed, perhaps after realizing how serious I was and that I wouldn't be too much of a liability. I overcame his last reservation when I told him he wouldn't have to re-rig all of his reels of 80-pound test, as I would bring my own rods and reels loaded with 20-pound tournament Ande.

He asked me when I wanted to come to Freeport and laughed when I asked if tomorrow was too soon. He told me to c'mon over, he would meet me at the airport.

The next morning, Wednesday, March 11, dawned sunny and cold with strong, 20 to 25 mph winds out of the northwest as I jumped on a plane for Freeport. A rather bumpy takeoff and then a crosswind landing half an hour later made me realize that it might be a rough day offshore.

Pete met me after I cleared customs, and we threw my rods and boat bag into the back of his truck. I had thrown in some extra clothes and made a one-night reservation at the nearby Port Lucaya Resort Hotel, just in case we needed a second day.

On the way to his dock a few miles away, Pete and I got to know each other. Pete was a very fit fifty-two-year-old, about five feet eight inches, without an ounce of fat on him (he still wore jeans with a 32-inch waist). He told me that his dad, who had died the year before, was a horticulturist who had moved to the Bahamas from

## Fish #7: The Wahoo

England when Pete was one year old. Pete and his five brothers and two sisters grew up and went to school in Freeport. The ocean was a big part of the boys' education. Fishing, diving, and conching were daily pursuits.

Pete was married until 1974, when he went through a less-than-friendly divorce. Shortly thereafter, he met an attractive, dark-haired, London-born woman named Linda, who had moved to Freeport. They were soon married, and now they lived together in a bayside home.

Pete fished 280 days a year on his Cummins diesel-powered 28-foot SeaVee, for wahoo from October through April, and then for Allison tuna and dolphin the rest of the year. He trolled lures of his own making on five or six lines, with two on downriggers, 12 to 14 mph. His boat was spartan, equipped with a compass, a GPS, and a depth finder that he used to stay in about 350 feet of water, where most of these critters live.

We pulled up at his dock, jumped aboard his fueled-up boat, and headed for the high seas. Our voyage out took us through about five miles of large bays and narrow channels where the water depth never exceeded five feet. Sparse mangrove islands dotted the coves, offering good refuge for pelicans, herons, and other shorebirds. Pete said the cormorants had recently discovered this part of the Bahamas and were now there in great numbers.

En route, Pete told me that we had two options: west or east. West meant a twenty-mile run to the open sea, which would have us trolling directly into the 25 mph winds; east meant an eight-mile run through a man-made channel that would have us fishing in the lee of Grand Bahama Island. He said he would make the decision when we reached the ocean and saw the size of the seas. Either way, he said, we would be covering about eighty miles trolling at high speed. His trick, he shared, was to cover as much water as possible due to the relative scarcity of the species. He said that the 12 to 14 mph trolling speed not only helped cover a lot of ground but was also important in getting bites from wahoo, which are capable of speeds up to 60 mph.

One look at the angry ocean and we turned east. Pete seemed disappointed. He said he'd been having most of his recent luck out west (fifty-two wahoo in two days the prior week). We motored north for a few minutes and then entered the wide, eight-mile-long, cement-walled canal that dissects the island of Grand Bahama. It was built in the late 1960s by the Bahama Port Authority, which owns most of the island and seems to run it as well. There are many small offshoot canals running at right angles, neatly forming peninsulas for high-priced residential development that had apparently been happening very slowly. As we sped by miles of undeveloped water lots, I wondered whose dream had led to this expensive dredging and what costs and/or regulations were delaying construction at a time when economies throughout North America were so strong.

Soon we came to the end of the canal, and I noticed there was some development near the ocean—big homes, which I guessed to be five thousand square feet and up.

As we turned left into the ocean out of the harbor, several large flocks of royal terns scurried by overhead. The strong northwest winds were largely blocked by Grand Bahama, which is heavily covered by tall Caribbean pine forests planted twenty years ago by the omnipotent Port Authority.

## Fish #7: The Wahoo

We were motoring along about half a mile off the deserted beaches in about sixty feet of water. I asked Pete how far out we had to go to get to his magical 350 feet. He said, "About a quarter of a mile." I couldn't believe it—three-quarters of a mile offshore, and we'd be in depths of three hundred feet. One mile offshore, by the way, and we'd be in water over one thousand feet deep!

The water was clear, dark blue, and almost totally waveless under cloudless skies. Pete put the 250-diesel engine in neutral and started rigging up. Needless to say, he was totally unsatisfied with my tackle. He took both of my Shimano LTD 20s off my rods and put them on lightweight 5-foot standup rods, custom-made for him by Tom Greene from Fort Lauderdale. Next, he cut off my leaders and retied Bimini knots to create shortened 2-foot double-line leaders that he tied to small black anodized-steel snap-swivels. Finally, he snapped on his special homemade multicolored skirted lures, each with two Mustad stainless-steel 7/0 salmon hooks—the sharpest I'd ever touched. Pete explained that he'd used his twenty-some years of professional experience to develop this lure, mainly out of plumbing supplies like PVC pipe caps. Seeing his knowledge and enthusiasm for his tackle, I wisely decided to leave any fancy-schmancy, to-date unsuccessful, store-bought wahoo lures in the bottom of my boat bag.

Pete told me to take the wheel and keep us in 350-foot water as he dropped five lines back. Then he took over, throttled up to 12 mph, and handed me a small fighting belt to strap on. I liked his positive attitude.

When I'd started the day, I had been uncomfortable about spending time with a stranger who made his living from the sea—not chartering weekend warriors like me, but spending hours alone on a small boat in a big ocean stalking and catching elusive wahoo that he sold to fish houses for $2.75 per pound—in other words, a real commercial fisherman. Our worlds seemed so far apart. I wondered what we'd ever talk about and if he would be ready to kill me after the first hour.

To my surprise, conversation came easy. We talked about fishing, our lives, our wives, our pasts, and our dreams for the future. We were surprised to discover that we both had been passionate squash players before concentrating on fishing. In fact, one of our discussions on international squash tournaments was interrupted by the *W* word—in fact, two *W* words. One, then both downriggers went off, and both custom rods bent over double. The lines were smoking as they flew off the reels. "That's them!" Pete said.

"How can you tell?" I asked.

Pete explained that at this depth, few fish would attack those high-speed lures with the exception of barracuda, which were not common on this east side.

I grabbed one rod and started taking back some line after the fish slowed down, thinking that I could be back in Islamorada for cocktails. All of a sudden, the fish stopped fighting—or perhaps should I say that half of the fish stopped fighting—and popped to the surface as a bloody, bitten-in-half carcass.

I reeled it in, fearing the truth but still asking Pete, "Shark?"

"No, another wahoo. Here, give me that rod and bring in the other fish."

I grabbed the other rod and was relieved to feel good tension accompanied by the characteristic wahoo head shake. Ten minutes into the battle, the fish went limp and popped tailless to the surface.

## Fish #7: The Wahoo

"Uh-oh," said a mildly disgusted but still diplomatic captain. "Head and shoulders. That's why I fish 80-pound test. So I can get them to the boat fast and avoid that happening."

The next half hour was about the quietest I spent with Pete Rose. I felt about two feet tall. I'd finagled my way onto his boat with my 20-pound test tournament line and cost him about 15 pounds of wahoo at $2.75 a pound. I was trying to figure out a formula to offer to buy our catch for the day when one of our outside flat lines went down. I pulled in a wahoo of approximately 15 pounds and then another, probably a 12-pounder; happily, both were untouched by other wahoo.

Our spirits were up, and we took a break. Chocolate milk for Pete, 7-Up for me. Pete had packed some salami, cheese, and bread for lunch, which we both forgot about, thanks to fishing action and good conversation.

The day went by quickly. Before I knew it, we'd trolled all the way east along the shores of Grand Bahama to Deep Water Cay and back. We'd caught several fish, about half of which had been able to avoid what I was now calling "wahoo fratricide."

Two days of this wouldn't be tough to take at all. Pete Rose was a great guy—fun to be with and share thoughts with. That night, I set my alarm clock for 5:30 a.m. and went to sleep with Pete's words ringing in my head: "We're finished practicing. Tomorrow we're going west to get the job done, regardless of the weather."

Let me tell you about a difference between charter-boat captains and commercial fishermen. The former have two shots at canceling—because they or their parties have a deathly hangover, or they or their parties decide the weather is too foul. The latter go, come hell or high

*Captain Pete Rose, obviously not happy about the pounds of wahoo he lost by bringing along Bubba and his light tackle.*

water. No fish, no money—it's a pretty good incentive. During one of our conversations, I asked Pete if rough weather ever kept him on the beach. He responded with a look as if I were speaking Russian.

When I checked out of the pleasant Port Lucaya Resort Hotel, the northwest wind was really crankin'. I wondered how good an

## Fish #7: The Wahoo

idea this was. As expected, my host was waiting for me in his boat with a "let's get started" look on his face. We retraced the first leg of the previous day's trip; then, instead of turning right and going east, we turned left and went west, directly offshore. Pete said the wind had really laid down. I wondered which wind he was talking about. The sea was choppy but manageable—I guessed the waves to be five to seven feet.

About eight miles north of West End, we reached Sandy Cay, a small but beautiful uninhabited sandy island surrounded by wide beaches and heavily shaded by mangroves, palms, and casuarina trees. Off the northern end of the island was the half-submerged wreck of a 65-foot Haitian boat that had brought 110 passengers to this spot a number of years ago. They had all been saved, but what a frightening passage that must have been!

We went on for about half a mile, then Pete throttled back and turned the controls over to me, telling me to steer into the wind while he set up the lines. This day, perhaps in deference to the heavy seas, Pete chose to troll four lines instead of five. He said that we would try to cover fifty miles, twenty-five out and twenty-five back, and that our best action would be at seven, eleven, fourteen, seventeen, and nineteen miles. Don't ask me how he knew that. I facetiously asked him what happened at thirteen miles. He answered, "I'm kind of superstitious; I won't look at that number." *Touché*, I thought. In these growing seas, maybe we'd hit a rock or something at mile thirteen.

As we throttled up to 12 mph, a pair of porpoises greyhounded up from behind us, swam past our boat, and then turned on their sides in our prow wash for a few minutes before heading north into the waves as if to say, "C'mon guys, right this way."

"Good sign, Pete," I said, obviously not having any idea what I was talking about.

"Absolutely," Pete affirmed, probably humoring his new friend.

Exactly five minutes later, the downriggers went off. We landed two wahoo in ten minutes, 10 and 12 pounds each—small fish, but a good start.

Then it happened—action at each of the predicted miles. At one point, we were ten for ten—ten hookups, ten fish—a fact that I foolishly pointed out to my superstitious pal. Just like that, our luck turned. Anything that could go wrong, did. Lines crossed, leaders broke, hooks were pulled, and wahoo were eaten on the way to the gaff. To make matters worse, the barracuda that Pete had predicted on this route showed up on our lures every time we strayed inadvertently into water less than three hundred feet deep, usually when I was at the helm.

As the day went on, the winds and seas picked up noticeably. Pete said that he didn't bring rain gear unless it was going to rain. So as not to appear to be a wuss, I stowed my Helly Hansen rain gear. We were both soaked.

It was noon as we passed by Memory Rock, twelve miles from Sandy Key. It's a small rock that sits above a sandbar about six feet above high tide with a light standard attached. It was actually a large rock before the US Navy started using it for target practice before WWII. The bombs they dropped whittled away the rock and also left some underwater bomb holes in the area that are great for catching mutton snapper.

We passed thirteen miles, with Pete scanning the horizon and refusing to confirm the fact by looking at his GPS. I smiled and

# *The Angler's Scrapbook*

Sunrise, Islamorada. The beginning of a new fishing day.

The author fights a tarpon on one of Islamorada's classic flats.

A hard-fighting sailfish takes to the air.

A lit-up dolphin goes airborne.

A good-sized bonefish is ready for release.

Above: Nicole Ellis

Right: One of the toughest fighters in the seas: a big blue marlin.

Below: A 100-pound tarpon jumps off the bow of the author's skiff.

Above Right: The baits, lures, flies, and plugs that worked are: top row (left to right), balao (sailfish), razorbelly pilchard (barracuda), Chernobyl Crab (bonefish), brushtail jig (permit); middle row (left to right), Banjo Frog (bass), Goombay Hooker (wahoo), Tarpon Drudgery (tarpon); bottom row (left to right), Spit'n Image (dolphin), Skirted balao (white marlin), and Silverado Rattletrap (snook).

# The Top Ten and Their Requirements

SAILFISH

Met Requirement:
8-pound test, any weight

BARRACUDA

Met Requirement:
8-pound test, 25 pounds

BONEFISH

Met Requirement:
On Fly, 9 pounds

PERMIT

BASS

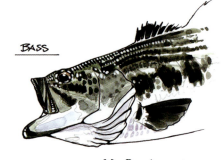

Met Requirement:
Spin, 20 pounds

Met Requirement:
Plug, 6 pounds

**WAHOO**

Met Requirement:
20-pound test or less, 25 pounds

**TARPON**

Met Requirement:
On Fly, 100 pounds

**DOLPHIN**

Met Requirement:
Spin, 25 pounds

**MARLIN**

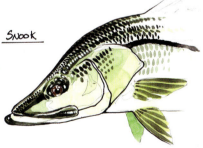

**SNOOK**

Met Requirement:
White Marlin: Any, 20-pound test OR
Blue Marlin: Any, 50-pound test or less

Met Requirement:
18-pound Snook OR
8-pound trout, plug

*Watercolors by Tim Borski*

# The Winners

Barracuda, 25 pounds.
Captain Rusty Albury

Sailfish, 53 pounds. Captain Rusty Albury

RIGHT: Bonefish, 9 pounds 2 ounces.
Captain Rusty Albury

ABOVE: Black Bass, 6.17 pounds.
Captain Rusty Albury

LEFT: Permit, 22 pounds.
Captain Robert Trosset

Wahoo, 30.4 pounds. Captain Pete Rose

Tarpon, 110 pounds. Captain Gary Ellis

LEFT: Dolphin, 29 pounds. Captain Rusty Albury

BOTTOM LEFT: White Marlin, 77 pounds. Captain Alan Starr

BOTTOM RIGHT: Snook, 24.8 pounds. Captain Ron Hueston

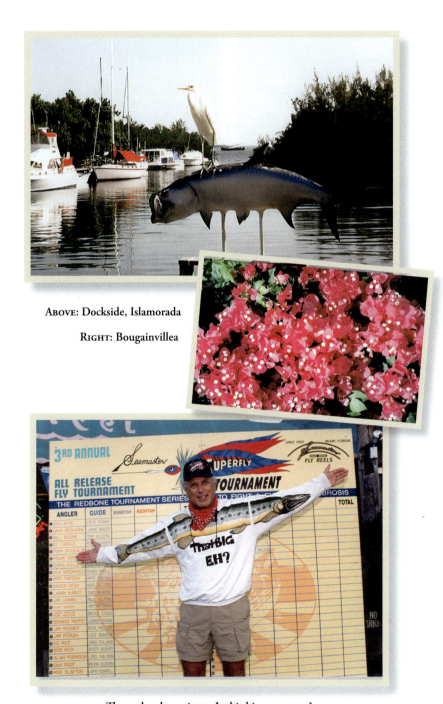

Above: Dockside, Islamorada

Right: Bougainvillea

The author hams it up. Is this his next quest?

wondered where he would be tomorrow, Friday the thirteenth. Pete said that mile fourteen was our best shot. I glanced at my watch, wondering if I'd be sulking back in the Keys tomorrow.

The GPS said fourteen miles, and right on cue, both downriggers went off simultaneously and both lines broke. "What happened, Pete?" I asked.

"I don't know," he said. "Maybe two wahoo bit and crossed lines, breaking them. Keep an eye on the flat lines."

No sooner had the words left his lips than both flat-line rods bowed, accompanied by the highest, loudest screams I have ever heard from fishing reels. Both Tom Greene custom rods bent until their tips nearly touched the gunwales. I dove for the rod on my left and could barely wrest it from the holder. I held up the tip as the obviously big wahoo on the other end screamed off, running shallow against the SeaVee motoring along at 12 mph. I glanced at the other rod, still in the rod holder, and noticed that about half of the line on the reel was already out. Just then my fish came out of the water and we saw him in the distance. He was huge. "What should I do, Pete?"

"Just what you're doing, Bob. Stay with the fish that you know."

The two fish turned left and ran for shallower water. Pete countered their move and turned the boat the opposite way and headed for the depths to avoid any 'cuda that might be in the shallows. A good move. Unfortunately, it put us broadside to waves that now looked monstrous in the afternoon sunlight. The spray soaked us. "Sorry about that!" Pete yelled. I didn't even notice.

Both big fish continued to run left and right and, of course, buttonhook. When that happened, Pete gunned it to pull away and give me a chance to retrieve some line. At one point the lines crossed. "Am I over or under?" I asked.

"Move your rod right next to the other rod. It's the only way to know."

This move was contrary to my instincts, but I followed instructions.

"Over or under, Pete?" I pleaded.

"I don't know," he said, "but you've got to make a decision and cross over or under and around that second rod with your rod, and you've got to do it now or you're going to break off both fish. If you choose wrong, the tight lines rubbing against each other will break for sure. Make your choice!"

"I don't know if I can, Pete!"

"You've got to make your choice and make it now!"

*Great*, I thought, *this'll be a wonderful end to the trip.* I started to take my rod over the top and around the other rod and got cold feet. *"Dammit!"* I went the other way, under and around, and held my breath as both lines sprang free of each other, still intact.

"Yes!" yelled Pete as my heart started to beat again. I was back in the fight. Within ten minutes, I had my fish within thirty feet. As Pete grabbed the gaff, the fish surfaced with a fresh burst of energy, and we could see why. He was being chased by a monster wahoo of at least 100 pounds. As Pete and I watched in horror and disgust, the big predator ate our fish in three bites, leaving just the head.

"Dammit," Pete said. "Forget about it. Put the rod down; I'll bring it in. Grab the other rod."

I picked up the other rod. I had loaded it with 600 yards of line at World Wide the day before, and I was glad that I did. There

## Fish #7: The Wahoo

were only a few turns of line left. This big fish had dumped more than 500 yards of line. There was some pressure but no motion, no pull, and no characteristic head shakes. I shared this foreboding news with Pete as he pulled in the head of a wahoo that must have been a 40-pounder.

I braced my knees against the transom and reeled in the dead weight as fast as I could, anticipating what I was about to see. Pete looked over nonchalantly ten minutes later as I brought whatever I had left up to the transom. We looked into the clear Bahamian water and there he was—a 30-pound wahoo totally intact, bleeding heavily from the gills! Pete was so excited, he jumped in the air, yelling. He grabbed his 4-foot gaff, gaffed the fish behind the head, and pulled him aboard in one strong, fluid motion. The bleeding fish barely moved as he hit the deck. Pete whacked him on the head to make sure he was dead. Even mortally wounded, wahoo can deal serious injuries with those sharp teeth. I'm sure that the blow was redundant. This big fish showed no sign of life.

Pete and I were both jumping up and down and high-fiving. I gave him a big bear hug. I'd been after this lunker for six months, and this was an exciting time. I had found a real pro, and it was fun sharing this hunt and this moment with him. I was more than pleased that for all the thousands of wahoo Pete had caught, he still felt the excitement of this catch.

I asked Pete a bunch of quick questions like, "What happened? Was he dead when we landed him? Why didn't he get eaten by his own like so many of the others?"

Here's how he answered. The fish had been gill hooked. While he had bitten the first hook, the second or trailing hook had lodged firmly in his gill. The pressure of the hook had destroyed his gill plate, causing massive bleeding, which pumped through his lungs during his frantic flight, after which he died. We had sped to deep water (700 feet), thus avoiding the barracuda that are always drawn by the scent of blood in the shallows. By running off more than 500 yards of line, the fish had escaped the other wahoo that were no doubt in the pack, one of which had feasted on his friend. Pete showed me that the hole inflicted by the gaff was nearly bloodless, meaning that the fish's heart had stopped pumping before he was gaffed. As I grabbed a camera, Pete asked me if I wanted him to clean the blood from the gills. I said no, that I thought it told a lot about the fight itself—with apologies to any squeamish readers.

As I write this, I think of the words of Dave Barry, the popular *Miami Herald* syndicated columnist: "Hobbies of any kind are boring except to people who have the same hobby. Auto racing is boring except when a car is going at least 172 mph upside down. Talking about golf is always boring. (Playing golf can be interesting, but not the part where you try to hit the little ball; only the part where you drive the cart.) Fishing is boring, unless you catch an actual fish, and then it is disgusting."

As we iced the fish in the forward fish box, Pete asked me if I wanted to head in. I said no and suggested that I drive while he caught some fish. He shared with me that our earlier misadventures had lost five lures and he was getting low, at which time I dug out my own lures, albeit cursed, to keep us going. As we rigged up, two porpoises appeared out of nowhere and began circling our boat playfully while we bobbed up and down in the growing swells.

*Fish #7: The Wahoo*

*Me and my Met wahoo.*

We cruised for another four miles before turning around and trolling back toward Memory Rock. The rolling swells behind us made it difficult to keep the speed constant. Ironically, we didn't hook another wahoo, although we did hook half a dozen barracuda that Pete reeled in and released with incredible speed. Pete was gentleman enough not to suggest that these 'cuda were all my lures were worth, but I know he was thinking it.

We finally packed it in and started our ride home, which by my calculations was about eighteen miles away. En route, I complimented Pete on his effective lures and suggested that he ought to sell them in Johnny Morris's World Wide Sportsman catalog. Pete said, "No way," explaining that the business of lure building, no matter how lucrative, would cut into his fishing time. Here was a man who had his priorities in order. Of course, by now you know me. I wouldn't let up.

"What do you call these lures, Pete?"

"They don't have a name."

"That's no good. You can't sell lures without a snappy name unless maybe you call them No-Name Lures."

"I don't think so, Bob," he said politely. "They're only made at home out of bathroom plumbing supplies."

"Well, you're from Great Britain; you could call them Handmade Loolures. Get it, a trip to the loo, right?"

"I don't think so," Pete said, laughing.

"I've got it. How about Pete Rose's Own Hall of Fame Legend Lures, in honor of your controversial namesake?"

"Wouldn't he get mad?" Pete asked.

"Who cares?" I countered. "He's got enough to worry about;

anyway, don't you think he'd like to see his name linked with the hallowed halls of Cooperstown?"

We both laughed, and I added, "Seriously, Pete, I brought along the Met Hall of Fame entry form for this fish, and it calls for us to identify the lure by name. You've got to tell me what to fill in by the time we get to your house." I'm sure that Pete Rose needed this assignment like he needed a hole in the head.

The trip to the Roses' dock was a pleasant downwind shush to Sandy Cay and a smooth glide over the bonefish-loaded shallows adjacent to West End. Along the way, Pete told me about the trip to Key West that he and Linda were planning for an international light-tackle offshore tournament in April. I wondered how anyone would ever beat them.

We showed off our prize catch to Linda before confirming its weight of 31 pounds on Pete's IGFA-certified scale and wrapping it carefully in four garbage bags for my 5:30 p.m. return flight to the mainland. Over a cup of hot tea at the dining room table, I pulled out the Met entry form for proper recordkeeping and Pete's signature.

"OK, Pete, the time has come. Name that lure."

"No problem," Linda piped up. "Goombay Hooker."

"Fabulous," I nearly shouted. "How did you come up with that?" I hadn't noticed it was the name written in eight-inch letters on each side of Pete's boat.

I said goodbye to Linda, and Pete and I loaded my stuff into his truck. On the way to the airport, I tried to pay Pete for a great two days of fishing. He looked hurt and refused the money.

"C'mon, Pete, it's only fair. Not only did you catch me my prize, but I had a great time."

*Pete Rose and his wife, Linda, with my wahoo and the Goombay Hooker Lure.*

## Fish #7: The Wahoo

"So did I," he said. "Look, let's just say you paid me with consulting help on marketing our Goombay Hooker Lures."

"You mean you'll make and sell them?"

He paused, smiled, then said, "I'll think about it."

Have you ever been in the presence of someone who does his something better than anyone else? The something doesn't matter—running, singing, talking, working, playing, acting—they just do it better than anyone else. That's how I felt about wahoo fishing with Pete Rose. I was absolutely in awe of his skills. I've never learned so much about fishing in two days.

While time on his boat flew by, I distinctly remember one conversation as if it took place yesterday. I asked Pete about the negatives of his job, and he answered thoughtfully, "Well, one negative is those pesky blue marlin."

"What do you mean, Pete?" I asked.

"Well, in April and May, as the wahoo are migrating, I get a lot of marlin hookups that I just break off."

"Oh, really?" I blurted out as my eyes opened to a diameter of four inches each and I felt myself getting goose bumps.

"Yeah," he said. "Those big fish are a real nuisance. One day last April, I had four on in one morning."

Guess where Bubba would be headed in April to look for species number eight?

*The Dolphin*

CHAPTER 10

# FISH #8
# The Dolphin

*In addition to its brilliant coloration,
the dolphin strikes explosively, fights frantically,
and performs beautifully in the air.
The attack of a dolphin school at
a trolled bait is one of the top thrills
in Gulf Stream fishing.*
—A. J. McClane, *McClane's Field Guide
to Saltwater Fishes of North America*

---

"No, I'm not going to kill Flipper. I'm going fishing for a dolphin-fish—a cold-blooded fish, not the warm-blooded mammals that are also called dolphin." This is how I have to begin every conversation with nonfishing friends before I go dolphin fishing.

Everyone who has fished saltwater knows that the name *dolphin* is shared by two distinctly different members of God's kingdom, but no one seems to know why this came about. Perhaps the best, if not the only, guess as to the confusion comes from author/angler Peter Goadby in his beautifully photographed book *Saltwater Gamefishing*. Referring to dolphinfish by one of their other names, Peter points out that "mahi mahi were known and recorded by long ago mariners. Perhaps the name 'dolphin,' confusing it with the marine mammal dolphin, came from its habit of swimming around the bows of sailing ships, particularly when the ships were becalmed in the doldrums."

It seems hard to believe that anyone could mistake what A. J. McClane referred to as "the riotously colored" dolphinfish for the brown or gray mammals also called *porpoises* that conservatively outweigh the fish by 200 to 300 pounds apiece. Given the generous ancient mariners' grog rations and, in the absence of a better explanation, I'm going with Goadby. I just wish that dolphinfish anglers would universally adopt one of the other names used to describe dolphinfish, such as *mahi-mahi, dorado, coryphene* (in France), *papagallo* (in Italy), or *siira* (in Japan). It could save us a lot of onshore explaining. Besides, dolphin mammals don't even take bait. They're too smart for that. (Well, that's not quite true either. Three years ago, while fishing for snook with Mindy and Rusty in Snake Bight Channel off Flamingo, I hooked up what appeared to be a 300-pound porpoise that grabbed a small hooked jack crevalle that had eaten my bait. The animal took off like a freight train. I palmed the bail at once, breaking him off to avoid tiring him out in those shark-infested waters. That's the first and only time I've hooked or heard of someone hooking a porpoise. Rusty said that it was probably a young

### Fish #8: The Dolphin

*This is Flipper. Flipper is not my target species.*

male that had been kicked out of the school and was feeding in the murky channel without the advice and counsel of any elders.)

Up north, almost every community organization and charity sponsors a summer golf event, affording avid amateur golfers a virtual tournament circuit. In the Florida Keys, those golf outings are replaced by dolphin tournaments with names such as Marathon Dolphin Scramble, Coconuts Dolphin Tournament, Holiday Inn Dolphin Tournament, Holiday Isle Dolphin Tournament, Tavernier Creek Dolphin Rodeo, Caloosa Cove Dolphin Tournament, Original Ladies Dolphin Tournament, Governor's Cup, Port Largo

Residential Homeowners Dolphin Tournament, Italian Fisherman Dolphin Tournament, and so on.

Dolphin, *Coryphaena hippurus*, are the ideal species for these tournaments. They are found in incredibly large numbers offshore in relatively shallow waters, especially during the summer months.

There is no mistaking the arrival of a school of dolphin in the ocean. They swarm in, looking for food, all lit up in iridescent shades with their green backs, yellow underbellies, and flecks of blue on their sides. Their pectoral fins often take on a brilliant shade of neon purple, giving them a surrealistic look against the clear, dark blue water that they search for and thrive in. The appearance of a dolphin school is as breathtaking for an old salt as it is for a novice angler. I've heard dolphin called the Dennis Rodmans of fishing. I don't think that's fair. They're brighter than Dennis Rodman. I'll let you define bright any way you like.

While many species eat to live, dolphin seem to live to eat. They have a very high metabolic rate and seem to be in perpetual motion, searching for food in large or small schools. Studies have shown dolphin growing from 1 to 2 pounds to more than 30 pounds in less than eight months. Their life span is about four years (quite a contrast to some of the 100-pound tarpon that are believed to be more than thirty-five years old).

The offshore captains divide dolphin into three basic categories: *schoolies*, *gaffers*, and *slammers*. Schoolies are the smallest dolphin (up to about 10 pounds) and are, of course, found in huge schools. This category is sometimes divided into *shakers* and *bakers*, the former so small that you shake them off the hook, the latter barely large enough to keep, as their fillets aren't much larger than a few strips

## Fish #8: The Dolphin

of bacon. Gaffers range between 10 to 20 pounds and are apt to school with five or six other dolphin of the same size. Slammers, the prize catches that weigh anywhere from 20 to 60 pounds, travel with one or two other fish. These are the fish that tournament anglers search for. The biggest slammer caught in several of the weekend dolphin tournaments can win its lucky captor $10,000 or more. One-hundred-pound dolphin are possible but very, very unusual.

It is almost easier to list what dolphin won't eat than what they will eat. Any small live bait, lures, spoons, and feathers all work just fine. The key to capturing a dolphin's interest and triggering a bite is motion. Drifting works but trolling works better—and you can't troll too fast. These critters, with speeds up to 50 mph, can hit a lure trolled at 20 knots and still swim circles around a boat.

When hooked, dolphin rarely dive deep for long, preferring to fight on the surface and in the air, flipping, cartwheeling, and violently shaking their heads. While these fish are smaller than several of the targeted offshore fish such as sailfish, marlin, and tuna, pound for pound they fight just as hard, if not harder.

One of the best dolphin-catching tricks is to search offshore for some large, floating flotsam and jetsam. Large boards or planks or other debris that have been in the water for at least twenty-four hours become encrusted with plankton that attract all types of small, hungry baitfish, which in turn attract schools of ravenous dolphin. Floating weedlines have the same up-the-food-chain effect.

Another dolphin-catching trick is to watch for birds. Dolphin create such a frenzy when they drive bait to the surface that there are plenty of leftovers for seabirds, which fly over them and then dive on the water when the dolphin are near the surface. Debris is hit and miss, but diving birds are a sure sign of dolphin unless they are following blackfin tuna or bonito. The more birds, the larger the school of small fish. One or two diving birds means slammers. If the birds are flying in the same direction as the current, they are chasing schoolies, which always hunt with the current. Birds flying in the direction opposite the current are no doubt following big slammers, which always swim against the flow.

Once they have a dolphin on the line, some anglers bring him to within twenty or thirty feet of the boat and leave him in the water. Because dolphin are curious and social and swim in groups, they will often school up with the hooked fish to see what is going on, giving the anglers a chance to cast for more hookups. This method offends many people's sensitivities. Not mine. It's a proven way to trick and catch a great fighting fish and may well figure into my search for a 25-pounder on spinning gear. Remember, by Met definition, *spin* means artificial lures cast, not trolled, to a fish.

Actually, we forgot the definition of *spin* one spring. Rusty and I were fishing for blackfin tuna in 1997. We were on our way to a popular tuna spot called the Hump, about twenty-five miles off the coast of Plantation Key. Our live well was full of razorbelly pilchards. About twenty miles out, we spotted seabirds diving on a board and pulled over to take a closer look. There, very visible below the board, was a pair of large dolphin. I rigged up a light spinning rod and threw a hooked pilchard in front of the larger of the two. The dolphin ate it immediately and then fought for twenty minutes before we gaffed him and threw him in the fish box—a nice 26-pound bull dolphin.

"That takes care of another species," Rusty said.

## Fish #8: The Dolphin

"Boy, that was easy," I thought as we got ready to resume our trip to the Hump. I looked down at the board, now fifty feet away, and noticed that the other dolphin had left the board and was swimming back and forth, ten feet behind our boat.

"Look at that, Rusty."

"Go ahead and feed her," Rusty said.

I rigged up again and threw a bait to the fish, but she wouldn't eat. She just kept circling the boat. Rusty tried a Millie Bucktail with no luck.

"Rusty, she's looking for her mate."

"Don't be ridiculous," Rusty snapped as he fired up the Mercury engines. "Her hunger is just overcome by her curiosity about our boat."

Rusty was probably right. After all, he was the expert. As he put the Ocean Master in gear and got the boat up on plane, I looked out to see the single dolphin following in our wake.

Later that afternoon, as we were weighing the dolphin and doing the paperwork at Islamorada Bait and Tackle, Rusty got a strange look on his face, pulled out the Met rulebook, and said, "Oh, darn it," or words to that effect.

"What's the matter?"

"*Spin* means artificial. We used bait."

Rusty was crushed. I couldn't even bring myself to tease him.

"Oh, well," he said. "I'll take him to the cleaning table and fillet him for dinner. You want some?"

"No," I said, thinking back on our afternoon's adventure and the second fish that had followed our boat. "He's all yours."

I went for a full year without hunting dolphin, as we spent the summer up north and then concentrated on other, more available species in fall and winter. The summer months are the best time to find dolphin in the warm ocean waters around Islamorada and the Florida Keys. As we headed into May 1998, Rusty and I felt pretty good about our chances. We decided to use a strategy that we felt would optimize our odds for catching a blue or white marlin or a 25-pound dolphin on any given day—both fish I still needed for the Met. We called our tactic the modified run and gun. We planned to troll four small skirted balao on 20-pound test lines, looking mainly for white marlin, but we also rigged the largest balao we could find on a 50-pound test center flat line, hoping that if a blue marlin came up, he'd choose that bait. We would put one engine in gear and troll at around 2,000 rpm, which would give us the equivalent of about 8 mph on the ground.

We'd try to stay in seven to eight hundred feet of water and watch for diving birds or debris that could indicate that dolphin were around. We'd also keep an eye out for weedlines, which provide dolphin not only with food but cover from larger predators, and shade as well. (My cousin Donny from Palm Beach told me that on calm summer days up there, he and his pals often spread newspapers on the water and position their boat close by to watch for the arrival of dolphin searching for food.)

Besides the five rods trolling balao behind the boat, we planned to keep two spinning rods rigged with 10-pound tournament Ande and lures in the forward rod holders so that if we spotted promising debris, I could pitch artificials and hope to jig up a curious 25-pound dolphin.

As in most southern waters, small schoolie dolphin are prevalent, but larger fish also seek small fish on debris. In fact, large

## Fish #8: The Dolphin

dolphin will often hang around the fringes of schools, looking for a fish that gets separated. Other species love to feed on schoolies as well. Many marlin hookups take place when surprised anglers are fishing for schoolies on light tackle.

We put our strategy to work over Memorial Day weekend in 1998, sixteen months after I'd started this quest. The weather cooperated, with the strong El Niño winds that had hurt fishing all winter subsiding to gentle breezes out of the southeast and southwest. The wind shift brought clear skies and temperatures in the mid-90s to South Florida. When the wind blew out of the southwest, it also brought the haze of smoke from the huge fires that were burning largely out of control in Mexico.

The trolling part of our strategy was singularly unsuccessful. Rusty and I spent a lot of hours pulling dead balao through some stiflingly hot, humid days. We started early every day and were drenched in sweat by 9:00 a.m., hoping for some summer showers to cool us off. We brought along guests on most days, whom we hoped had a high tolerance for hot weather and tedium. My son Barney joined us a few times, as did his friend Summer LePree and my pal Rodney Lloyd, who was mistaken so often for Kenny Rogers that we started calling him the Gambler.

The debris and weedline part of the strategy was more successful, and we caught a lot of schoolies to fill our freezers and break up the monotony. The big dolphin seemed to be scarce. We did catch a few trolling, but the ones that I cast to were very finicky.

Patience is an important commodity for any angler. It's mandatory when you have targeted very specific species as opposed to anything that will bend a rod. As important as patience may be, however, I believe it's only the second most important attribute for an angler. The first is optimism. It's the one characteristic that brings us back and keeps us in the sport. Think about the most avid anglers you know, no doubt yourself included. These are the most optimistic people around. We have to be, or we wouldn't even get up in the morning to go out there, wherever *there* might be.

Izaak Walton best articulated the necessary prerequisites for those who would fish in his landmark book *The Compleat Angler*, published in 1653, saying, "He that hopes to be a good Angler must not only bring an inquiring, searching, observing wit, but he must bring a large measure of hope and patience, and a love and propensity to the art itself; but having once got and practiced it, then doubt not but angling will prove to be so pleasant that it will prove to be like virtue, a reward to itself."

I've learned something else too. We all spend a lot of time waiting for our successes, and then we talk about them incessantly on shore as if we're trying to find converts. None of us ever talks about our failures. How many anglers do you hear talking about the bad things? Granted, we all talk about the one that got away, but only in the larger context of what we'll do differently to catch him next time out. You never hear an angler dwell on an unsuccessful fishing trip. They might make a few passing remarks—"Boy, the fishing was terrible . . ." "I got skunked . . ." "I never even saw a fish . . ."—but then they're planning their next outing.

And so it went as the hot summer days lengthened around us aboard the *Fish This!* Many days, the fishing was terrible. I got skunked. I didn't even see a fish. But I kept coming back for more. We fished for seven days and didn't even see a marlin or large dolphin. I tried to

Fish #8: The Dolphin

*Barney caught a 300-pound hammerhead shark in a rainstorm.*

console myself by thinking of the first sentence of Hemingway's *The Old Man and the Sea*: "He was an old man who fished in a skiff in the Gulf Stream and had gone eighty-four days now without taking a fish." Even though that worked for me, I still turned to the Conch for more consolation—which was always a big mistake.

"Rusty, we've been trolling around for a week now with rather limited success."

"This is nothing," Rusty responded. "I talked to Captain Skip Neilsen yesterday, and he told me we might troll around for a year and never see a marlin."

Me and Rusty trolling around in tight quarters for a year? What a thought. Probably only one of us would survive.

We decided to try another strategy. We started looking for birds swarming over schools of small blackfin tuna and bonito, which we hooked with small spoons and feathers. Then we rehooked these fish on our 50-pound test lines, slowed the engines, and drifted them behind the boat, hoping a hungry marlin would swing by. While this never happened, one day we did feed a 300-pound hammerhead shark, which Barney brought up to the boat after an hour-and-a-half battle. This fish was mean and huge. He had to be. The large bonito he gobbled down weighed 10 pounds.

We went back to plan A—run and gun. The eighth day of our quest dawned picture-perfect—not a cloud in the sky or a ripple on the sea. It was so calm, in fact, that my bride, Mindy of the queasy stomach, decided to join Rusty and me for the search.

We saw Rusty's truck at Islamorada Bait and Tackle and pulled in. He was picking up some new jigs and asked me what I was looking for. I told him I wanted to find a pilchard-shaped rattle bait with two treble hooks that TV celebrity/writer Mark Sosin was autographing, called Spit'n Image.

The Conch spoke: "There ain't no way no fish is gonna eat that!"

"Rusty, there's a triple negative in that sentence."

"A what?"

## Fish #8: The Dolphin

"Never mind," I said as I paid for my new acquisition. Mindy and I headed for the boat.

As we motored out of the channel at Indian Key, the day had a special feel to it. I'd never seen the ocean so calm. It looked like a giant pond. The smoke and haze from fires in Mexico made it impossible to distinguish the sea from the horizon. We ran south for twenty miles, crossing the wakes of two ocean freighters heading in opposite directions, before we found a large, well-defined weedline that looked like it ran from Miami to Key West. We let down the outriggers and started trolling. Twenty minutes into our troll, we spotted a huge palm tree floating upside down with about six feet of stump sticking up in the weedline. Rusty idled up and cut the engines. There were schoolies everywhere. We pulled in our trolling lines, grabbed spinning rods, and started throwing at them. Talk about finicky eaters—they seemed to have lockjaw. Rusty even threw chunks of bait that we watched float down to them and then out of sight, untouched. Mindy took out a fly rod and started experimenting with different flies while Rusty and I went through all the artificials in our tacklebox. Nothing worked. Then I remembered—my new Mark Sosin–autographed Spit'n Image lure! I tied it on with Rusty *tsk, tsking* and Mindy laughing in the background.

"Pick a direction, Everett."

"Ten o'clock."

"Fine," I said and hurled the lure. No sooner did it hit than—*bang!* A 5-pounder slammed it. I chuckled uncontrollably as I reeled the fish back to the boat and threw again with the same result. In fact, every cast I made with Spit'n Image delivered a dolphin. Not only that, but it apparently turned on the bite. These previously tight-lipped fish were now slamming everything. Mindy's flies and Rusty's jigs were getting hit on every throw. The schoolies were fighting one another to get into our fish box!

Within twenty minutes we had caught about a dozen and a half schoolies and put our rods down for a water and iced-tea break. By now, we were floating as part of the weedline with dolphin, filefish, rainbow runners, and other assorted small fish resting in the shade of our boat. We watched as juvenile needlefish and flying fish tried to look invisible in the sargassum grass. Rusty even reached into the water and scooped up a juvenile flying fish in his hand to show us what they looked like up close.

We sat there for twenty minutes, feeling like we were a part of nature and watching the fish, before starting our trip south. I asked Rusty if we had a safe on board where I could lock up my new Spit'n Image lure for safekeeping. His silence was my answer. We got to about forty miles offshore before Rusty pulled back the throttles in the most beautiful dark blue water any of the three of us had ever seen.

"It's like looking into a giant dark blue sapphire," Mindy said.

"Mindy, if you don't mind, I'm the wannabe writer here. I'll make up the imagery. By the way, is it all right with you if I use that line?"

"Be my guest," she laughed.

So there we were, with the ocean so blue it was like looking into a giant dark blue sapphire. We put the twenties out with a fifty in the center and started trolling back the way we'd come. We broke out huge Italian subs from The Trading Post Deli and relaxed, savoring our lunch.

The beauty and joy of the day made the quest seem much less

## Fish #8: The Dolphin

important. We talked about the difficulty of catching each of the Met species. Rusty kept saying, "You just have to put in the time. It can happen in a minute. All we need is a break."

We cruised on after lunch for an hour and a half, Rusty at the helm and Mindy and me chatting in the bow. Then we got that break Rusty had been talking about. He yelled from the tower, "Bob, look ten o'clock, thirty feet!"

There was a gaffer swimming parallel to us, apparently unaware or undisturbed by our presence.

"Is he big enough, Rusty?" I asked as I grabbed my Spit'n Image–rigged spinning rod and jumped up on the gunwale of the bow.

"There's only one way to find out. Throw on him."

I did throw. The lure landed one foot in front of him, and he crashed it—missed! He kept on swimming. I retrieved the lure and threw again, right on his nose. He ignored it.

"Get down!" Rusty yelled.

As I jumped down to the deck, he gunned the engine and then pulled it out of gear. I thought he'd lost his mind.

"What are you doing?" I yelled.

"Big fish on the center 50. Looks like a marlin," Rusty shot back. "I gunned it to set the hook for you."

"I knew that," I told Mindy. "I knew that." I ran back to the cockpit to fight what I hoped was my blue marlin. But my marlin performed a magic trick and turned himself into a large acrobatic dolphin. Now remember, a trolled dolphin hookup on 50 wouldn't count for the Met. I needed to throw to the fish and catch him on 16-pound test.

"Here, Mindy, fight him," I said, handing her the rod and putting a fighting belt around her waist. Then I grabbed my spinning rod and jumped up on the transom to see if her hooked fish had company, which he did. Mindy's fish, swimming about fifty feet away, looked to be right around 25 pounds. Swimming on each side were two fish, one smaller and one much larger.

"Throw right on the big one!" Rusty yelled. "And make it good. You don't want to give the smaller fish a shot at the lure."

I knew the drill, and I knew the consequences of a bad shot. I also knew that this was my Met fish. I snapped open the bail and let it go. The Spit'n Image lure hit the big fish in the nose.

*Perfect.* Just like room service.

Before I had a chance to laugh at my analogy, the dolphin crashed the lure without even changing speed or direction. The explosion in the water was huge, my spinning rod bowed, and we had a hookup. I felt the tight line and whacked the fish, just for good measure. She exploded out of the water, a big cow dolphin at least five pounds heavier than Mindy's hooked bull. This fish would make the stick—if only I could bring her in.

Now both of the hooked dolphin took off swimming and jumping together, followed closely by the unhooked fish.

"Should I break mine off?" Mindy asked, not wanting my Met entry to break off on her line.

"No." Rusty made a command decision. "We're going to catch both of those fish. Just be careful."

Mindy's fish dove back the other way, so we switched sides. She went under, I went over. We did this maneuver three more times before Mindy used the big Penn 50 reel and standup stick to pull her

## Fish #8: The Dolphin

bull closer to the boat and away from the battle. Rather than follow, my fish dove away from the boat, stripping line as she went, probably to a depth of 50 to 75 feet.

"Be patient," Rusty warned. "Don't try to overpower her. She'll come back up. They always do."

Right then, I thought of a trick that Robert Trosset had taught me in Key West. In spite of the excitement, I tried to make my hands as gentle as I could, feeling the fish with the rod tip while backing down on the pressure to make the fish stop running. Here's the theory. The fish feels pressure and runs. You take away the pressure and she stops running. It works, and it was working this afternoon. The fish stopped diving, and I gently brought her back to the surface within ten minutes. We had hooked up at 2:50 p.m. and, after two more deep runs and a few jumps, I had her to the boat at 3:15 p.m. Mindy's fish fight was over, so she grabbed the camera as Rusty grabbed the gaff. I lifted the fish and Rusty tried for the gaff. He missed her! The fish sounded as the gaff handle hit her harmlessly on the dorsal fin. The fish felt the metal and went ballistic. Rusty didn't feel the fish on the gaff and went ballistic.

"Mindy, I can't decide who's more upset, Rusty or the fish," I cracked. We both started laughing in spite of our situation. Rusty was not laughing. I'm sure he was thinking of what my reaction would be if this fish went free.

"Relax, pal," I tried to reassure him. "She's still solidly hooked. You'll get her next time."

I was right about that. In five minutes, I had her back up to the boat. Rusty aimed again, gaffed her behind the pectoral fin, and lifted her from the water to the fish box in one fluid move. She was so large that her tail hung out of our large double ice chest.

*Mindy and I display our two big dolphin aboard the* Fish This! *Note the shape of the head of her bull versus that of my cow.*

*Even in black and white, you can notice the color change of my Met dolphin as it dies from the back forward.*

## Fish #8: The Dolphin

There was no doubt about it—we had fish number eight. We exchanged high-fives all around, then decided to head in. It was 3:25 p.m., we had an hour run ahead of us, and we wanted to get this fish to the local Met check station, Islamorada Bait and Tackle, before it closed at 5:00 p.m. We knew that if we waited until tomorrow, loss of blood and natural dehydration could cost us our Hall of Fame entry.

Mindy found one can of Coors light beer from a previous trip, and the three of us shared it, toasting each other on the way home. This fish had been a long time coming. Her capture had been a team effort, and that beer tasted great.

The cow dolphin that had weighed 30 pounds on my boatside Boga grip weighed 29 pounds at the Met check station. Islamorada Bait and Tackle owner John Preast; his wife, Becky; and staff members Jack and Bill, who had sold me the Mark Sosin lure that morning, were all there along with my pal Ron Wagner, who loves their free coffee.

"What'd you get that big fish on?" Bill asked facetiously.

"Gee, I'm not sure, Bill," I pretended. "What was that lure, Rusty?"

"I don't remember," he grumped. And we left it at that.

We threw the fish into the back of Rusty's truck and squeezed into the cab. Rusty turned on the engine and the welcome air conditioner and said, "Just a minute, I forgot something." He ducked into the Bait and Tackle, and I saw him walking toward the lure counter. In two minutes, the Conch reappeared clutching a small paper bag. I smiled at Mindy and decided not to ask him what he had purchased.

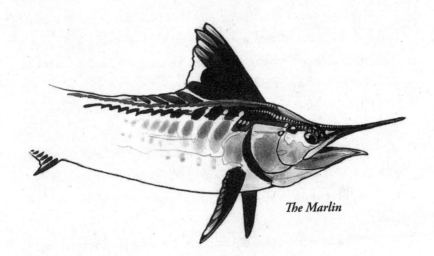
*The Marlin*

CHAPTER 11

# FISH #9
# The Marlin

*Perhaps nothing compares in angling to seeing a thousand-pound fish leap fifteen feet in the air, shaking its head violently to dislodge the hook as its ten-foot body cartwheels in the air to crash against the water. Nothing in angling is as physically challenging as bringing such a fish to the gaff. And nothing in angling takes as much moral courage as releasing that extraordinary predator to live and fight again.*
—Herbert A. Schaffner, *Saltwater Game Fish of North America*

---

I COULD FILL this chapter with what I don't know about marlin. Rusty told me that there are four species: blue, white, black, and striped, of which the first two—blue and white—are found in the waters off the lower Keys. I did some research and turned up some information on a fifth species. According to *McClane's Field Guide to Saltwater Fishes of North America*, the hachet marlin, while uncommon, is found in the waters off the mid-Atlantic states ranging down to South America. At any rate, I believe the best place to find a blue, white, or hachet within the Met boundaries may be off the western shores of the Bahamas.

Warren Schintzius, a Buffalo native who moved to Fort Lauderdale after college and started a yacht brokerage business, apparently discovered the secret of treating his clients fairly and had a reputation for honesty and dependability.

Warren kept a boat in the Bahamas and fished there whenever he could. When asked for advice on how we could catch a blue marlin, Warren didn't hesitate. He suggested we call Captain Bob Smith in Bimini. "There are younger captains with newer boats, but Bob Smith knows where to catch marlin," he said. With that advice, I called Captain Smith and reserved the dates of June 4 and 5 with his wife, Bonita ("Bonny" for short).

Unfortunately, this meant that I couldn't fish the Don Hawley Tarpon Tournament. I told Mindy that this would leave the field open for her, fishing with Craig Brewer, to win it. (Of course, she did.)

When I called Captain Smith back to go over the details of our trip to Bimini, we had a conversation that went roughly like this:

"Captain Smith, I'm looking forward to fishing with you."

"What you want to catch?"

"A blue marlin."

"No problem, Mon. What else?"

"A wahoo."

"No problem, Mon. What else?"

"A dolphin."

## Fish #9: The Marlin

"No problem, Mon. What else?"

"How about a white marlin?"

"No problem, Mon. What else?"

"Aah, I think that'll do it," I said, not wanting to appear piggy.

"OK, Bob, I'll see you Tuesday night."

This guy sounded great. It felt like I was ordering takeout from a seafood restaurant.

Warren had suggested we stay at the Big Game Club, where the anglers from many of the private fishing boats stayed, so that Captain Smith could pick us up there in his 41-foot Hatteras, the *Miss Bonita II*.

I called Rusty to give him the departure time, and he asked if his dad, Russ, could join us. I told him that would be great, and Rusty said, "Good, 'cause I invited him last night."

I was thrilled that Russ, or Uncle Russ as he is known in Islamorada, would be joining us, as he was one of my favorite people in Upper Matecumbe.

Russ Albury was a sixty-five-year-old widower who had lost his wife two years before to cancer. He was a big bear of a man with a gentle way and a keen sense of humor. Before he became a locksmith, Russ owned and operated Islamorada Tackle and Marine. In this role, he was consulted daily by the leading anglers, offshore captains, and backcountry guides. As you can imagine, he built up a wealth of information about fishing in the Florida Keys and some darn good stories as well. I knew Russ would be a great addition to our crew.

Late Tuesday afternoon Russ, Rusty, and I flew to South Bimini, cleared immigration, and took the taxis (land and then sea) to the Big Game Club on North Bimini. Their docks were about half full with a variety of large watercraft, predominantly sport-fishing boats. Interspersed among the Hatterases, Ocean Yachts, and Bertrams were several high-speed cigarette boats and sailing vessels. My seatmate on the water taxi told me that these were great waters for fishing, sailing, and diving.

The Big Game Club lived up to its name. It was, in fact, pretty big and pretty gamey. Built in 1947, this hotel, with its fifty guest rooms, two bars, large dining room, and cracked tennis court, was sandwiched between the shoreline and the main drag connecting Alicetown to the only other town in Bimini, Baileytown. Its walls were full of memorabilia, ship ensigns, and hero pictures of big, dead fish and beaming anglers. The brick courtyard surrounding the pool was full of beautiful red, purple, and orange bougainvillea in bloom. Unfortunately, the Big Game Club suffered from a problem that many properties in the islands had: It is extremely hard to maintain an aging facility. In the case of Big Game, that week they had about half of their water pressure. For the two days we were there, neither of our toilets worked unless we manually filled the reservoirs using wastebaskets full of water from the showers.

But we weren't there to flush; we were there to fish, and the day broke with a beautiful sunrise in a near-cloudless blue Bahamian sky. The temperature was in the high 70s, with a gentle 7-knot breeze blowing out of the west. Captain Smith's tackle, as it would turn out, was very adequate—in fact, more than adequate for the fish that we wouldn't encounter on this two-day expedition.

The offshore fishing in Bimini, in a nutshell, turned out to be awful. The first morning, as large flocks of laughing gulls flew overhead, we trolled dead mullet and mackerel "off the

*Fish #9: The Marlin*

*Captain Bob Smith on the bridge of the* Miss Bonito II.

edge," in more than two hundred feet of water about two miles off the western shore of Bimini. All told, we managed to have two barracuda cut our baits in half. At noon we took a break for lunch, changed to lures, and increased the trolling speed. The result was one dolphin attack. Russ showed us some vintage fighting style, and a 22-pound cow dolphin was no match for him or our 50-pound, marlin-ready tournament Ande. She would make a great dinner for us that night, boiled in aluminum foil and served the island way at the Red Lion restaurant right next door to the Big Game Club.

In spite of the slow fishing, Captain Bob Smith turned out to be a treasure. He was a remarkably spry seventy-five-year-old native of Bimini who had been fishing these waters for more than sixty-one years. Bob's first fishing job, when he was fourteen, was catching bait for captains. He told me that he used to bring bait to Hemingway's captain on the *Pilar*, where his job was to keep Papa's fighting chair constantly turned toward a hooked fish.

Of course, I had to ask him what he remembered about the man. Bob said that Hemingway was well liked in Bimini. In those early days, before he was widely published, Hemingway was known as a two-fisted drinker who loved to carouse and brawl and generally burn the candle at both ends. Bob said that he had a passion for arm wrestling with competitors like Bimini's own William Bryant—who, boxing under the name Yama Bahama, once beat the boxing champion from Cuba, Kid Gavilán, known for his patented "bolo punch."

Captain Smith said that these arm-wrestling matches would often erupt into drunken brawls, with both men throwing roundhouse punches at each other. Then, as quickly as the fights began, the two combatants would be hugging each other, drinking and singing with their arms around each other's shoulders like nothing had ever happened.

Captain Smith had caught a lot of fish in his life. Perhaps the highlight of his career was being inducted into the IGFA Hall of Fame, an honor brought to him in person by the Bahamian ambassador himself.

*Fish #9: The Marlin*

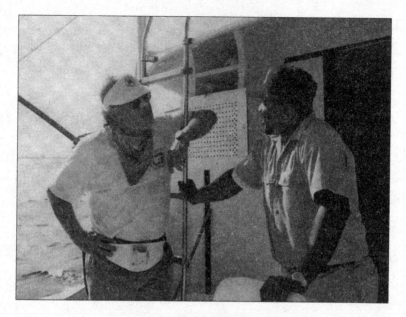

*Mate Dale Robins and I talk sports.*

I asked him how long he planned to fish, and he said until he could no longer climb the six-step ladder to his seat on the bridge. Watching him scurry around the boat, I imagined that wouldn't happen for a long time.

His current mate, Dale Robins, had studied under Bob's long-time mate, Stanley Laverity, before taking over two years before when Stanley retired. Dale was a thirty-two-year-old ball of fire with a passion for sports. He played third base and batted cleanup for the Bimini Athletics baseball team. Dale and I whiled away the long, slow, sunny hours of the first day, quizzing each other on American sports trivia and talking baseball strategy, two of my favorite subjects as well.

*Catching Big Fish*

During the trip, I shared with the captain and mate that my passion was saltwater fly fishing. Captain Smith surprised me by calling ashore and lining up his brother-in-law Ansil Saunders to take me bonefishing that afternoon. In fact, when we got in, Ansil was waiting on the dock with a beautiful 14-foot wooden skiff that he had made himself. Happily, I had brought along my Loomis 8-weight fly rod and Islander reel, and we were in business.

As he cranked up his 40-horse engine, sixty-two-year-old Ansil told me that they had some big bonefish in Bimini. In fact, as the black writing on the pocket of his white captain's shirt proclaimed, Ansil Saunders was a world-record holder. In 1971, he guided an American named Jerry Lavenstein to a 16-pound, 3-ounce bonefish, which he caught on 12-pound spinning tackle for a world record that still stands.

I climbed down into Ansil's skiff, and we headed for the flats. About five minutes into the ride, we pulled up to a giant sixty-foot mud. As I finished rigging up, Ansil told me to throw into the head of the mud about fifty feet away. I really wasn't interested in catching one of the "schoolie bonefish" that I assumed were making this mud, but I knew what Ansil was trying to prove and decided to humor him. I made one false cast and threw my Clouser Minnow fifty feet to the far front edge of the mud, stripped the line twice, got a hookup, and held the rod up high. As a 3-pound schoolie pulled some line, I turned to Ansil and said, "OK, Captain Saunders, now that I know that you can find fish and you know that I can catch fish, can we please go find a few grown-up bones?"

Ansil laughed and said, "OK, it's just that I see a lot of people with fly rods these days, and I like to know what I'm up against."

*Fish #9: The Marlin*

*Ansil Saunders—Guide to the World's Largest Bonefish.*

We both laughed. As we continued our journey, Ansil told me that he was waiting for the tide to rise, allowing us to get onto his favorite big flat, appropriately named Big Flat. Ansil said we had a few minutes and asked if I would mind catching him a few dinner fish. I smiled and said sure, guessing that if I hadn't known how to cast, those few minutes would have been used for a fly-casting lesson. I stowed my Loomis and Ansil pulled out an old spinning rod rigged with a green tube lure. All of a sudden, I knew what he had in mind for dinner and wondered if this captain had friends or relatives at Deep Water Cay. It looked like Bubba was getting the chance to be the breadwinner again.

It didn't take long. My first cast produced 10 pounds of angry barracuda. It took about ten throws to catch two smaller fish for the captain's neighbors. On the way to Big Flat, Ansil started calling me Cuda Bob. I think he liked me.

A twisting waterway, full of snappers, took us half a mile to a huge lagoon where the water was about six inches deep and the tide was just beginning to rise. Everywhere you looked were schools of bonefish on the move, with fish tailing in twos and threes.

I climbed out of the boat and started tracking a school of fish quartering at me from the west. "Cuda Bob," Ansil said in a loud whisper, "you walk like a large elephant!"

Now, where in hell had this Bahamian seen a large walking elephant? Anyway, I changed to my dainty gait, caught the lead fish in the school, then six others in the 5-pound range in the next hour before the fish followed the rising tide off the flat.

Ansil and I were giggling like schoolboys. It was fun to see the way even experienced older guides delighted in watching their

## Fish #9: The Marlin

parties or, in this case, their new pal, catch fish.

As we packed it in, Ansil told me about some of the people he had taken out in his little boat, including Martin Luther King Jr. twice, the second time three weeks before the leader of the American civil rights movement was murdered in Memphis.

Dr. King wrote the acceptance speech for his Nobel Peace Prize while sitting in a lawn chair on the bow of Ansil Saunders's skiff on the first day they went out together, after telling Ansil that he was "totally consumed by the beauty and life of this place."

As we headed for home, I asked Ansil what he had talked about with the famous Dr. King. Ansil said, "I shared with him the 151st psalm."

"But, Ansil," I said, "there are only 150 psalms."

"I know that, Cuda Bob. The 151st psalm is the one I wrote!"

"Boy, I'd really love to hear that, Ansil," I said.

"I'll do it for you right now," he replied, taking a right turn and idling his little homemade skiff out of the setting sun and into the shade of a nearby mangrove island.

He had me sit on the bow, holding the boat against the mangroves as he stood up, cleared his throat, and started reciting his 151st psalm from memory. It was really quite moving, talking of creation and bearing witness to the unassailable evidence of the existence of the Lord from this outdoorsman's everyday experiences.

As the first verse drew to a close, some of the Lord's creations, the no-see-ums, discovered us and attacked from everywhere.

"That's beautiful. Thank you, Ansil," I said as the pesky gnats bit every exposed inch of my body.

"There's more," Ansil said, seemingly oblivious to the insects, which now seemed to be growing in size as well as number.

Ansil's psalm celebrated land and sea, sunrise and sunset, fish and fowl, and I wondered if I would ever see the Big Game Club again or if I would be devoured by Bahamian no-see-ums half a mile from Alicetown.

Ansil's articulate and heartfelt testimony finally ended. It was truly beautiful, and I told him so as I gave him a friendly congratulatory handshake and we headed for home. The 151st psalm was the perfect way to end the day.

Day two of our Bahama escapade was slower than the first. No strikes, no takedowns, no fish—the first time I've ever been totally skunked offshore. We did have three rubber bands break from wear on the outriggers, which was exciting. And at one point, Rusty jumped up and yelled that he'd spotted a large, dark shadow under one of the flat-line baits that must have been a large blue marlin. Actually, I think it was a hallucination, caused by some questionable fried chicken he'd wolfed down earlier.

I shouldn't complain about this slowest of slow days on the water, as it gave me a great opportunity to all but "compleat" this little island story. No one likes getting skunked, but when it happens, as it always will, what better place than in these storied waters, chasing the progeny of the same big fish that Hemingway loved and hunted and celebrated in his writings.

Long after our second fishing day had ended and we were heading home, I thought about Captain Bob Smith, Dale, and Ansil, wondering who would take their roles in keeping the ancient spirit of Bimini alive.

As we were carrying our rod cases through customs, I had a

## Fish #9: The Marlin

sinking feeling about how tough this Met Hall of Fame requirement was turning out to be, and I wondered if I'd ever really do it. Just then, the customs officer asked us, "What's the matter, boys? Not enough big fish for you in Islamorada?"

At that moment, I didn't have an answer for her, but I knew that Rusty and I would suck it up, climb back aboard the *Fish This!*, and continue the quest with pleasant memories of a not-so-successful island fishing trip.

In all likelihood, the marlin I had the best shot at was the blue, *Makaira nigricans*, because of its distribution throughout relatively warm ocean water in general and the Met region in particular. While white marlin, *Tetrapturus albidus*, seemed to be more abundant, all the offshore captains said that they were without a doubt the most difficult marlin to hook. Apparently, white marlin are notorious for picking up and carrying around baits in their mouths without swallowing them.

Besides being my largest target species, the marlin may have been my most difficult, because its numbers have been seriously depleted. Not only are marlin prime targets for trophy hunters, due to their size and fighting skills, but commercial long-liners also target them for the quality of their meat. Blue marlin females range in size to more than 1,800 pounds, while most of the males weigh between 180 and 300 pounds. Long-liners claim that they catch most of their big blue marlin on the high seas, where they spawn in spring and summer, miles out of range of the sportfishing fleet.

The blue marlin, or "the man in the blue suit," as it is affectionately called, is most readily recognized by its long, low, blue dorsal fin that matches the dark blue color of its upper body. This color fades to white on the belly. The fish also shows a series of lighter-colored vertical bars on its sides, which seem to be more pronounced when the fish is engaged in battle. The marlin's bill, or spear, is shorter and thicker than the bill of a sailfish.

A large, scythe-shaped tail gives this fish incredible speed, which leads to the first tip on how to catch one. Fast-trolling skirted dead bait—bonito, herring, balao, and strip bait—is very effective. Marlin are not easily fooled. They will often swim in a boat's wake for many agonizing minutes, moving from one trolled bait to another as if checking restaurant menus. Slowing the bait or jigging will result in an instant refusal. I have yet to hear of anyone catching a marlin on drifted live bait, at least in the Met region. I think that marlin are just too smart for that.

While conservation seems to be spreading in the world of sailfish, such is not the case with marlin. All of us have seen far too many photographs of dead blues hung on dockside winches, with their weight painted on their flanks. It seems as if many anglers believe that this ultimate fish must ultimately be killed for total angler satisfaction.

As with sailfish, there is a good marlin tagging program that gives great satisfaction to everyone on the catching boat. While the life-or-death decision to release marlin rests in the consciences of anglers, I think that the captains have a major responsibility here as well. They are the vested experts whose livelihood ultimately rests with the plenitude of the fish population, and they should act accordingly on their boats.

Due to its large size, tenacity, and stiletto-like bill, the marlin isn't the only endangered species in a fish fight. Marlin can inflict

## Fish #9: The Marlin

serious injury and even death on offshore crew members, no matter how experienced they might be. Just in this past year, two experienced crew members were killed trying to wire marlin. Wiring is the process of taking a few wraps of the leader around one hand, which allows the mate to grab the marlin with his other hand, either to remove the hook or to haul the fish on board. Both deaths occurred in incidents where the fish surged away from a boat and sounded, tangling line around the mate's wrist and pulling him overboard, literally attached to the sounding marlin. The mates drowned while everyone in their boats watched in helpless horror.

Happily, killing a marlin would not now be mandated in my quest. Two weeks before my first offshore marlin search, I called Sue Baker at Met headquarters.

"Sue, I've been doing a lot of thinking about the Met. In the same spirit that we don't have to kill tarpon, I'm wondering why we have to stick marlin, or sailfish for that matter."

"Hold on, Bob, before you go any further, I've been trying to call you. At a rules committee meeting two nights ago, it was decided that Met Hall of Fame billfish entries need only be measured for length, photographed, and released."

This was welcome news. I started to ask Sue if I had anything to do with their decision, but then I thought better of it. Her answer wouldn't really have mattered. At the end of the day, if catch and release is going to work, it must have a broad-based constituency. In other words, saving the resource must be a success that has many fathers. As I thanked Sue for this good news and hung up the phone, I felt renewed excitement for my search for the muscular marlin.

June in the Bahamas is not the only month or place not to find marlin. Rusty and I put in some long days in the Keys pulling lures and dead baits in deep water, where we replicated our lack of success off Bimini. Many of the offshore captains suggested that marlin seek warm water and are best ambushed in the Keys during late spring or fall when they are migrating through the region. With this information in hand, Rusty and I positioned our boat in Key West and fished four fall days off the legendary Wall, a well-known fishing spot twenty miles southeast of Key West on the way toward Cuba.

On one of these excursions, our spirits soared as we turned on the VHF and heard of multiple marlin hookups from a fleet of offshore boats returning in a caravan from a very successful billfish tournament in Cuba. Apparently, the Cubans had relaxed their rules about Americans entering their waters to fish, while the State Department seemed to overlook this practice. Exhibition baseball games and some fishing tournaments were manifestations of at least a moderate warming of relations between the two neighboring countries. Unfortunately, a new administration soon reinstated their previous restrictions.

Rusty and I had no better luck in these waters than off Bimini. We had a few pretty good takedowns, but not by anything we could positively identify as a member of the marlin family. With the coming of winter's cold water to the Keys and the Bahamas, we decided to put off marlin fishing until spring. In April, remembering Pete Rose's comments about those "pesky blue marlin," I called him and set up a two-day fishing excursion to Freeport. I asked Pete if he minded if I brought Rusty along and he said, "No problem."

Pete's wife, Linda, picked us up at the airport and drove us to the boat where Pete was waiting. We handed him four offshore standup

## Fish #9: The Marlin

rods and Penn reels loaded with tournament Ande (50-pound test), jumped aboard, and were off by 9:00 a.m. As Pete waved goodbye to Linda, he said that the north wind, which seemed to be blowing at about 20 mph, meant that we should fish out to the east of the island.

The seas were calm in the lee of the island, we were comfortable all day, and we caught no fish.

That night we went out to dinner with Linda and Pete, who told us that he wanted to get an early start the next day. He was planning a two-and-a-half-hour run to the west that would put us in an area where he'd been seeing a lot of big blues. He said that we would pass Matanilla Reef, turn right, and troll toward Walker's Cay.

We said good night to the Roses, and Rusty suggested a nightcap. I, of course, went along only to keep him company. As the Conch ordered his third brandy, I suggested we ought to hang it up and get some sleep, as Pete was picking us up at the marina dock at 6:00 a.m.

"Look at the wind blowing those palm trees," Rusty said. "No way in hell we'll be fishing offshore tomorrow!"

We walked back to the hotel and went to bed. At 5:30 a.m., the wind whistling in the halyards of the sailboats at the marina dock woke me from a deep sleep. I threw on my clothes, found some coffee at the office behind the checkout desk, and walked out to the dock, just in time to see Pete Rose's 28-foot Goombay Hooker idling into the harbor. Rusty was nowhere to be seen. I called his room and woke him up.

"What?" he answered, less than cheerfully.

"Pete's here and we're waiting for you," I said.

"You've got to be kidding," Rusty answered.

"You know I never kid about fishing," I laughed as the phone went dead.

"Where's Rusty?" Pete asked as he pulled up to the dock and threw me a line.

"He's on the way down," I said. "We went out last night, and I'm afraid he got overserved."

We waited fifteen minutes for Rusty to finally show up. He was bundled in foul-weather gear and looked like he was still asleep.

"Morning, Ev," I chirped in the most obnoxiously upbeat, cheerful voice I could muster.

Silence was the response as Rusty climbed aboard and looked for a spot to stand in the middle of the boat.

We motored out of the harbor under a full moon with the wind blowing out of the northeast at a steady 25 mph. I noticed that we were the only boat up and about. Soon, we were offshore and heading due west. We passed West End, Sandy Cay, and eventually Memory Rock with the sun rising at our backs. The waves were well defined and running about five feet. Pete's SeaVee slid over them with ease, and, for the most part, we stayed dry. Pelicans flew by, mostly traveling east in formation. I wondered to myself where they were coming from and going to.

After running for two hours at about 3,300 rpm, I looked ahead to see what appeared to be a white wall against the horizon in front of us.

"What is that?" I asked Pete.

"That's Matanilla Reef," he replied. "Well, actually it's waves breaking on the reef itself, which in some places is just a few feet

## Fish #9: The Marlin

below the surface. Those waves come the entire length of the Atlantic Ocean, and Matanilla Reef is literally the first thing to get in their way."

"Wow. That's quite a sight," I said.

"Yeah, but wait till you see it up close," Pete answered.

Now Rusty seemed wide awake.

"How far do we have to go to get around the reef?" Rusty asked.

*Good question*, I thought.

"Oh, we don't go around it, Rusty. We kind of pick our way through it," Pete said.

I looked over at Rusty. He looked as if he'd just seen a ghost.

The closer we got, the higher the wall looked. When we got within a hundred yards, Pete pulled the throttle back, turned 90 degrees to the left, and started studying the waves.

"Do you carry a life raft?" Rusty asked Pete.

"No, I've never needed one."

The waves seemed to break all at once over the reef. It was a frighteningly beautiful sight—a fifteen- to twenty-foot wall of white water accompanied by a constant roar, the likes of which I'd heard only at Niagara Falls.

"Rusty, isn't this the most beautiful thing you've ever seen?" I asked my pal.

Rusty said nothing.

Just then, Pete apparently saw what he had been looking for, turned right, brought the boat up on a slow plane, and headed right toward the wall of water.

"Is this safe?" I whispered to Rusty.

"I don't know, Bubba," he answered.

Pete stood quietly behind the wheel and steered through the waves. It looked like we were going through a white-walled canyon. Then, all of a sudden, we were out the other side in the midst of the darkest blue water I'd ever seen. I glanced at the depth finder—seven hundred feet, eight hundred, nine hundred, then all zeros. Just like that, we were in water a thousand feet deep, gently sliding over widely spaced waves rolling to about ten feet.

"Rusty, take the wheel, will ya, while I set up the lines," Pete said nonchalantly.

"Routine," I whispered to Rusty.

"Yeah, right," the Conch sneered.

We would end up fishing to within a few miles of Walker's Cay before skirting Matanilla Reef and heading for home. There would be no "pesky blue marlin" this day, although we had a great time catching four good-sized wahoo, probably on their way to Bermuda.

As we *shooshed* down the face of the waves on the way back to Freeport, I thought about the big marlin I hadn't caught that day, and it didn't really seem to matter. He was out there; I knew I'd find him. In the meantime, I had seen one of the most breathtaking sights in nature and experienced a day on the water that I'll never forget.

We put marlin fishing aside as summer arrived and we moved up north. Then, when fall came, I concentrated on snook and didn't think much about marlin until Mindy came through with a great Christmas gift. She had done some research and found the name of Jim Sharpe, whom many of the Keys captains identified as the king of marlin fishing in the Florida Keys. I was

## Fish #9: The Marlin

familiar with him as the author of *Dolphin: The Perfect Gamefish*, which I keep in my library as a reference book on how to catch those colorful critters.

I called Captain Sharpe and set up a three-day trip with him in January. He gave me several days to choose from and said that the time of month based on phases of the moon was far more critical than the warmer waters of spring and fall. He told me that while the marlin might not be as plentiful, he felt that we would still have an excellent chance to raise some fish.

I have to admit I was skeptical, although I did find his enthusiasm infectious.

The big day arrived and I made the fifty-six-mile drive south to Summerland Key, where Jim kept his boat, the *Sea Boots*, a Key West–built, 43-foot Torres.

If the fishing had been nearly as good as the conversation and storytelling, I might have picked up stakes and moved to Summerland. Unfortunately, we didn't see as much as a scale or a tail during three days of fishing. Each morning, we dutifully put out the lines and then retrieved them at the end of the day with nary a takedown. We moved around a lot, trying many locations with no success.

On the third day, I confided to Captain Sharpe that after fishing for marlin in the Bahamas and throughout the Keys without even seeing one, I was beginning to despair. I wondered if they were a figment of the imagination, like the Loch Ness Monster or the classical snipe that we hunted in our youths.

Two weeks after returning home, I got a nice follow-up letter from Jim Sharpe, thanking me for agreeing with him that

*Catching Big Fish*

*Fishing on the Sea Boots was a family affair. Here Captain Jim Sharpe puts his arm around his wife, Barbara, who came to greet him, and his son Jim Jr. (kneeling), who, with mate Todd Baad (right) put their angler, Dr. Rosie Morrison, on this 520-pound blue marlin.*

PHOTO CREDIT: Jim Sharpe

## Fish #9: The Marlin

marlin in the Keys were a worthwhile adversary. I think he missed my point. As far as I'm concerned, marlin in Lake Erie are also a worthwhile adversary as defined by scarcity and/or nonexistence.

I whined to Suzan Baker, wondering aloud if the marlin had become extinct in the region since the time it had been included in the Met Hall of Fame requirements. Sue treated my entreaties with a bemused lack of interest. I was beginning to wonder if she was becoming hard of hearing or if I, in fact, was becoming invisible.

I decided to put the marlin search on hold and concentrate on the snook, the only other species I needed to qualify for the Hall of Fame. I figured I'd find that big marlin in late May or June. Then I got a call from my neighbor Johnny Morris. He said that he'd been talking to one of the Islamorada offshore captains, Allan Starr, who had just returned from the annual Bacardi Billfish Tournament in Bimini and reported that there was an excellent marlin bite. Knowing of my quest, Johnny asked me if I wanted to join him for a weekend excursion on his boat, a beautiful "fighting lady," yellow-colored 46-foot Merritt, called the *Tracker* after one of his popular bass boat brands. I jumped at the opportunity and started getting my tackle together.

Halfway through the week, though, Johnny called to say that something had come up—and he couldn't make it. However, he still wanted me to use the boat and the reservations he'd made for us on Cat Cay, an island two and a quarter miles long and half a mile wide located on the western edge of the Great Bahama Bank, eighteen miles southwest of Bimini.

I felt hesitant to accept his kind offer but thought about the

Catching Big Fish

*Johnny Morris loves catching bluefin tuna such as this 827-pound monster around Cat Cay.*

Photo Credit: Bass Pro Shops

## Fish #9: The Marlin

quest and said, "Oh, no, John, I couldn't.... Well, OK. Thank you very much." I just couldn't resist.

Allan Starr was about five feet ten inches tall with a full head of jet-black hair and a twinkle in his eye. He was thin and gave the impression of being fit—which he quickly disproved with stories about his various maladies due to a life spent abusing his health and well-being. He told his stories in the voice of an old prizefighter.

Allan's grandfather was a fisherman who moved his family from Portugal to Massachusetts. Somewhere along the way, he Americanized the family name from *Estrella* to its translation, "star," adding an *r* to form *Starr*. Allan's dad also made his living on boats.

Allan was born in New Bedford, from which the *Pequod* set sail, but his family soon moved fourteen miles to South Dartmouth, where he grew up. He worked on fishing boats during the summers on nearby Cuttyhunk Island. He told me that he learned his trade crewing for Carl Veeder, who is generally regarded as the father of light-tackle striped bass fishing. He spoke in reverent terms about Carl, talking about how he'd developed new fishing techniques and lighter tackle, putting himself at a disadvantage to the fish that he caught and released with frequency.

As a youth, Allan Starr had a quick wit, but he was not a varsity scholar. He joined the Coast Guard when he was seventeen and served for eleven years before receiving an honorable discharge. He then went into sportfishing as a paid captain for a number of boat owners. He also had intermittent jobs in marinas or for boat builders—but always within the smell of saltwater. With a lifetime of experience on boats and fishing, he trained a lot of young men—such as Davy

Jones, who was crewing for us that trip, and even Alex Adler—on the finer points of the business. Many of the young Keys captains credited him with giving them their start. They said that Captain Starr could be a tough taskmaster who loved to go fast, and work and play hard. As he sped toward six decades with one wife, two exes, two daughters, and two granddaughters, in spite of bad knees, scarred lungs, and an irregular heartbeat, Allan Starr showed very few signs of slowing down.

Fittingly, Allan had a passion for fast wooden sportfishing boats. He said that if the Lord wanted men to have fiberglass boats, he would have planted fiberglass trees. Captain Starr knew where the fish were, and he liked to get to them fast, fish them hard, and get home fast. It was not a coincidence that he fished a 52-foot Jarrett Bay called the *Reel Quick*.

In late January, Allan's team won the most prestigious offshore tournament in Islamorada, the Presidential. As he celebrated the win at the bar at Cheeca, Allan was informed that there had been a protest over the timing of his last sailfish catch. Tournaments have a time at the end of the day, usually 3:00 p.m., when lines are to be out of the water. A fish may be caught after that time only if it was hooked before 3:00 p.m. In this case, an old nemesis claimed that Allan's last hookup happened after 3:00 p.m.

Captain Starr was called on to take a lie detector test. Not surprisingly, he failed the test, in spite of the sworn oaths of his crew and anglers. I'm convinced that a combination of Canadian Club and digoxin pills, for his heart, had a lot to do with that result.

A month later, Allan put this disappointment and embarrassment behind him by winning the Poor Girls Sailfish Tournament.

Fish #9: The Marlin

*There was never a dull moment with Captain Allan Starr.*

He apparently had some pretty choice messages for a few of his offshore competitors on his VHF radio.

A month after that, Allan was gunning the *Reel Quick* into the channel at Bud and Mary's to clear the shallow bar at the headpin, which at the time was covered with only two and a half feet of water due to a huge low vernal equinox tide. All of a sudden, a boatload of teenagers shot in front of him and then literally stopped in his path. The experienced captain had only one choice. He pulled back the throttles and jammed the big boat into reverse to avoid running over the four in the skiff. The big Jarrett Bay came off its plane and jammed hard aground. The impact drove the struts that support the propeller shafts through the cold-pressed epoxy hull. Fortunately, Allan was able to get the *Reel Quick* back to Bud and Mary's under its own power. While the boat sustained considerable damage, fortunately no one was hurt.

When Allan called his boss to report the damage and get the timetable for repairs, he was informed that the boat was being immediately decommissioned (put up for sale) and that his services would no longer be required (he was fired). Captain Starr's quick reactions had saved four young boaters and gotten him fired all at once, making him available for our Bahama trip while he was looking for a "new situation." In spite of this unfortunate episode, I think a lot of people in Islamorada would agree with me that there were very few captains as conscientious or with anywhere near the knowledge that Allan Starr had of big boats.

That Saturday, after a twenty-minute run to the northwest, Allan throttled back the boat and yelled down to Dave and Rusty, who had tagged along, to put out the lures. We had rigged four custom standup rods and Penn International reels with 50-pound green tournament Ande and different-colored soft trolling lures. In the hope of catching a blue marlin, the two outriggers were set at about fifty yards and the two flat lines at twenty yards. I glanced at my watch. It was 9:36 a.m.

"What if a white marlin comes up, Cappy?" I asked Allan.

"I'm going to show you that right now, Bubba, and then we're going to have a dry-run rehearsal."

"Like a fire drill?" I asked.

"Exactly."

### Fish #9: The Marlin

As we were talking, Dave rigged up a dead balao on one of the 20-pound standup rods with an orange-and-black plastic Mold Craft soft-head skirt for improved visibility. He stood the rod up in the holder behind the Tracker's fighting chair and put the skirted bait in a pail of water to keep it fresh.

I climbed down to the cockpit and stood next to Dave as Captain Starr turned into Coach Starr and gave us our game plan. It went something like this: "If a blue hits one of our four baits, it will be an automatic hookup. Just leave the rod in the rod holder, count to five, pick it up, point the rod tip at the fish, reel up the slack, and strike him.

"If a white comes up, it will probably be on one of the flat lines. They're real finicky eaters and probably won't hit those big lures. Dave, I want you to reel in the flat line the fish is looking at. While he's doing that, Bob, you grab the 20-pound rod and throw the balao back to where the flat-line lure was, then lock it up. When the fish takes the bait, put the reel in free spool till you know it's time, then lock it up and strike him."

"How will I know when it's time?" I asked.

"I can't tell you that," Allan said. "You'll just know, and you'll catch him, or you won't know, and you won't catch him."

*Great*, I thought, feeling like Luke Skywalker trying to make sense out of a lesson from Obi-Wan Kenobi.

"Is that all, Captain?" I asked.

"No, I want you to practice the drill. Fish on the left flat!"

Dave grabbed the flat line and reeled in the line as I fumbled to pull the 20-pound rod out of the rocket launcher and fling the bait back about forty feet to where the teaser bait was.

"Good," Allan said. "Now do it again to make sure we've got it right."

The physical part was easy, but I still wondered how I'd know when the time was right to set the hook. In truth, my reflexes were slow due to lack of sleep. You see, while the rest of the crew had slept last night in Coconut Grove, I had spent the night fishing for a big snook from sundown to sunup at Government Cut in Miami, our last catch being a 16-pounder at 6:30 a.m., just before I had to head for the airport. I'd felt pretty good until the hot Bahamian sun began to beat down on us. I felt the sweat beginning and hoped for a quick catch so I could take a nap.

I started to think about Santiago's epic battle against the huge blue marlin in *The Old Man and the Sea*. Fish fights like that still happen today. I thought about an incident that had taken place in the Bahamas just a week before. An Islamorada offshore captain, Ronnie Riebe, was fishing a sixty-year-old retiree, Tommy Resha, in Riebe's charter boat, a 46-foot Bertram, the *Abracadabra*, in five thousand feet of water ten miles offshore of Hopetown in the Bahamas, when they hooked up a giant blue marlin. Tommy fought that fish, which they guessed to be between 1,200 and 1,500 pounds, for thirty-two hours and forty minutes! When they finally took up the drag in a do-or-die measure, the fish broke off just four feet from the boat. Tommy, by the way, was fishing 100-pound test line with a 400-pound leader. The fish towed the 25-ton boat twenty-five miles from where the hookup took place.

I was fishing with 50-pound line with a 100-pound leader and was wondering how my equipment and I, with no sleep the night before, would stand up to such a challenge. Fish like the one Tommy

## Fish #9: The Marlin

Resha fought, weighing over 1,000 pounds, are called *granders*, and it's every angler's ultimate dream to catch one on his favorite tackle.

As the sun beat down on us, I thought that I would be pleased to save my grander for another, more well-rested day. I hoped instead for a smaller, more manageable fish.

There's an old saying about being careful about what you wish for. It was 9:45 a.m. and we had turned 180 degrees and were cruising south at about 8 knots, settling into the fisherman's familiar vigil, watching the water, when, like a dream, there he was.

"White marlin on the left flat line!" Allan yelled. "Do it, Dave! Go, Bob!"

The fish was up, looking right at the teaser bait. Dave started cranking it in. The fish disappeared. I threw the skirted balao overboard and free spooled it back to where we'd seen him.

"He's gone, Allan!" I shouted.

"Lock it up and watch for him," Allan said. "He'll come back."

Sure enough, there he was, moving on the surface bait from left to right. As we watched, he dove on the bait and I felt the line come tight.

"Good, he's in your hands, Bubba. Do it!" Allan yelled.

I pointed the rod tip down and free spooled the reel, keeping my right thumb on the monofilament, heavy enough so that the line didn't backlash and light enough so that the flying line didn't burn my thumb. "One-a-thousand, two-a-thousand," I counted out loud for no particular reason other than to sound like I was in control and knew what I was doing.

At seven-a-thousand, I felt the fish surge as if he had tried to swallow the bait and felt the hook.

That was it! I jammed the reel into the strike position, felt the line come tight, and whacked the fish. The line was still tight. I whacked him again. The stiff rod doubled over and line flew off the reel faster than I'd ever seen it fly before.

"Good job, Bubba, you've got him!" Allan shouted. "Dave, Rusty, get those other lines in."

The white marlin came out of the water, jumping, spinning, cartwheeling, tail-walking, trying to rid himself of this thing embedded in his upper lip.

Someone slapped a fighting belt with a built-in gimbal around my waist so I could steady the rod butt. Allan jammed the boat into reverse to follow the fleeing fish. I dug my knees into the transom as the saltwater spray splashed up and over our stern.

The fish was still jumping and appeared to be about 250 yards away, running from us fast.

"He's going to spool me, Allan!" I shouted.

"Oh, no, he's not," Allan said, giving it the gas in reverse.

Diesel fumes mixed with cold salt water splashed over me into the cockpit.

All I could do was hold on, keep the rod tip up, and pray that nothing bad would happen.

Then the fish stopped jumping and the pressure on the line eased, allowing me to reel in some major slack as Allan slipped the boat into neutral. I knew that the fish was still on, but it was clear to all of us that the tide had turned.

Then he got a second wind and took off again, but not with the same fury or force.

A line from Hemingway's short story "On the Blue Water"

## Fish #9: The Marlin

popped into my mind, and I applied it to myself: "There is a great pleasure in being on the sea, in the unknown wild suddenness of a great fish."

As the fish slowed again, I was able to pump him by lifting up and reeling down to retrieve more line, cranking with my right hand and guiding the line on the reel with my left to keep it from piling up on one side or the other.

Fifteen minutes into the fight, the fish started sounding.

"Talk to me, Cappy," I said.

"You're doing fine. Don't change a thing," Allan responded as he maneuvered the boat to keep the transom pointed directly at the struggling fish.

Dave, who had been standing quietly just behind me and to my left, whispered, "You might try transitioning from the lift up to the reel then down a little more slowly, so that you don't give him back any line."

I tried it and it worked—excellent advice to remember when fighting a big fish, where every foot of line counts. From then on, I really felt that I had gained the upper hand. The white marlin dove deep, but I was able to keep some pressure on and eventually lift him. He came up to the surface but was unable to repeat his dramatic aerobatics, allowing me to take in line and bring him closer to us.

The fish gave us some anxious moments when he dove deep and tried to swim under the boat, but Captain Starr bumped the throttle and jumped the boat ahead, keeping the line away from the propeller blades.

Twenty-five minutes after it began, we had him up to the side

*Rusty grabbed the leader of another Met species.*

of the boat. Rusty grabbed the leader, making the catch official. Then he stepped in front of me, wired the fish, grabbed his bill, and lifted as Dave grabbed his tail and helped hoist him aboard. After Rusty removed the hook, we measured the marlin, took some

*Fish #9: The Marlin*

***Rusty and I hauled our white marlin over the transom to measure it.***

pictures, and put the fish back in the water. The whole release took about thirty seconds and the marlin swam away, unharmed.

The fight had started nine minutes after we put the lines out and ended thirty minutes later at 10:15 a.m.

The fish measured 74 inches (6 feet 2 inches) long with a girth of 29 inches. Using the formula of length times girth squared, divided by 800, we estimated the fish to weigh just under 78 pounds.

Just like that, I had my ninth species. After hugs and high fives all around, I went below to change out of my wet shirt. I have to admit I didn't reemerge until well after noon. As soon as I sat down on the couch to rest my eyes, I was out like a light.

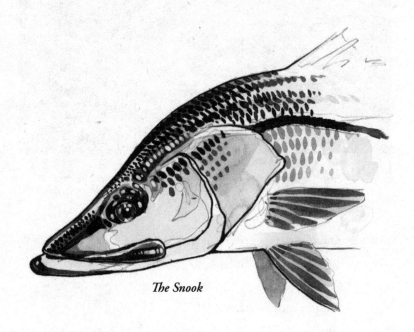

*The Snook*

CHAPTER 12

# FISH #10
# The Snook

*The snook is a back-street fighter, without match. The linesider hits harder than any other inshore game fish, pulls like a bonito and jumps like a tarpon. And it does it all in tangled little mangrove creeks too narrow for an alligator to turn around.*

—Frank Sargeant, *The Snook Book*

---

Beginning with my first trips to the Keys, I remember arriving back at the dock and encountering people waiting for the returning fishing skiffs. They would surreptitiously saunter up to our guide or one of us anglers and almost whisper, "Got any?" sounding like druggies looking to score.

Our guides would always say, "Naw, we were bonefishing," and the disappointed dock people would walk away. One day I asked what they wanted, and my fishing partner that day told me they were looking for snook. "It's a great-tasting species of saltwater fish," he said. "They aren't allowed to be caught and sold commercially, so there is almost a black market for them. They taste that good."

I suppose that with only four or five trips south a year, my pals and I always considered ourselves bonefish and tarpon purists and never invested the time to go snook fishing. After we tasted one prepared four different ways by Gary Ellis's wife, Susy, we quickly became regulars in the snook search.

Snook have firm white meat that lends itself to almost any type of preparation and sauce. My favorite is broiled with meunière sauce, but baked, fried, or even blackened snook is hard to beat. The taste of fresh snook can turn the purest catch-and-release angler into a meat fisherman. We often used to try and plan a late afternoon stop in the backcountry at a favorite honey hole to try to catch a dinner snook.

Ironically, the snook's culinary popularity is a relatively recent phenomenon. For years, people used to grill snook with the skin on, but they found them to have such a soapy taste that they were called soap fish. Then one day, a hungry local took the skin off his snook and discovered one of the most delicious fish in the world.

In spite of this discovery, the snook has not only survived but also flourished in great numbers due in part to its heartiness, habitat, and tenacity but also smart conservation rules that protect the fish from anglers during the summer spawning months. Snook can be taken in South Florida only six and a half months a year. They are also protected between December 15 and January 31 for an interesting reason. During these winter months, when the water gets really cold, snook will almost go into a coma, floating to the surface to keep warm. In this condition, they can be literally scooped out of the water by hand. The winter fishing ban is therefore put into place to protect these defenseless fish. During the season, there is also a bag limit of two snook per angler, and they must measure between 26 and 34 inches, with only one fish allowed over 34 inches. In other words, an angler can take only two fish, and both must measure over 26 inches, with only one over 34 inches. Those rules are constantly changing to protect the species.

Snook, *Centropomus undecimalis*, are found in abundance around South Florida and range throughout Central and South America as well. Fond of brackish water, they are prevalent throughout the backcountry in canals, under bridges, and in spots where they are sheltered from sharks and other predators, such as the mangroves of islands and shorelines. They are also found in streams and estuaries, where saltwater collides with freshwater.

Some of the largest snook are found on the ocean side, where they even take up residence under docks and in inlets. Jupiter is famous for big snook, and it was on my list of destinations if I couldn't find my 18-pounder in Florida Bay.

There is a popular theory that many male snook over 19 ½ inches long undergo sex reversals. This theory is supported by a huge change in the ratio of females to males in fish of above this size as well as the capture of several snook in the middle of the reversal process. In actuality, sex reversal in several saltwater species is not uncommon. Researchers call this "protandrous hermaphroditism." The fish are males first—with all immature fish having developing testes—and transform into females as they grow!

Snook vary greatly in color, depending on their habitat. Their backs are often dark gray, green, or even black with silver undersides. The most predominant feature of a snook is the thin black line that extends from gill plate to tail on each side of the fish. Combine this with its underslung jaw, and the snook is readily identifiable.

Most snook, at least in the middle Keys, range between 8 and 12 pounds. A 16-pounder is a noteworthy catch, and I have heard of some snook caught in central Florida that weighed between 30 and 50 pounds.

No fish that I've ever fished for crashes baits with the ferocity of snook. Many people have likened their strike to that of the black bass. Both species seek cover and survive by ambushing prey. The similarity with bass does not end there, as both fish are topwater battlers that, when hooked, will spend as much time out of the water as in. Like bass, snook will often jump from the time they're hooked until the time they are netted.

I've had my best luck catching snook with pinfish, although pilchards and shrimp also work well. Two of the best older guides in the middle Keys, Captain Billy Knowles and Captain Hank Brown, earned reputations catching snook along the mainland shoreline almost exclusively on finger mullet. In fact, Hank and Billy were affectionately known as the Kings of East Cape. If those two weren't catchin' 'em, nobody was.

Certain lures and plugs are very effective with snook. Around Islamorada, we use Hank Brown's Hook Ups and jigs as well as Paul Tahera's Back Bone Jigs. Surface lures and plugs are effective and fun too. A snook strike on the surface is unforgettable. Bagley Mullets, Rapalas, Bombers, and Rattletraps all deliver great results.

Snook will crash flies as well. I like to fish them with an 8-weight

## Fish #10: The Snook

rod and medium-sinking 3-inch flies tied on 1/0 or 2/0 hooks. The snook's favorite color seems to change from season to season. In the fall of 1997, I had my best luck with dyed-green bunny hair.

There are five basic fishing techniques for catching snook: (1) deep channel dredging, (2) mangrove flipping, (3) nighttime stalking, (4) oceanfront beaching, and (5) bridge or pier fishing.

Some of the best channel fishing is along the mainland coast of Florida Bay. Along with East Cape, Snake Bight Channel just east of Flamingo is a dynamite snook spot. The trick here is to throw your bait way upcurrent and drift it back past some of the runoffs like you do with Atlantic salmon. The snook will usually strike as the line comes tight at the end of the drift. Channel fishing is effective because, caught in the open, these wily battlers have no mangrove roots or other structures where they can break you off. Recently, however, we had been losing a lot of hooked snook to bull sharks in the murky water of Snake Bight. Last spring, as I was reaching into the water to grab a nice 9-pounder that Mindy caught, what looked to be a 150-pound bull shark grabbed the fish right out of my hands and swallowed him in one bite, leaving me counting my fingers. Mindy, by the way, quickly opened the bail, free spooled for five seconds to give the shark time to ingest the snook, closed the bail, and tried to set the hook. She fought the surprised shark for ten minutes on 8-pound test before bringing back just the snook's head.

I learned a lesson that day. From now on, please call me Bubba the Netter. It's a better nickname than Lefty.

Casting up against the mangroves is also a popular technique for hooking snook. We often see snook stacking up like cordwood under the mangroves and in the mini channels that surround many of the backcountry Keys. The bigger the snook, the farther he seems to be able to lie up under the mangroves, shaded from the sun or his predators, the shark and large barracuda.

These laid-up snook will usually leave their cover for a bait drifted close under the overhang. Anglers are well advised to heavy up on the equipment and tighten the drag to the max. When snook feel a hook, their first reaction is to dive back into the trees, where the roots will quickly break the strongest line.

The first part of the fight is the most important, as you have to whack the fish hard and put the wood to him to drag him away from the cover. If you don't, it will be a short fight. I have talked to some anglers who have had success with snook another way. They use light tackle and try to finesse the fish out of the mangroves before he knows he's been hooked. Either way, once the fish is out of the mangroves, he'll do some airborne runs but always with an eye to return to his mangrove sanctuary.

Almost every regular Keys fisherman has a favorite snook hole. Captain Gary Ellis took so many snook off the northeast shore of Palm Key (one mile off Flamingo) for two seasons that everyone started calling it Ellis Island. It became a popular spot that many have fished, but few as well as Gary. Then one day, Gary soured on killing snook and started releasing every one he caught. Within a few weeks the snook disappeared from Palm Key and have not returned in two years. It's a spooky little story; but that's how these waters are.

I believe that all the fish that stack up on the bottom of the channels or under mangroves during the heat of the day come out to feed when the sun goes down. Nighttime and strong current make ideal conditions for snook fishing around bridges and pilings as well

## Fish #10: The Snook

as on the backcountry flats, although the latter are far less accessible in the dark.

Being on the water at night can be mystical and mysterious, as all sounds seem to be magnified. In the words of *The Phantom of the Opera*, nighttime shadows heighten each sensation, and snook become things that go bump in the night. Loss of visibility may in fact even the odds for the angler with artificials. Whether fishing bait or lures, movement is very important.

Snook are definitely good nocturnal feeders, and sacrificing a shoreside evening to fish them can be very rewarding. Two words of caution: Leave your running lights on and bring your bug spray.

Oceanfront snook are probably the largest and most difficult to feed. My pals up in Central Florida say the best time to fish them is in June and July at the beginning of the spawn, when the egg-laden females linger in the coastal waters before dropping their eggs and heading into the brackish waters of the estuaries. The problem, of course, is that these fish are out of season. Frankly, I don't believe that catch and release of off-season snook would negatively impact their population. That notwithstanding, I have decided on another strategy for catching my 18-pound snook in fall, when they are in season.

While bonefishing on the ocean side, I have seen some monster snook around docks as well as bridges. Some of the old-timers have told me that these fish are waiting for the fall mullet run that takes place from the first of October almost to Halloween. Finger mullet school in the shallows, attracting large, hungry snook that have cruised the flats throughout September, appearing oblivious to any offerings. I've scouted some good spots and plan to throw my Bagley

Mullet either with or without the assistance of some netted finger mullet to stir up the resident snook.

Rusty and I began our hunt for an 18-pound snook in October 1997. We loaded my two Loomis plug rods, each equipped with Shimano Calcutta 251 reels, into my skiff with a collection of brightly painted plugs and an 8-foot cast net in the hope that we could fill our live well with finger mullet. Our first trip out, we left the dock at Max's just before sunrise in hope that we could be set up by first light. As predicted, the fall mullet run had just started, and two throws of the cast net filled our live well with frisky 4-inch-long finger mullet.

Rusty motored right to a dock just south of Cheeca Lodge, where we had been seeing huge snook. We poled up within sight of a pod of fish. Rusty stuck the end of his push pole into the mudflat, tied off the skiff, got a scoop full of mullet, and started bouncing them off the deck into the water.

"Why are you doing that?" I asked. Rusty explained that this dazed the mullet and made them easier targets for the snook. I started casting my plugs on 12-pound gray Ande line into the middle of the dizzy mullet.

We might as well have stayed in bed. The big snook around the dock ignored us, our bait, and my plugs. I cannot tell you how frustrating it was to watch 20-pound snook swim lazily over, under, and around my Bagley Mullet. I changed lures. Nothing worked. After about an hour, as we were stowing our rods and preparing to pull up stakes, one of the neighbors clad in a pink bikini walked out on the dock and handed us two cups of hot coffee. As we were leaving, I said to Rusty, "That was better than fishing in the swamp."

## Fish #10: The Snook

"Yeah," he said. "Nice scenery."

Our next stop was Palm Key, off the shore of Flamingo. After a forty-minute ride, we arrived just as the tide was beginning to fall—good conditions for Ellis Island. Rusty poled up to about thirty or forty feet from the shore so I could cast to the edge of the mangroves, where we knew the snook would be, and started pitching our captive mullet one by one into the overhanging branches. As each mullet hit the water, there was an explosion as a large snook bolted from its hiding place to gobble up the free meal.

"Showtime," I said as I grabbed a rod and clambered to the bow to start casting. "This is going to be easy."

"Yeah, right," the Conch whispered under his breath as I let go with my first shot. I threw upcurrent as close to the mangroves as I could and let the falling tide whisk my plug by the nooks and crannies that we now knew held large, hungry, but wary fish. I cast for twenty minutes in silence, without so much as a bite.

"What's up with this, Rusty? Am I invisible or what?"

"Hey, it's not going to be easy," Rusty said. "These big snook have been around for a long time and are pretty smart. There's also a lot of live bait around, and these fish know the difference. The people who set up the Met requirements knew what they were doing."

So there I was again: Rusty was smart, the snook were smart, and the Met rules committee was smart. The mullet and I were the only dummies around. This Met quest was beginning to try my patience and trash my ego.

Our next stop was a large grass flat with many large bare sand patches or indentations. Rusty said that these potholes hold fish that wait there for the falling tide to bring them baitfish.

"As I pole us over to the flat," Rusty said, "throw your plug over the far side of each pothole and retrieve it slowly."

Rusty was right. Many of my casts resulted in strikes. Within an hour I had caught a dozen fish—a bunch of small redfish, two small snook, and three trout. The bite turned off as the tide stopped falling, so Rusty and I headed for home. As we sped over the shimmering water of Everglades National Park, Rusty suggested that I might want to try some of the mainland waterways west of Flamingo, where Billy Knowles and Hank Brown fished.

I decided to give it one more shot in my home waters. Craig Brewer invited me to go out on his new Maverick Mirage—kind of a sports car of a backcountry skiff—built "to go real skinny," as the guides say, in about seven and a half inches of water.

On our fishing day together, Craig tried several spots, including some channels near Flamingo. Throwing into a deep hole on the side of one of these waterways, I felt the familiar crash of a large fish that nearly dumped all my line before we could get on the engine and gain ground on what turned out to be a 14 ½-pound snook. It was a great fish. I was getting closer.

On the way into the Lorelei Basin, we saw Captain Billy Knowles putting his skiff away and decided to have some fun with him. As Craig pulled up to his dock, I reached into the live well and hauled out my fish. Holding the snook up with both hands up, I said, "There he is, Captain Billy, my 18-pound Met fish."

Billy scowled, "Son, that fish doesn't weigh over 14 ½ pounds."

I hate it when they do that.

"Son," Billy went on, "your best shot at that 18-pounder will

*Fish #10: The Snook*

*Captain Craig Brewer and Bubba showed Captain Billy Knowles a 14 ½-pound snook. Captain Billy was not impressed.*

be in Chokoloskee this spring. If you catch him around here before then on a plug, it will be dumb luck."

As fall gave way to an El Niño–warmed winter, I gave up on big snook fishing to concentrate on other species more common to the waters around Islamorada. In fact, I really didn't think about snook until Christmas. While watching the present-unwrapping ceremonies, Mindy handed me an envelope that contained a loving note with the following message: "This card is good for two days of snook fishing in Chokoloskee this spring." What a great gift! I was confident that two days in this fishing mecca would be more than I would need.

Chokoloskee is a small encampment of a fishing village in the Ten Thousand Islands of the Everglades adjacent to Everglades City on the Gulf of Mexico about a two-and-a-half-hour drive from Islamorada. It has changed less than any community I know of in South Florida.

Once a haven for people wanting to escape someone or something—often the law—life there has always been spartan. What the area lacks in amenities, it makes up for in one commodity: fish—very, very big fish.

Snook season in South Florida was open for a few months in the spring before closing down on June 1 to allow for spawning before continuing in the fall through December.

A good friend of ours, Captain Steve Huff, was one of the premier backcountry guides in South Florida who, with his wife, Patty, moved from Duck Key in Marathon to Chokoloskee, where he fished the Ten Thousand Islands better than anyone.

We called Steve and learned that the best time to fish snook would be the last week of May after Memorial Day on the new (first quarter) moon. The theory was that the targeted nocturnal feeders would be feeding in the morning like hungry dogs.

Unfortunately, but not surprisingly, Steve Huff was booked for that week, but he put us in touch with one of his protégés, a young captain named Tim Brady, who had an opening for us for a few days right after Memorial Day weekend. Steve also suggested that we book a cottage at the historic Rod and Gun Club in Everglades City on the Barron River.

As the time approached, I asked Mindy if she wanted to join me, and she suggested that instead, I should invite our

*Fish #10: The Snook*

*Count on Steve Huff to catch the big ones, in this case a 150-pound tarpon.*

PHOTO CREDIT: *Sandy Moret*

youngest child, Barney, who would be home from his freshman year at the University of Miami and would love to have the time with his dad.

She was right. The day after Barney arrived home, we were off to Chokoloskee for two days of fishing. After an early dinner and a great night's sleep at the Rod and Gun Club, we lathered up with bug spray and met Captain Brady at his 18-foot Maverick skiff at the dock in Chokoloskee at dawn.

We fished hard all day, throwing plugs toward and sometimes into the mangrove-covered shoreline. Final tally for the day: four small snook, trout, and an assortment of other fish. Tim, a soft-spoken pro, seemed a bit disappointed by the disappearance of the big fish. He suggested that we leave an hour earlier the next day so we could be fishing for a while before sunrise.

While Barney and I were disappointed as well, we were both happy to have some time together. Sitting on the big wooden chairs on the widest porch at the club and chatting about life, I was very impressed to see that my son was growing up to be a thoughtful young man and not only the athletic youngster who'd started college six months ago at Miami. I think that we both realized that our love and friendship transcended any outcome of our fishing outing. And this was a good thing, because the fishing the next day went from worse to worst.

Starting an hour earlier turned out to be a giant mistake. As we started casting in the dark, it was apparent that the fish weren't biting, but the swarms of mosquitoes that early settlers called swamp anglers *were* biting. They came in huge numbers and seemed to thrive on the copious amounts of Cutter and OFF! that we'd lathered on

## Fish #10: The Snook

*While I was hoping for a big snook, Captain Tim Brady put us on some nice redfish (note the distinctive spot on its tail).*

our bodies. And Captain Tim seemed to be totally immune to the mosquitoes and impervious to our pain.

Barney and I tried to laugh off the bites and kept on casting as the sun rose and the swamp anglers went away—nature's own insect repellent, I guess. The fishing sucked, and it was getting awfully hot as we stopped at an island for a swim and some lunch. Our memories, however, live on about that great father/son trip and the chance it gave us to celebrate our friendship even in the face of adversity, including the hiding fish and swarms of swamp anglers.

June arrived, and snook season came to a close until the next September. Rusty reminded me that I could substitute an 8-pound sea trout on a plug for the snook and keep on fishing through the summer, as trout were not out of season. I told him that I was a little reluctant to change targets, as I've always thought of snook as heroic battlers and trout more as family fun fish. Rusty said that he agreed up to a point, but that an 8-pound trout was extraordinary and could even turn out to be the toughest catch of the ten Met species. Challenge accepted.

The spotted sea trout, *Cynoscion nebulosus*, is actually not a trout. It's a member of the drum family (*Sciaenidae*), kind of a catchall extended *Seinfeld*-like family that includes croakers, black and red drum, kingfish, weakfish, and sea bass.

Found in coastal waters from New York to the Florida Keys and into the Gulf of Mexico, sea trout may well be the most popular saltwater gamefish in their range because of their abundance and willingness to do battle. Their favorite bait is shrimp, but they will strike all kinds of artificials as well.

Sea trout are often referred to as "family fish," and many children, like my son Barney, will always remember a trout as the first fish they ever caught. Sea trout shade from black backs to predominantly silver bodies, streamlined like their unrelated freshwater namesakes, and easily identified by numerous small, round, black spots on their backs. Unlike freshwater trout, sea trout have two sharp canine teeth in their lower lip that can puncture the thumb of an unsuspecting angler. They are often incorrectly called weakfish, which are actually their cousins. The name *weakfish*, by the way, does not refer to the fish's strength but rather its tender mouth. Like weakfish, spotted sea

## Fish #10: The Snook

trout are great table fare, barbecued, fried, or broiled.

Most of the sea trout I have caught have been in the 2- to 3-pound category. Like just about everyone else who fishes in Florida's coastal waters, I have a few "secret" trout holes that I keep in reserve for guests who haven't done a lot of fishing. What these popular fish don't have in to-the-death fighting skills, they make up for with topwater acrobatics. They are found in the ocean, bays, canals, and rivers—wherever there is current and plentiful food in the form of crustaceans.

Trout spawning begins in spring and continues through November. While most of the trout population lives in backcountry estuaries, some fish make their way to the ocean, where they tend to grow to some pretty good sizes. As they grow, sea trout seem to shift their food preference from shrimp to small fish.

While small trout are abundant, trout of more than 5 pounds are scarce and getting scarcer, and I was clueless as to where to find one. I asked several of the Islamorada guides where they would go to catch an 8-pound trout, and they all laughed at me. I asked Rusty about his trout experience, and he told me that after a lifetime of fishing, his largest was 6 ½ pounds. Apparently, while big trout might have been around when Hy Hyman founded the Met Tournament in 1936, the old one–two punch of overfishing and poor conservation had certainly knocked down their sizes, if not their numbers.

Then I got serious. I bought *The Trout Book* by Frank Sargeant and picked up several back issues of *Florida Sportsman* from the library. Sargeant spoke about great trout fishing in the Indian River near Stuart, Florida. He also talked about big fish being found in the Banana River up around Cape Canaveral. Unfortunately, the Banana

River is out of the Met region; it is also a manatee preserve and is closed to powerboat traffic. I knew I could still fish it if I used a port in the region, but I decided that these logistics might be a little too funky and I would concentrate first on Stuart.

While scanning the back issues of *Florida Sportsman* for information on trout, I came across some interesting articles written by Mike Holliday from Stuart. His knowledge of trout was impressive. I called him up late on a Friday, told him about my quest, and asked if he wanted to go fishing. He said, "Sure. When do you want to go?"

"How about tomorrow?" I responded.

He said, "Fine, c'mon up, but one thing—I can only fish Saturday and Sunday mornings."

No problem. I jumped in the car and started the four-hour drive from Islamorada to Stuart. I arrived at the Marriott Indian River Plantation Hotel at midnight, checked in, and left a wake-up call for 3:30 a.m. The woman at the front desk looked at me like I were from the moon.

Speaking of the moon, it was full for our adventure, and the Indian River was lit up like broad daylight. Mike had suggested that an early departure would give us our best shot at big trout feeding by moonlight.

I walked down to the Marriott dock at 4:00 a.m., passing by some huge yachts and sportfishing boats. I had known that Stuart, which calls itself the Sailfish Capital of the World, had some great offshore fishing, but I'd never thought of it for light-tackle or shallow-water fishing. I reached the end of the pier as an older Maverick powered by a 115 Yamaha with a small American flag flying from the poling platform pulled up.

## Fish #10: The Snook

I introduced myself to Mike, climbed onto his boat, and stowed my gear as he motored out away from the pier and into the moonlit Indian River. As he brought the boat up on a plane, I turned my baseball cap around to keep it from blowing off and sat back to enjoy the ride. Before I'd had a chance to ask my new acquaintance even one dumb angler question, he pulled back the throttle and announced, "We're here!"

We were just two minutes from the dock. "We're where?"

"I want to fish this flat on the fall," he said. "It's small, but I've seen some nice fish moving by out here."

Mike shut off his engine and went to the bow to set up his trolling motor. I picked up my plug rod, rigged with a surface plug, and surveyed the scene. Under the light of the full moon, I could see what looked to be one hundred small white pipes sticking out of the water in what seemed to be even rows. "What are those?" I asked.

"Those are rows of PVC pipe," Mike replied. "Each one holds a mangrove shoot. As the mangrove grows, the PVC breaks away. These were planted by our local fly-fishing club."

How strange it was to have come from Chokoloskee, the mangrove capital of the world, to Stuart, where the locals were planting mangroves. Also, what a passion their fly-fishing club must have for their sport.

"It's very shallow here," Mike warned. "Throw your plug toward the PVC pipes and keep your rod tip up to keep it off the bottom." As we moved to within sixty feet of the mangrove shoots, we started to hear the familiar sound of big fish crashing bait. *This could be interesting*, I thought.

My first throw placed my plug about five feet from the pipes.

I'd retrieved it about ten feet when something exploded on it. The line came tight immediately, and I set the hook on a very large fish that obviously wanted no part of this game. The hooked whatever-it-was stripped 100 yards of line off my reel as I stood in awe, holding my rod over my head to avoid any mangrove shoots or irregularities on the bottom.

"Mike, if this is a trout, it's a big one," I said as the fish slowed.

"Bring him in and let's see," Mike replied, laughing.

After two more runs, I brought the fish to within fifteen feet of the boat. Mike shone his flashlight on him. The thin line down his side meant there was no mistaking this fish. It was a snook—a very large snook. Mike netted him and I grabbed a Boga grip out of my bag.

Snook have razor-sharp serrated bone structures behind their gill plates that can lay open your fingers or hand for multiple stitches. It is always best to grab them by the tail or the mouth as opposed to the gill. I slipped my thumb into the fish's mouth and lifted him so I could affix the Boga grip scale to the corner of his lip. Mike picked up his flashlight and the Boga told the story. My first cast in Stuart had produced an out-of-season 15-pound snook—the largest I'd ever caught.

Gently releasing the fish, Mike, always the gentleman, apologized that it wasn't a trout.

"What's the difference?" I said. "That's the largest snook I've ever caught! It was a monster!"

"Actually," Mike said, "by our standards, it's pretty ordinary. We see a lot of 30-pound snook up here, especially in fall when the mullet run begins in the inlet and the rivers." I made a mental note of this fact for my snook quest, in case we didn't find that big 8-pound trout.

*Fish #10: The Snook*

*Lifeguard, sportswriter, guide, and photographer Mike Holliday turned angler to catch this good-sized snook.*

As the sky began to brighten in advance of the sunrise, I got to know a lot about a very interesting young man. Mike, an only child, was thirty-eight years old, a Floridian who had moved with his mom and dad to Princeton, New Jersey, where his mother took the job of rare book librarian at Princeton University. He and his parents were avid readers. Young Mike fished often with his dad but longed to return to salt water. When he graduated from high school, Mike enrolled at Florida University in Stuart and studied marine biology. After college, he stayed in the Stuart area, fishing, guiding, and writing freelance fishing and hunting stories while working part-time as a lifeguard in the afternoons—which explained why he couldn't fish on Saturday or Sunday afternoons.

Mike was a good-looking guy, very well read and experienced in outdoor life. He lived with his wife, Palmer, who was expecting any day, and a couple of dogs, one of which he hunted with in fall. On the boat, he was soft-spoken but gregarious. His love and knowledge of the environment were always in the forefront.

We caught a lot of fish during the next two mornings, but none as notable as that first-cast snook. The biggest trout we landed was a 4 ½-pounder in the brackish bronze-colored water near the nuclear power plant.

Mike was very knowledgeable about his surroundings. What a contrast it was for me to come out of the swamp and fish the flats, channels, bridges, and docks of such a beautiful community as Stuart, with its elegant waterfront homes and finely trimmed lawns. Almost every house seemed to have a dock, complete with some type of watercraft tied to it. The number of fishing boats indicated that the locals were taking advantage of the resources.

"What other species do you have here besides snook and trout, Mike?"

"We catch a lot of pompano, big jacks, redfish, and tarpon."

"Small tarpon, like 30- and 40-pounders?" I asked.

## Fish #10: The Snook

"No, Bob, big fish—monsters, 100- to 140-pounders."

"C'mon, Mike, you're putting me on."

"No, really," he said. "They come in here in late fall and stay through the winter. In the old days, before the bridges to the Keys were built, a lot of trophy hunters came here for record tarpon. While those anglers are gone, the fish are still here. They don't get fished that much, as a lot of the locals like to fish for food, so our snook get beat up pretty good in the inlets. Some of us, myself included, still love fishing for tarpon on the fly."

"You know, Mike," I said, stating the obvious, "this place is really a well-kept secret. How come?"

"You're right, Bob. I think it's because everyone focuses on sailfish in the ocean, and no one thinks about what happens back here in the river. The locals fish the river a lot, but we don't get that many outside visitors. As a result, there are only a few full-time guides who live and work here."

On Sunday at noon, after another good morning of fishing, but nonetheless troutless, I thanked Mike Holliday on the dock and asked him to call me the next fall when the mullet run began.

The call came in September in the wake of Hurricane Georges: The big snook were in. My middle son, Ted, was getting married in October, but with his fiancée attending to details, I asked him if he wanted to sneak away for a day of father/son fishing before he got hitched. He said, "Sure. I'll meet you there."

Ted was a gamer. At twenty-nine years old, he had just earned an MBA while working full-time for the Buffalo Bisons baseball team. He was bright and a good athlete, unassuming and fun to spend time with. Every time I thought of Ted, I thought of the words

Howell Raines wrote in *Fly Fishing Through the Midlife Crisis*. When talking about his son, Raines said that he "had become a person whose company I would seek even if he were not my son." That's how I felt about Ted.

In Stuart, 4 a.m. came early. I introduced Ted to Mike, and they hit it off right away, chatting nonstop about a variety of subjects. Mike told us that the snook had been thick all week, but you couldn't prove it by our fishing that day. Ted started out by refusing to touch a rod for fear of catching my fish. I insisted that he pick up a rod and start casting. We were there to fish together, I told him, and I would be as happy to see him catch a lunker as myself. Throwing a jig on spinning gear, Ted hooked up some huge horse-eye jacks, but the linesiders were nowhere to be found.

As we tried new locations, Mike brought us up to date on what he had been doing. His wife, Palmer, had given birth to their first child—a daughter. Mike had also retired from his lifeguard job and accepted a position as outdoor editor of the *St. Lucie Tribune*. In his new job, he was looking for fishing stories for the *Tribune*. We pulled up to another spot, and I suggested that he put me on an 18-pound snook and write about it. Mike agreed that was a good idea as he started the trolling motor to put us within casting distance of a concrete breakwall.

"I've got two favorite ways to fish these snook," Mike told me. "When it's dark, I like to fish them under strong dock lights. The lights attract baitfish, which then draw snook. But during the day, the snook seem to use these walls to trap bait. I like to throw black and silver Bombers as close to the walls as possible. It can be very productive, even in the heat of the day. Try it."

## Fish #10: The Snook

"Go ahead, Bubba," Ted said. "I'm going to grab a soft drink from the cooler."

My third cast was my best. I plopped the big No. 7 Bomber right to the base of the wall almost with no splash. "A nine on that dive, Ted," I laughed.

A huge snook that was judging the entry from below also voted his approval, crashing the plug before I even had a chance to retrieve it.

"Bingo!" I yelled. "Is that him, Mike?"

"He looks good," Mike said as he pulled the boat away from the wall.

You have a much better chance of landing one of these hogs if you can get him out into open water, where there are fewer obstructions to break the line. This big fish knew the game. He headed left, right along the wall toward the corner that led toward a man-made channel. I had the drag tightened up pretty well. All I could do was hold the rod up and watch this speeding fish, while cheering for Mike to get out into the river fast.

The fish reached the corner and tried a right-hand turn. He was too late. I leaned on him and pulled him away from the cement. Feeling the pressure, he changed tactics and headed full speed right for the boat. The line went dead, and I thought I might have lost him.

"Keep reeling," Mike said as I put the rod tip in the water and reeled as fast as I could.

"Why are you putting the rod tip in the water, Dad?" Ted asked.

"I'm trying to put water tension on as much of the line as I can. By putting the rod tip in the water, I can cut down on the slack I give him, especially when he goes past the boat—if, of course, he's still on." My answer came quickly as the fish swam under the boat. The line came tight again as I swung the rod to fight the fish on the other side. He felt the line and came out of the water, shaking his entire body. I bowed to the fish by lowering the tip, to avoid him breaking me off because of too much tension.

"He's big," Mike said. "Hand me the net, Ted."

"What net?" my son responded.

We looked all around and, sure enough, the net was gone. Apparently, it had fallen overboard at some point during the morning's festivities and none of us had noticed.

"What do you do now, Mike?" Ted asked.

"Grab him by the tail, I guess," Mike responded as Ted and I looked at each other quizzically.

"It's never easy, is it, Cappy?" I said, getting my two cents in.

"You got that right, Bubba," he laughed.

Mike got his chance pretty soon. After five rapid-fire leaps, it looked like the big snook had jumped himself out. After a few more potentially dangerous lunges under the boat, I was able to lead the tired fish alongside. Mike knelt down on the floor of the skiff, rolled up his left sleeve, reached over, grabbed the snook by the tail, and hoisted him out of the water into the boat.

"Well done," Ted said, taking the words out of my mouth.

As Mike released the plug, I grabbed my Boga grip. The three of us held our breath—16 ½ pounds! A pound and a half light. What a letdown.

"You got a bonus, though, Bob," Mike said. "He's been tagged by the Department of Environmental Protection."

*Fish #10: The Snook*

*Captain Mike Holliday and my son Ted became pals and found some nice fish like this big snook.*

That was a new one for me. I didn't even know there was a snook-tagging program, but sure enough, there was a 2-inch-long wire tag extending from the fish's abdomen.

Mike explained that between 1984 and 1997, using live bait, the DEP had caught, tagged, and released more than fifteen thousand snook in Jupiter and Palm Beach Inlets. Then they ran a public relations / educational program, asking anglers to return the tags from captured fish so that they could study the migratory patterns of this species.

"If we send in the tag," Mike said, "they'll send you all of the information and even a commemorative T-shirt. I'm also going to keep the fish in case they want the carcass for research."

We photographed the fish (about fifty times) from every angle, put him in the live well, and headed over to a restaurant at Pirate's Cove Marina for lunch. Their dockside scale weighed our fish in at 16 pounds, 2 ½ ounces.

An hour later, storm clouds rolled in, and our day of fishing was done.

Two weeks later, I received a large envelope from Mike, which included a copy of the half-page story he'd written for the *St. Lucie Tribune* about my quest, complete with a three-column color photo of Ted and me with the tagged fish. He had also sent a T-shirt from the DEP along with the tag and a two-page letter from the agency detailing the personal history of our fish as well as some findings from the tagging program.

Of the fifteen thousand fish, the DEP had received approximately 3,600 tags from anglers. My 38 ½-inch snook had been caught and released in Jupiter Inlet in 1993, measuring 27 ½ inches. It now being 1998, this supported the research that snook grew about two inches a year.

The DEP letter went on to say that most of the tagged fish migrated north in fall and returned south in spring. Ironically, the fall move was to find warmer water in the depths of the ocean, where temperatures are slower to change. Northern spots such as Stuart

## Fish #10: The Snook

also provide the fish with easy access to flats and bridges, where large amounts of forage can be found all winter. The farthest northern migration recorded was 142 miles to Ponce Inlet, while the farthest known southern migration was to Indian Key Bridge in Islamorada, 193 miles away (my own backyard!).

The DEP letter contained good news about snook in South Florida. Research indicated that the snook population in Jupiter and Palm Beach Inlets, which was estimated in the mid-1980s at 7,500, was now hovering around 20,000 and "appeared to be fairly stable." This information came as a pleasant surprise, considering how many people had discovered how delicious these fish taste.

After receiving the letter, I found out that the DEP was planning to change the snook bag limit in Florida to two per day, over 26 inches and under 34 inches. This would make it impossible, not to mention illegal, to bring an 18-pounder to the dock. Accordingly, the Met would have to change its Hall of Fame snook requirement, perhaps going to length, girth, and photograph of the fish. And in fact, that's exactly what they decided to do. I got a call from Sue Baker telling me that they would accept the measurements of a snook along with a photo. For me, this was good news and would, no doubt, move the Met that much closer to catch and release of all Hall of Fame fish.

With the 1998 snook season ending in two weeks on December 15, I started to panic. If I didn't catch an 18-pounder by then, I would have to wait until the season opened again on January 31. I called Rusty for advice. He was on his way to fish in Flamingo in the Salt Water Flats Fishing Association championship against some of the top anglers in South Florida, and he said he'd ask around to try to get some ideas. The tournament had what was called a "slam format." Entrants targeted backcountry slams (redfish, trout, and snook), and the prize money was substantial. Rusty was feeling good about his chances, as the finals were being held in what we consider local waters. He felt he'd have the home-court advantage.

He fished the tournament and finished out of the money after catching a trout and a red in the first hour and then searching in vain for two days for a snook. (Ironic, don't you think?) While he didn't bring home the cash, he told me that he'd met some outstanding anglers, two of whom, Rufus Wakeman from Stuart and Ron Hueston from South Miami, had some ideas on where we could find our fish, even though May and September were considered better months.

I called Rufus and arranged to meet him at a boat ramp at 6:00 a.m. on the day after Thanksgiving. He closed our conversation by saying, "We'll fish all night to catch that bitch if we have to!" *There's something unique about Rufus*, I thought as I hung up. This was going to be fun!

I met Rufus at the appointed hour. He bounced out of his truck, a Grizzly Adams look-alike, about six feet, four inches tall, weighing well over 250 pounds with a full brown beard and eyes that sparkled in the overhead lights of the boat ramp. I'm six foot two, and he made me feel vertically challenged. His enthusiasm was all-encompassing. He stuck out his big bear paw of a hand to shake mine—I was expecting a bear hug!

Standing by his truck, he told me half a dozen stories before we even made a move to launch his 21-foot Maverick. I knew that we would not lack for conversation. I guessed Rufus to be in his mid-thirties, which he later confirmed; although he seemed surprisingly worldly for his age.

*Fish #10: The Snook*

*Captain Rufus Wakeman caught this IGFA record snook only to see it disqualified because it had been temporarily confined in his live well en route to be weighed and measured.*

PHOTO CREDIT: Rufus Wakeman

Rufus continued to tell me tales on the way to our first stop to "dog" the first bridge we came to. He cut his engine, lowered his bow-mounted electric trolling motor, and maneuvered the bow of his big skiff to point into the falling tide, keeping about thirty feet from the bridge so I could throw under the structure.

As I pulled out my plug rod, Rufus handed me a small DOA root-beer-colored plastic grub to tie on my line. He told me that DOA was a lure company started by a fishing pal of his named Mark Nichols and that their lures worked great. He said that he fished almost exclusively with them. For snook, he liked plugs that would get to the bottom, where a very slow retrieve with an occasional bump to lift the plug up and down worked best.

With my first throw under the bridge, something tugged my line and the fight was on. I yelled, "Rufus, that's him, that's him!"

All of a sudden, my line was going up in the air—five, ten, fifteen feet straight up.

"What's happening, Rufus?"

"You hooked the line of one of the fishermen on the bridge," he answered.

I detected a tad of muffled mirth in his voice. Remember, this guy was one of the top anglers in South Florida. In the morning darkness, I felt my face getting red. I thought to myself, *Great start—today may end up being titled "Rufus and Dufus."*

Rufus nosed under the bridge and I loosened the drag so that the bridge guy could untangle our lines. Then he yelled up to the guy, "Sorry, man, we didn't see your line."

"Oh, that's OK, Rufus," replied a voice in the darkness. As the two guys chatted like old pals, I wondered how they knew each other. I found out the answer later that day: Everyone in Stuart, Florida, knew Rufus Wakeman. As we moved around and worked the Indian River, fishing and sharing stories, my new friend stopped and talked to everyone—people on offshore boats, on sailboats, on docks of marinas, fishing off bridges, even marine patrols. He may

## Fish #10: The Snook

have been the most gregarious person I'd ever met.

As I threw under bridges, off points, and next to jettys, seawalls, and mangroves, Rufus also gave his cell phone a workout, calling friends and associates. Every conversation started with, "How was your Thanksgiving?" and ended with, "How's fishing?"

Rufus was a man of the people—a 250-pound charmer. And who among us hasn't wanted to find out where the fish are, how other fishermen are doing, and maybe a little bit about them as well?

The morning went by quickly. At first, Rufus didn't want to pick up a rod, fearing he'd catch my fish. I told him not to worry and encouraged him to have a go at it. I didn't have to invite him twice. He started fishing with a spinning rod, and the results were incredible. We caught ladyfish, snappers, jacks, a huge croaker, flounder, puffers, groupers, and at least one of all five species of snook (all small). According to Rufus, the five snook varieties were common, fat, sword, spine, and tarpon snook. He also told me their Latin species and genus names along with the names of every other fish and bird that we saw. In addition to being the unofficial mayor of Stuart, Rufus was a knowledgeable conservationist. We released everything we caught before stopping for lunch.

The rest of our fishing day was pleasant but uneventful. We fished all the way up north to Fort Pierce Inlet and caught a few 3- to 4-pound trout before working our way back to Stuart. At 9:00 p.m., after dogging all the local bridges, we hung it up.

Rufus started to apologize that we hadn't caught my 18-pound snook, and I cut him off right away. "Don't be silly, Rufus. I knew it was a long shot. I'm not disappointed, and I had a great time." I meant it. I'd met a world-class angler, an easygoing and outgoing good guy, a certifiable character, and a big-hearted galoot all rolled up into one Rufus Wakeman. He was more special than a big snook, any day.

Rusty called Ron Hueston to set up my next snook maneuver. He told me a little bit about my next angling partner as we fished together in Flamingo the next Sunday. (Among other species, we caught two snook that day, 11 pounds each.)

Ron was not "to manor born," like Rufus. Ron was the son of a Miami policeman and made his living driving heavy construction equipment. Someday he wanted to get his captain's license and become a fishing guide.

Given that Ron was from Miami, I assumed we'd be fishing one of the many Miami hotspots like Government Cut, the huge inlet for ocean vessels, famous for humongous sideliners.

"So I'm on my way to Miami, Ev?" I asked Rusty as we threw plugs against the mangrove-lined shoreline of East Cape, five miles from Flamingo.

"Nope," the Conch responded. "Chokoloskee."

"Damn, Rusty, I've been there, done that."

"Not at night."

Wonderful. Rusty had fixed me up to fish in the mosquito capital of the free world at night with someone I'd never met.

"Listen, pal, it's scary enough there in the daylight. Now you've got me set up to run around at night with a guy from Miami who drives a front loader?"

"Not exactly, Bubba. He lives an hour from Chokoloskee and has been fishing there for twenty years. And he doesn't drive a front loader, he runs a track hoe."

## Fish #10: The Snook

"Rusty, what about Miami, Government Cut, Joe's Stone Crab, South Beach? I thought you were going to set me up for a few days in Dolphin Country while Mindy fishes the Islamorada Ladies Bonefish Tournament."

"I thought so, too, Bubba, but Ron thinks that Chokoloskee is the only place in South Florida where you're gonna find your fish right now."

"OK, Rusty, but what do you know about him besides the big-equipment thing?"

"Not much," Rusty said. "But he's really into fishing. I've never met somebody so intense."

Now, think about it: Rusty, the most intense fisherman I'd ever met, talking about some guy being more intense than he was. I felt like I was signing on for a voyage on the HMS *Bounty*.

"Rusty, you know, you've never fished the Ten Thousand Islands. Maybe you should join me."

"My bags are already packed, Bubba."

We left at noon on Tuesday. During the two-and-a-half-hour drive in my Roadmaster, Rusty answered every question I asked about snook with, "Ask Ron."

We arrived and checked in to the good old Rod and Gun Club, where Patty, the receptionist/concierge/manager, did a passable job of pretending she remembered me. Looking around, I guessed that we were the only guests in the lodge—making me wonder what all the regulars knew about December fishing in Chokoloskee.

After checking in, Rusty and I had a cocktail before suiting up, applying a gallon of OFF!, and heading out at 7:00 p.m. to meet Ron at our prearranged rendezvous spot—the parking lot of the local Circle K.

Five minutes after we arrived, up pulled a dark green 1998 Ford pickup pulling a 17-foot Hewes Bayfisher skiff. The driver sprang from the cab so lively and quick, I knew in a minute it must be Captain Ron. He was about thirty-five years old; wire-thin; five feet, ten inches tall; dressed in worn blue jeans and a camouflage shirt; and had long, light brown hair tied in a shoulder-length ponytail.

Ron said, shaking my hand, "This is a tough time of year for snook. I was here last weekend with my brother, and we found three big ones. I'm not promising anything. Put your gear in my boat while I grab a coffee and a chili dog. What's your name again?"

"It's Bob," I said, wondering how long it would take Rusty to hitchhike back to Islamorada if I jumped in my car now and headed for home.

Ron was halfway to the door of the Circle K. Rusty looked at me and shrugged. "I told you he was intense." I laughed in spite of myself and thought this was going to be one for the books.

We loaded the boat as Ron came bounding out of the Circle K with his dinner in hand. He said, "Follow me" as he jumped into his truck and hung a right out of the parking lot.

We launched at the boat ramp at Chokoloskee Island Park with mosquitoes buzzing around our heads but not biting, as if to say, "Round one for you, but we know where you're going, and that bug spray won't last forever."

Ron sat behind the wheel with Rusty and me on each side. The light of an almost full moon sparkled off the water and shone on the mudflats and oyster beds that I hoped we would avoid on our skiff trip to wherever we were going.

*Fish #10: The Snook*

*Capt. Ron Hueston loves to fish in the swamp at night, and he's better at it than anyone else I know.*

As we idled in a muddy channel, the width of a typical bathroom, Rusty asked Ron how far we would be running to our first spot.

"About twenty miles," Ron said, as I crossed myself and committed my soul to the Lord—and I'm not even Catholic.

Ron gunned his 90-horse Yamaha and brought his boat to a

plane. His head turned from side to side as he plotted his course, occasionally shining his flashlight on rustic wooden channel markers. As I went from scared to death to amazed at Ron's acuity in these dark waters, I wondered what was going on in the Conch's mind. I was sure that Mr. Macho Man wouldn't volunteer anything, but he had to be impressed with this nocturnal navigation. Kind of professional respect, if you get my drift.

I thought I knew the waters around the Ten Thousand Islands from my fishing trip in May, but I was wrong. I only knew them in daylight, not in the dark. As we cut through the cool evening air, I had a strange thought. Have you ever done something that takes you out of your comfort zone and puts you a little bit on the edge of what you think is safe? Well, for me, this was it. At first it was exhilarating, then a little intimidating, and finally strangely relaxing. *Maybe*, I thought, *this is how—and even why—we choose our hobbies.* I was totally at ease within a few minutes, trying to identify stars as we sped in dark silence toward Ron's first spot, sitting two feet in front of a high-droning outboard engine that sounded impatient for us to reach our destination.

Thirty minutes from the dock, we pulled up to a point jutting out from the mainland. Ron shut down and lit up a Marlboro before he started rummaging through his oversized tacklebox. He handed me a Rattletrap plug.

"This is a special modified Silverado Rattletrap," he said. "To the best of my knowledge, I'm the only person who fishes them here. Tie it on while I move us closer with the electric motor. Then throw in toward the point and retrieve slowly as it falls with the current."

"Tell me when, Ron."

## Fish #10: The Snook

I watched the red ash of Ron's cigarette flare up as he smoked in silence, the only noise the gentle hum of his trolling motor. I thought about Florida citrus trees and wondered if cigarette smoke has the same effect on swamp angels that smudge pots have on frost. Rusty must've thought so because he lit up, too, although Rusty's smoking was often Pavlovian. He'd see someone light one up, and he lighted up too.

"Now, Bob, get started," Ron said a few minutes later.

I threw and retrieved. Nothing happened. I threw again and *wham!*—a major hit. I lifted the rod—there was nothing there. I brought in the line and checked the lure. It was OK, but the 60-pound leader was frayed six inches above the Rattletrap.

"Wow, look at that, you guys," I said.

"They're here," Ron pronounced in a major understatement.

I fished in silence for the next half hour until I got another huge hit. I had thrown about seventy feet and retrieved about ten when I felt a thump, accompanied by a giant splash. The fish on the other end of the line ran left thirty feet before there was a sickening snap and my rod straightened up. As a big snook, annoyed by the lure in his mouth, jumped again, three times in the moonlight, I looked down to see that my line had broken at the reel. Throwing in the dark, I had left some loose line on the spool. A backlash on the reel had created a kink in the line, and the snook had exposed my error. Thankfully, Ron and Rusty were sympathetic.

"Forget about it," Ron said. "It's early. You'll get another chance."

Rusty said nothing and just kept on slapping mosquitoes.

But I didn't get another chance. We moved and fished and

moved and fished until about 2:00 a.m. We caught some small fish and told some big tales, but Ron Hueston won the prize. I always thought that Butch Constable of Jupiter was the most dedicated snook hunter in the world: His telephone number was 561-74-SNOOK.

Ron Hueston, a recycled bachelor, focused on snook like a bounty hunter. They were his passion and his life, and he lived it to the extreme. At around 2:30 a.m., Ron said to me, "Gee, Bob, you've got a lot of energy for an elderly guy."

The silence became deafening. Rusty bit his lip.

"You ready to head back?" Ron asked, not knowing the button he'd pushed.

"No way," I said. "The night is young. I'm just getting started. You got any more spots?"

*Elderly.* I'd show him. I was ready to cast all night if that's what it took.

Around 4:00 a.m. Rusty said, "Let's head in, Ron."

"What do you think, Bob?" Ron asked.

"Well—OK," I said, trying to sound reluctant and wondering if there was a doctor in Everglades City who could treat a torn rotator cuff in my casting shoulder. We headed back to the dock, pulled the boat, drove back to the Rod and Gun Club, and hit the hay just as the sky was lightening in the east.

I woke up at 9 a.m. with the word *elderly* ringing in my head. Then I rousted the "kids" to go fishin'. A day in the swamp produced nothing but a consensus plan for snookin' that evening after the sun went down. After dinner we were going to head straight for the spot where we'd broken off the fish the night before, catch my fish, and

## Fish #10: The Snook

head home. As we approached Chokoloskee, we went past a blue bass boat powered by what looked like a 140 Suzuki.

"There he is!" Ron raged. "I can't stand that guy. He's fished here for thirty years and thinks he owns the place. He's pulled up on me in a lot of good fishing spots. I'll tell you straight up, that guy makes me nuts." (That's not exactly what he said; I've dropped a bunch of expletives.)

After a pleasant dinner on the screened porch of the Rod and Gun, watching the returning commercial crabbers on the Barron River, we headed for the dock again. We launched Ron's skiff and idled into the channel, full of high hopes for nailing my Met snook on another beautiful moonlit night with relatively no wind or mosquitoes.

All of a sudden, a boat pulled out into the channel, not twenty feet in front of us. There he was, the accursed blue bass boat. Somehow the three of us knew where he was headed. The bass boat jumped on a plane. We jumped on a plane. The race was on.

We passed him at the second furlong post. He passed us at the two-mile mark. We passed him again after twelve miles and built up what looked like an insurmountable lead. Now remember, this was happening at night, through tortuously narrow channels surrounded by sandbars and oyster beds.

We made a turn, circled a small island to the left, and suddenly seemed to be all by ourselves in the darkness. Pulling out at the other end of the mangrove-covered key, we could see our target point in the distance, still with no other boat in sight.

Then all of a sudden, there he was—the blue bass boat coming around the other side of the island about a hundred yards back in our wake. Having seen that 140 Suzuki on his transom, the five of us, three in our boat and two in the other guy's, knew what was going to happen. Ron had his Yamaha 90 turning 5,500 rpms, but it was no match for the big Suzuki. The now-hated bass boat went by us like we were standing still, sprinted down the final straight, and pulled up right in the sweet spot we had been talking about all day. Ron said nothing, shot by them at full speed, and then pulled the throttle back and stopped, about fifty feet past them.

"This is going to be good," I whispered to Rusty.

"We're here," Ron declared. "Start fishing, Bob."

Both boats maneuvered around quietly for about twenty minutes like two naval destroyers maintaining radio silence, until their captains' trolling courses inevitably brought them a little too close together. The bass boat guy fired the first salvo with a request for more room. Ron countered with a reminder of some previous navigational affronts. The other guy questioned if we were from another state and didn't know any other spots.

Ron still held his ground, and it appeared to be over as the other boat slid away to a distance of about sixty feet—just far enough away for us to be able to see the two giant snook they hooked jump out of the water before they netted them into their boat.

As they engaged the Suzuki and motored away, I whispered to Rusty, "I think they got the last word." I looked up at Ron, who was running the electric motor and had been chain-smoking since we'd met in the parking lot of the Circle K the previous night. I thought I saw smoke coming out of his ears.

We moved to several more spots and, before I knew it, it was midnight and I hadn't had a bite all night. I figured I was zero for

## Fish #10: The Snook

1,300 casts. The old panic started to come back as I felt an anxiety attack coming on, and I prayed out loud, "Please, Lord, let me catch a snook on the next cast and I—I won't tease Rusty for ten days."

I cast again as Rusty and Ron laughed. I had retrieved ten feet of line when the bite came. After a short fight, I reeled in a nice 10-pounder. As Ron reached down and grabbed the fish, I said, "Thanks, Lord, but I was only kidding." Needless to say, that was the last snook I caught that night. I decided right then and there that that was the last time I'd be facetious about prayer on a boat—or on shore either, for that matter.

We tried a few more spots before calling it a night at about 4:00 a.m. Ron had really given it his all and probably would have stayed out all night, but Rusty had had enough, and I figured the bite was over.

On the way back to the dock, I calculated that I had been throwing plugs in the Ten Thousand Islands for more than twenty hours over the past two days. My back ached, my right arm was throbbing, and my fingers were numb. As we sped along, Ron broke the silence. "Sorry we didn't get him, Bob. You did OK for a man of your years."

"Thanks a lot, Ron," was all I could think of to say.

After about four hours of sleep, Rusty and I said so long to Ron as we got ready for our two-and-a-half-hour drive home.

Ron said, "Bob, if you don't get that fish by May, call me and come on back as my guest. Stay in my trailer. We'll get him, I guarantee it."

"Thanks, Ron, I'd love to."

In spite of my frustration, I would have liked to spend time with Ron again. He was the most focused guy I'd ever fished with, and he was great at it. Rusty called it "intense" fishing; I would say "extreme" is a better descriptor. There weren't that many big fish around, and Ron had put me on my target fish two nights back and I'd lost him. I reflected on this as we motored out of Everglades City past Jungle Erv's Airboat Tours.

We drove for about half an hour in silence with Rusty behind the wheel and me scribbling notes.

"I'm going to write a book," Rusty commented.

"On what?" I asked.

"Fishing rules of the road," he said.

"Got a title, Rusty?"

"Yeah, *A Guide's Guide to Etiquette*. What do you think?"

"Rusty, I think there's a market and sincerely believe it will be a bestseller." Then I fell asleep.

Back home in Islamorada that evening, Mindy and I were getting ready for dinner when the phone rang.

It was Rusty. "I've got some bad news and some bad news," he said. "Which do you want to hear first?"

"The bad news," I bit.

"Ron just called. He talked to a friend of his named Doug who was putting in at Chokoloskee at eleven o'clock last night when that guy in the blue bass boat pulled up and threw two big snook on the dock. One weighed 14 ½ pounds, the other weighed 21 ½ pounds."

"Thank you very much for calling, Rusty," I snarled.

"Wait, Bubba, that's not all. Doug headed to our spot and caught a 19 ½ pounder."

"Is that it?" I groaned.

## Fish #10: The Snook

"No, man, the fish had a special modified Silverado Rattletrap implanted in his lower lip."

"Good night, Rusty," I said, hanging up, pouring a scotch, and rejoining Mindy.

"Was that Rusty?" she asked.

"Yes."

"What did he want?"

"You don't want to know, Mindy. You just don't want to know."

Thus ended the year. Snook season shut down for two months. Just before it reopened in February, I told my sad Chokoloskee tale to a friend, Randy Towe, who, like Rusty, guided offshore and backcountry out of Islamorada. Randy said, "I think I can find that fish for you within an hour of here."

"Let's go," I said, and we set up a trip for the next weekend.

I met Randy at the dock at the Lorelei and was a bit surprised to see that he was not in his skiff but in his 26-foot center-console SeaVee. He explained that we were going to run across Florida Bay to the Gulf and up the shore past East Cape toward Lostmans River, about twenty miles south of Chokoloskee.

It turned out that Randy had the coordinates of some shallow wrecks that held a lot of big snook during the winter months. His plan was to anchor up close to the wrecked hulls so I could throw Rapala Bombers toward them and try to pull out an 18-pounder.

Randy was right. He did find some big fish for me. The only problem was that I just could not pull them away from the structure. I hooked up three big fish this way, and each in turn dove for the wreck and broke me off. No matter how much drag I used, I couldn't turn them. It felt like trying to stop a freight train. Then the

*Captain Randy Towe finds nice fish like this big snook offshore in the backcountry.*

PHOTO CREDIT: Randy Towe

tide stopped, and the bite turned off. On the way home, we tried throwing lures around many of the wooden poles in the Gulf that denote the boundaries of Everglades National Park but found no one home but jack crevalles.

By now we were moving into March, and I was getting frustrated. Rusty told me to cool my jets. "Wait till May, Bubba. The big ones will be following the warm water into the inlets and rivers to begin spawning."

I knew the Conch was right, but I was impatient. Then I read a report in the *Miami Herald* about some guy catching a 30-pounder

## Fish #10: The Snook

on live bait and I was off to the races again. I called Bouncer Smith, a legendary 250-pound-plus guide from Miami, to see if he had any free time. Bouncer was out, so I talked to his wife, Ruth, who, it turned out, was from my hometown of Buffalo. We played "do you know" for about an hour on the phone while agreeing on how to fix the city's image, who has the best chicken wings in town, and what the Bills needed to do to win a Super Bowl before the Big Man came home and picked up the phone. When Bouncer came home, I introduced myself and told him what I needed. Without a pause, he said, "I can't help you. I can't find you fish over 18 pounds that you can catch on plug equipment."

"Then I'm dead," I said, cutting to the chase.

"No," Bouncer said. "I'll give you the name of a guy who can't catch one under 18 pounds."

He had my attention.

"This guy isn't a guide, but he loves catching big fish and he might take you with him. His name is Dave Justice. He grew up down here, and while he's moved to North Carolina, he still comes back to Miami to visit his folks and catch big snook. No one is better at catching big snook in these waters than Dave Justice."

With that recommendation I called High Point, North Carolina, and got Sufix USA, manufacturers of quality fishing line, where Dave was employed as head of sales and marketing. He couldn't have been more enthusiastic and told me that he was coming south for the Miami Boat Show and would be happy to take me out.

"Isn't it too early in the season, Dave?" I asked.

"No way," he said. "I catch them there year-round. There are a couple of things, though."

*Great*, I thought. *The old conditions.*

"We have to go out at night, we'll probably catch him from the shore, and you have to swear that you won't tell anyone about any of my spots."

"No problem," I promised. "Anything else?"

"Yeah, we'll probably get chased by a few dogs and security guards. You all right with that?"

"Oh, no problem," I assured him, brushing away his admonition with an air of nonchalance as if being chased by dogs and security guards were a regular nightly occurrence for me. Anyway, how bad could it be? Hadn't I stared down death in the dark passages of Chokoloskee? I thought about how far I'd come since first hearing about the Met Hall of Fame at the Islamorada Fish Company Restaurant and Bakery. We agreed to meet at Dave's parents' house in Miami in two weeks.

The big day arrived. I drove up from the Keys and met Dave at 7:00 p.m. so we could be on the water by sundown. He had invited a pal of his, Alex Rodriguez, who, it would turn out, was a student of Dave's on the art of catching big snook. (First Pete Rose, then David Justice, and now Alex Rodriguez—I was beginning to wonder if all great fishermen in South Florida shared names with great Major League Baseball players).

I found out a lot about those two guys on our drive to the boat ramp. Dave had left Florida to become a full-time guide in Tennessee five years before. Two years after that, he moved to High Point for a "job he couldn't refuse" with Sufix, selling their expansive range of braided monofilament and fluorocarbon fishing lines. He also marketed his own line of weighted fishing lures, especially designed for linesiders, and even had his own weekly fishing talk show.

*Fish #10: The Snook*

***Captain Dave Justice's dad had plenty of reasons to be proud of his son's incredible fishing prowess.***

Alex lived in Miami, where he had started his own company building and selling low-end furniture. He also trained guard dogs, a fact I made a mental note of while wondering if we might run into any of his alumni that night.

After we'd gotten to know one another a bit better, Dave and Alex started talking about their snook-catching escapades. It seemed that both of them had grown up fishing from the shores and bridges around metropolitan Miami. They mentioned that some of the best snook fishing in the area was from shores that—how shall I say this?—weren't generally open to the public. They shared some great stories with me about encounters with security guards, laughing about how they'd managed to catch big fish right out from under the noses of the rent-a-cops.

Knowing that I had to use very light tackle (15-pound test), Alex had brought along his skiff, figuring it would be far easier to pull a large fish away from a hazard-infested shoreline.

"I hope we'll still get to walk a few of your favorite shores," I lied, hoping to be accepted as one of the guys.

"Oh, sure," Dave replied, smiling as we launched Alex's skiff at a beautiful new ramp at Venetian Causeway.

We spent the next twelve hours casting and moving from secret spot to secret spot throughout the waterways of Miami, including the Miami River and Government Cut, where the big wakes of large vessels bound to and from the ocean reverberated off the seawalls and created an almost constant roll for local fishing boats and their crews.

Dave showed me his technique of letting his heavy lures (½ to 1 ½ ounces) hit the bottom, reeling in a foot of line, then lifting and lowering the rod to let the lure bounce across the bottom. This method was especially productive with snook, which are bottom feeders. David, the teacher, used this method to his advantage and caught a dozen nice snook, all under 14 pounds. Alex, the assistant professor, caught six fish but won for the largest snook release with a 16-pounder. Bubba, the student, caught a couple of small snook, two barracuda, a 15-pound tarpon—and the bottom on too many occasions to count. Dave and Alex kept their patience and sense of humor and cheered wildly for me when I hooked and landed one of the biggest stingrays I've ever seen. Just for a few minutes, in the early stages of the fight, we thought I might have my lunker on, but changed our opinion after the ray didn't come up to fight on the surface, as most snook do.

## Fish #10: The Snook

Throughout the night, David and Alex kept up a stream of easygoing banter punctuated with stories of monster snook they had caught at each of the roughly fifty spots we tried. We also did a little shoreline fishing, with equal measures of no success with the fish and no confrontations with the law.

At about midnight, we pulled the skiff close to South Beach Park in time to see the security guard rousting a few shoreline anglers who, in his mind, no doubt, had turned into loitering vagrants as the clock struck twelve. As the last couple of anglers in sight headed for the gate, Alex called out to the guard, "Hey, Bill, how's it going? Do you still have that chip on your shoulder?"

"How you doing?" he responded. "Everything's fine. I just have to use my deep, gruff voice to get them moving faster. How's fishing?"

Who would have known that Bill the security guard had used that same deep, gruff voice to shag Dave and Alex out of the park two nights earlier?

"Ask him what he had for dinner," I whispered to Alex. "I'll bet it was leftover pizza."

"No, a corn dog," David chimed in.

"No, no, cold cuts," Alex opined before asking Bill the question.

"Tuna on white bread," the guard responded good-naturedly.

Hey, what can I tell you? Fishing all night with friends—old and new—can make you a little punchy.

After our night of fishing, Dave had to go back to work in North Carolina and I went off to Cat Cay, where I caught my marlin. I called Alex Rodriguez a week later to see if he wanted to try some more night fishing. He said that he'd love to but that someone had snuck into his yard and stolen the engine off his skiff. I started to ask him what had happened to his guard dogs, but I thought better of it.

With continuing reports on large snook being caught in the Indian River, I decided to concentrate on the Stuart area. Even though they were mainly taking live bait, I figured I might get lucky on a plug. Besides, this area offered a bonus in that you had an excellent chance to land a big trout while you were searching for a snook.

Returning to Islamorada, I reflected on my quest and realized that with two weeks left until June and the end of snook season, time was working against me. If I didn't get this fish right away, I would have to wait until snook season opened in September.

Some words popped into my mind: "Bob, if you don't get that fish by May, call me. We'll get him, I guarantee it." Ron Hueston had told me this as we'd said goodbye in Chokoloskee. *Guarantee* was a strong word. I gave him a call.

Ron said he'd love to go fishing but had a couple of problems. He was finishing up a construction job in West Palm Beach and taking exams for his captain's license, and he couldn't fish until May 25.

I told him, "OK, but I sure wish we had a little more time. You know I have to get this done before June?"

"No problem, Bubba. We'll do it the first night. I guarantee it. If not, we'll fish every night through the Memorial Day weekend."

I shuddered as I took down his instructions on where to meet.

"I'll see you at the Circle K between 5:00 and 6:00 p.m. on Tuesday night. The tide will be perfect for what I want to do. By the way, you don't mind a few mosquitoes, do you?"

"No, Ron, I don't."

"Good," he said, "'cause they'll be bigger and thicker than anything you've ever seen in your life."

## Fish #10: The Snook

*Great.* I started to wonder how badly I wanted this and if my second choice might get the job done. Then I remembered a quote I'd read in Nick Lyons's *The Quotable Fisherman*. It was from H. G. Tapply's *The Sportsman's Notebook*: "Fishing always reaches its peak at a time when the bugs are thickest. And bugs are thickest at the places where fishing is best—so whenever and wherever you enjoy good fishing you can expect to find mosquitoes, black flies, midges, or deer flies, all lusting for your life's blood." Well, no pain, no gain, I figured. I called the Rod and Gun Club to make reservations.

I asked several members of my family if they wanted to join me, and they all invented excuses. I called Rusty with an invitation. The Conch scoffed. I was on my own.

When the big day came, I was about ten minutes from the Circle K when my cell phone rang at 5:25 p.m. It was Captain Ron.

"Bob, I'm at the Circle K, ready to go. Where are you?"

"Ron, I'm about ten minutes out. You told me to meet you between 5:00 and 6:00 p.m."

"I know, but you're going to be late. Five-thirty is between 5:00 and 6:00 p.m., and you're going to be five minutes late."

*Great point*, I thought. Five thirty was indeed between 5:00 and 6:00 p.m. This guy was intense.

"Sorry," I said. "I'll step on it."

"Good," Ron replied. "We've got a perfect tide, but we have to get out there right away."

When I pulled up in the parking lot, Ron was pacing by his truck. "Let's go," he said.

I hadn't had anything to eat all day. "Do I have time to grab a couple quarts of water?" I asked.

"Yeah, but hurry," he said, walking inside the Circle K with me, probably to make sure I didn't sneak a corn dog.

"They're here, Bubba, just like I told you they would be. I went out by myself last Saturday and got three over 20 pounds in my first five casts."

Ron knew how to get my attention. Some might have been skeptical, but I remembered that Ron Hueston was candid and straight-up. I felt the excitement growing as I threw my stuff and myself into his truck for the five-mile drive to the ramp at Chokoloskee Island Park.

As we launched his skiff, I asked where we were going.

"I'll tell you when we're in the boat," he whispered, looking around to see if anyone was eavesdropping.

As we motored out the little winding channel between the mudflats and oyster bars, he confided, "I want to start at Gomez Point in the mouth of the Faka Union River on the way to Port of the Islands."

We ran about ten minutes to the Gulf of Mexico, turned, and headed northwest up the coast toward Marco Island. With no breeze, the Gulf was as calm as a millpond. While it made for a pleasant run, I had been hoping there might be some wind tonight to blow away some of the swamp angels that I knew would be waiting for us. Brown pelicans flew by us, traveling by themselves or with a mate as if they were getting in one last late afternoon hunt before sunset. Along the mangrove shoreline to our right, large white herons stood silently staring into the tannin-colored water, watching unsuspecting little baitfish.

The temperature was still in the 80s as we idled down into the mouth of the main channel of the Faka Union, which is posted as a slow-speed manatee zone. As if on cue, a large manatee, or warm-blooded sea cow, swam in front of the boat and stuck her dark snout out of the water as if to thank us for obeying the signs. She was quite a sight and looked to be about ten feet long. Under other conditions, I would have loved to turn off our engine and watch her, but I knew that was not in the cards for this night.

Ron told me that the river led to a place on Route 41 called Port of the Islands, where a housing development was going in on land that used to be the old Bermuda Ranch.

He turned off his outboard a few minutes later and used his electric trolling motor to position us about sixty feet from a large oyster bed on the northwest shore of the river. It was about 6:15 p.m. The entire boat trip had taken only twenty minutes from the dock.

Ron said the conditions were ideal. We had arrived in time for the end of the falling tide with a moon, one quarter before full, already high in the sky. "We're in the right place at the right time with the right tide," he said. "The early evening feed should be starting now."

Following his instructions, I'd brought along three plug rods of varying lengths and stiffnesses, each outfitted with a Shimano 251 Calcutta reel spooled with 12-pound clear Ande, and 40-pound leaders.

"Which one should I start with?" I asked.

Ron gave me the answer I'd expected: "The largest and strongest." He handed me one of his special Silverado Rattletraps, which I tied on with an improved clinch knot that he, of course, inspected.

I surveyed the area for hazards besides the oyster bed and noticed a submerged tree branch about eighty feet offshore in about three feet of water. As if he'd read my mind, Ron said, "They'll go for that branch. You'll have to guide them away from there."

"You mean muscle them away?" I asked.

"No, guide," Ron corrected. "When these big fish run toward a hazard, the natural instinct will be to pull in the opposite direction to stop them. But I want you to put your rod in that same direction and guide the fish or lead him away by slightly changing his direction. You do that and I'll tell you straight up—you'll get a fish a lot bigger than the Met calls for. OK?"

"OK," I agreed.

"Then start casting," Ron instructed.

I cast to the right side of the oyster bed, gathered in slack, and let the weakening outgoing tide propel my plug past what I hoped were large snook waiting to ambush unsuspecting mullet. The mullet, I noticed, were beginning to crash noisily around us. Like every angler who has ever thrown a line, I asked myself the silent question, *Are they here?*

My answer came suddenly and fiercely as I began the slow, steady retrieve that makes the Rattletraps swim best. *Bang!* A huge fish sprang from ambush and mugged my Silverado, breaking the silence of the water. I lowered the rod tip, reeled in slack, and set the hook with moderate force. The startled fish felt the metal and went airborne forty-five feet away, immediately identifying herself as a snook by the dark line down the length of her body. I knew it was a female due to her large size.

"Is that her, Ronny?" I shouted, barely able to contain my excitement for getting this thing done and getting out of the swamp before the you-know-whats showed up.

"I don't know," Ron said. "I'll let you know when I lift her. Get her over here."

Ron, by the way, never carried a net. He thought it's bad for the fish and took too much time, as the treble hooks of his plugs often got snared in the mesh. He preferred to reach into the fish's mouth and remove the hooks as quickly as possible, keeping the fish in the water.

This snook went left toward the oyster bed, then right toward the branch. Using Ron's instructions, I led her around the obstacles and had her up to the boat in five minutes. Ron grabbed the fish as I grabbed my Boga grip scale. I held my breath—16 ½ pounds. I felt sick.

"Don't worry about it, Bubba," Ron consoled, releasing the fish. "I don't want you doing this with just an 18-pounder. We'll get her."

I was excited. I threw again. *Bang!* Same thing, but this time the fish looked a little bigger. The Boga grip scale confirmed it—17 ¼ pounds. I glanced at my watch. It was 6:33 p.m. My hands were shaking. *Reload.* I threw a third cast in the same general direction. This time a huge fish made a hole in the water as she slammed the plug. I tried to set the hook but felt only slack line.

"Reel it in fast and throw right at the bubbles, Bob," Ron said. "She didn't feel the hook and, by the way, that's your fish."

By now the shaking had stopped. My hands felt totally numb. I took in a deep breath, aimed, and let it fly, cast number four. The plug landed fifty feet away, right in the middle of the circle of bubbles made by fish number three. She hadn't left. *Wham!* She ambushed the Silverado again. I dropped the tip, took up the slack, and slammed her, snatching my rod back as hard as I could. I felt the hook set. The big snook on the other end of the line obviously felt it too. She went right five feet, then exploded three feet out of the water, violently shaking her big head to free herself.

"That's her," Ron blurted out, in one of the greatest understatements ever uttered on the Faka Union River as this monster fish showed herself completely, twice more.

"Keep your rod tip down. It will keep her in the water. By the way, you don't mind me giving you advice, do you?" Ron asked, almost shyly.

"It's your game and your home field, Ronny," I said as I lowered my rod tip. "You're the coach. Please talk me through this."

"Fine," he replied as the fish, no doubt realizing she was firmly hooked, headed back toward her chosen ambush spot near the oyster bed.

"Rod tip down and lead her left."

This went against my natural instincts, but I tried it and it worked. I was taking line! The big fish knew it too. She reversed her field and took off toward the submerged branch sixty feet away.

"Lead her right, quick. Lean on her while I motor out into the river. This is the critical part of the fight, right here, right now." I followed Ron's instructions. The snook made a beeline for the branch.

"I'm in trouble, Ron."

"No, you're not. Lead her. Guide her. Do it!"

The snook knew where she had to go. She had to reach the branches to go free. She was four feet from escape. All of a sudden, she was slowing. She was a foot from the branch. She was at the branch. She was sliding past the branch—on my side! I'd guided her

## Fish #10: The Snook

toward me and taken away her escape. I knew it, Ron knew it, and the fish knew it.

"OK," Ron said. "Now relax and don't horse her. We're in the middle of the river. She has nowhere to go. It's your fight to lose."

I tightened up on my grip as the fish came toward the boat. She tried three more runs but not with her earlier strength. I was able to turn her each time. I was winning.

"I'm winning, aren't I, Ron?"

Ron's response was not what I'd expected, and it struck fear into my heart.

"Shark!" he yelled, pointing to the right.

I looked over to see a big blacktip moving at warp speed directly toward our hooked snook, about twenty feet from contact.

"Free spool!" Ron shouted.

I jammed the line-release lever with my thumb, setting the line in free spool. I figured that Ron wanted to give the fish a chance to flee the predator with no line pressure, but I feared that this tired fish wouldn't have a chance against a shark that looked to be a fresh and hungry six feet of teeth.

As we both watched, the snook did a very strange thing. She stopped. Absolutely stopped in her tracks with no movement. Even her gills seemed to stop moving. The big blacktip shark didn't stop. It looked like he had my fish. He was moving full speed in the attack mode. All of a sudden, he was a flying foot away from his prey, and then—he was a foot past her. Then ten feet past, then twenty, and still going.

"Get her in fast," Ron said.

"What happened?" I asked as I brought the fish closer.

"Sharks are almost blind, and they work off sonar," Ron explained. "That shark was zeroed in on the snook's frantic movements in the water. When you free spooled her, the fish relaxed, the movement stopped, and the shark swam by."

"But did you know what the snook was going to do? And did the snook know why she was doing it?"

"Those are questions you'll have to answer for yourself, Bubba," Ron said, chuckling.

Standing on the bow, I had the snook ten feet from the boat when she made a last-ditch run for the motor and trim tabs suspended off the transom. After the shark, I wasn't about to lose this fish to the boat. I ran around the gunwale to the transom with the rod tip in the water.

"What are you doing, Bubba? I've already raised the engine," Ron said, laughing.

Then the fish circled again toward the bow and the trolling motor.

"It's already up too." Ron smiled as he leaned over the gunwale to apply the "claw of justice." I led the fish to him. He grabbed the fish by the mouth, kept her in the water, and started nonchalantly disengaging the hooks.

"Ron, what are you doing? Get her in the boat!"

No need to kill a good fish, Bubba. Get your camera, or tape measure or scale, whatever you want to do first. This is your Met fish."

I went for the scale first and there it was—24 ½ pounds. Six and a half pounds over the Met's required weight.

We measured her length at 40 inches and girth at 21 ½ inches. Ron put the fish back in the water after each procedure,

*Fish #10: The Snook*

*Success at last! Captain Ron Hueston shows off my final Met target, a 24 ½-pound snook.*

holding her by the lip and looking around for the return of the big blacktip shark.

Ron was impatient during the photo shoot. "We've got to get this big fish back in the water fast so she can live," he said. I'd noticed how passionate he was about protecting the welfare of these big fish.

After the last picture was snapped, he lowered the fish back into the river and swept her back and forth, working water through her gills. She responded and, with a slap of the tail, pulled away from Ron's gentle grasp and swam off toward the oyster bar.

Just like that, it was over. I glanced at my watch. We'd hooked up at 6:33 p.m. and released the big fish twelve minutes later, at 6:45 p.m. She was my tenth and last species, and we'd caught her before the mosquitoes even knew we were there.

I gave Ron a big hug and a handshake.

"Thanks, my friend," I said.

"No problem," Ron said. "I told you straight up we'd get one. Now let's go fun fishing."

Fun fishing? He called a night in the swamp fun? I was thinking about some champagne toasts and a steak on the barbecue.

"Ron, maybe we should—"

"You're not going to wimp out on me, are you, Bubba? We're going fishing, aren't we?"

"Well—well—of course we're going fishing, Ron. I was going to say, 'Maybe we should try a lot of spots tonight,'" I lied. *No big deal*, I thought. *Just how bad can those mosquitoes be?*

I soon found out. As a beautiful South Florida sunset gave way to darkness, the swamp angels took over. Every time we slid in toward a mangrove island, they engulfed us. The bug spray was barely effective. We'd doused ourselves with the entire can before the night was over. It's impossible to cast a plug rod with one hand, retrieve line with the other, and slap mosquitoes all at once. I eventually just quit slapping as they simply covered me up. If they'd been bees, I'd have been a hive.

At 3:00 a.m., as the tide once again went slack and the bite turned off, we decided to pack it in. We had caught and released a total of fifteen snook, all over 14 pounds on a night that Ron called "slow." My Met fish was the largest, although Ron did catch one at

## Fish #10: The Snook

2:30 a.m. that weighed 23 pounds. Nine and a half hours after the adventure began at the Circle K, Ron motored us back to the ramp, leaving the fishery to the swamp angels.

When I got back to the Rod and Gun Club, I called Mindy to give her the news and share my excitement.

"Congratulations!" she said. "It will be nice getting you back again."

Strange. I didn't know I'd been away. Then I fell asleep.

When I woke up in a few hours, my first call was obvious.

"Good morning, Rusty," I said. "I'm on my way home so you can have the chance to shake the hand of a Hall of Famer."

"So, you caught a few fish? Big deal. I'll see you when you get here. What do you want to fish for tomorrow?"

EPILOGUE

# The Calendar

*Now small fowls flew screaming over the yet yawning gulf;
a sulken white surf beat against its steep sides;
then all collapsed, and the great shroud of the sea
rolled on as it rolled five thousand years ago.*

—HERMAN MELVILLE, *Moby Dick*

THE MIAMI ROD and Reel Club is gone now, and with it the Met Fishing Tournament—both victims of vexatious municipal taxation, some membership apathy, and change itself. An increase in annual property taxes from $6,500 to over $2,000,000 can be seen as nothing but confiscatory.

Once the club was torn down, Suzan Baker and a few other members attempted to hold the organization together with some monthly dinner meetings, but they fizzled. All that remains now are the fading memories and timeworn stories of some aging former members.

*Epilogue*

The great fish of South Florida and the western shores of the Bahamas, however, remain just as cautious and wily as ever, challenging anglers' patience, perseverance, and GPSes! Benefiting from better fisheries management and the increased practice of catch and release, they are once again growing in number and size to challenge the best of anglers.

I've been honored to play my part in the conservation movement in practice and in influencing the Met and other tournaments to release more fish and keep only those that anglers plan to eat. Also, I owe a debt of gratitude to the Met for supplying me with the challenge and the discipline to compete, find, and catch and release some very big fish with different types of tackle, but you don't need a tournament or a prize to create a fishing challenge for yourself and or friends. My quest took me twenty-eight months of fishing on and off to accomplish. I do think that it could have been accomplished in a shorter period by an angler armed with the proper amount of information, perseverance, and access to knowledgeable local guides.

At the end of the day, catching big fish is all about planning and perseverance. To develop a plan, you need information, and that can be a problem. There are a lot of people out there who know a great deal about a few species in their locality.

The difficulty is gathering specific information about all ten target fish throughout the region so that you can formulate a good game plan for catching them. As Yogi Berra once said, "If you don't know where you're going, you'll wind up somewhere else." The best time to put together a game plan is obviously before the game begins. Then, once you start, it takes a great deal of patience to stay with your plan. The temptation, which I succumbed to often, was to go

## Epilogue

off on fliers, responding to news of an unexpected abundance of a species in different venues.

In retrospect, these fliers are OK but are more fun if you keep in mind that they are high-risk ventures. Keeping the quest in perspective and keeping your sense of humor are important. This isn't life and death for the angler, nor is it for the fish now that we've all bought into catch and release.

It's also important to line up the people you plan to fish with and line them up early, especially any specific guides you want to engage. The more talented they are, the earlier they get booked up, and you can find yourself out of luck, especially on those narrow-window-of-opportunity species like snook. By the way, due to the new length restrictions on snook, they were ultimately replaced with cobia on plug gear as an alternative for the Hall of Fame requirement. While I have never fished for them, I have done a little research and added them to my calendar.

I believe someone can catch big fish on specific tackle as I did in less than twelve months, and I hope it happens. As my modest contribution, I have prepared the following calendar outlining from my own experience the best times and places to catch each species. This calendar is, of course, debatable and not designed to offend or disregard any great fishery. It is designed as a starting point for building a game plan.

Finally, I hope that you enjoy my book, whether you fish or not, and that if you do embark on a fishing quest, some of the book's content will add to your enjoyment of our wonderful sport.

Tight lines,
*Bob "Bubba" Rich*

*Epilogue*

# Where to Go

## Hall of Famer's Calendar

| | JAN | FEB | MAR | APR | MAY | JUNE | JULY | AUG | SEPT | OCT | NOV | DEC |
|---|---|---|---|---|---|---|---|---|---|---|---|---|
| Sailfish | Stuart | Stuart | | | | | | | | | Stuart | Stuart |
| Barracuda | | | | | Florida Keys | Florida Keys | | | | | | |
| Permit | | | | Key West | Key West | | | | | | | |
| Bonefish | | | | Islamorada | | | Islamorada | | | | | |
| Bass | Lake Okeechobee | Lake Okeechobee | | | | | | | | | | |
| Wahoo | | Bahamas | | | | | | | | | | |
| Tarpon | | | | | Islamorada | | | | | | | |
| Dolphin | | | | | Islamorada | Islamorada | | | | | | |
| Marlin | | | | | Bahamas | | | | | | | |
| Trout | | | Fort Pierce | | | | | | | | | |
| Cobia | | | | Key West | | | | | | | | |
| Snook | | | | | Chokoloskee | | | Chokoloskee | | | | |

### SAILFISH

Stuart deserves its nickname, Sailfish Capital of the World. Its proximity to the Gulf Stream makes for short boat trips to the fish. Other areas such as Palm Beach, Miami, Islamorada, and the rest of the Keys also produce a lot of sailfish.

### BARRACUDA

These predators are always abundant in the Keys and other locations throughout South Florida and the Bahamas. I found the big offshore Keys fish fairly easy to find, while their Bahamian cousins were easy to find in the shallows.

## Epilogue

### PERMIT
Forget about catching these wary gamefish on the flats if you have limited time. Head for the wrecks off Key West; you can fun-fish them at your leisure once your quest is over.

### BONEFISH
Large bonefish could be called the major industry of Islamorada. So many are caught and released at local waterside weigh stations during tournaments that the downtown stocks are continually replenished. While they are very savvy, many still get caught year-round. I've had my best luck in fall.

### LARGEMOUTH BASS
It's hard to argue with Lake Okeechobee's reputation for plentiful stocks and large fish. This species is prolific, however, and can also be found in quantity in freshwater throughout the region.

### WAHOO
The Keys' population is spotty compared to the number of these lone wolves in the waters off the Western Bahamas. Also, they are much less pressured there as they gather for their late-spring migration north to Bermuda.

### TARPON
If Homosassa were in the Met region, it would have been the place to go twenty years ago, without question. The Indian River guides in Stuart can make a great case for their fishery, but the place to find Moby Tarpon is Islamorada.

*Epilogue*

**DOLPHIN**

The number of summer dolphin tournaments and the number and size of the fish caught say that Islamorada is the place.

**MARLIN**

Head straight for the Bahamas. While their numbers are down, they're still much higher than in the Keys.

**TROUT**

Fish out of Fort Pierce and work the waters as far north as you can go while still being able to return to a Met region port the same day.

**COBIA**

They get on the wrecks in Key West in spring and in the harbor as well. West Palm captains give good reports on spring fish tracking along with cruising stingrays looking for food.

**SNOOK**

Let the big debate begin. Folks in Stuart and Jupiter certainly have a good argument, but I've got to give the nod to Chokoloskee, swamp angels and all.